THE WORKING
SPRINGER SPANIEL

THE WORKING SPRINGER SPANIEL

Keith Erlandson

SWAN·HILL
PRESS

First published in the UK by Flycatcher, an imprint of
Robinson Publishing 1995

Reprinted by Excellent Press 1997

This edition first published in 2002 by

Swan Hill Press
An imprint of Quiller Publishing Ltd
Wykey House, Wykey,
Shrewsbury, Shropshire, SY4 1JA England

Reprinted 2005, 2006

A copy of the British Library Cataloguing in
Publication Data for this title is available from the
British Library.

ISBN 1-904057-18-7
      978-1-904057-18-5

Typeset by Palimpsest Book Production Limited,
Polmont, Stirlingshire.

Printed and bound in the UK.

Contents

Preface   vii
1   Origins of the Springer   1
2   The Relationship between Dog and Man   10
3   Obtaining a Spaniel Puppy   15
4   Why We Must Dock   22
5   Spaniel Size and Efficiency   26
6   Hips and Eyes in Spaniels   31
7   Pre-Training Procedure   35
8   Training Equipment   41
9   Dogging Guns and Ammo   44
10   Early Obedience Lessons   48
11   Steadiness to Dummies and Retrieving   55
12   Introducing the Gun   64
13   Retrieving Real Game   68
14   Hunting and Steadiness to Game   74
15   A Breakdown on Game Scent   84
16   Perfecting the Hunting Method   91
17   Dropping to Shot   106
18   Working on Blind Retrieves   110
19   Jumping Fences   117
20   Water Work   120
21   Walking to Heel   123

22 Artificial Lines   126
23 Punishment   129
24 His Raison d'Être   134
25 The Importance of a Good Mouth   145
26 The Principles of Breeding Good Spaniels   151
27 Breeding a Good Litter of Puppies   158
28 The Working Cocker Today   164
29 The Fall and Rise, and Rise of the Cocker   171
30 Woodcock and 'Cocking' Spaniels   175
31 The Changed Face of Field Trials   180
32 Spaniel Trials in Britain   184
33 Past and Present   189
34 Fields Trials in Europe   193
35 Spaniels – A Continental Sportsman's View   219
36 Transatlantic Spaniel Trials: USA and Canada   225
37 Spaniels Today   231
38 A Review of Spaniel Championship Winners   236

Preface

It was not until I was asked to write this book that I realized that no definitive work on the working springer spaniel has been published within living memory. It is true that a book on the English springer spaniel was written 30 years before this book (*The Springer Spaniel*, by Dorothy Morland Hooper, 1963), with six revised versions since, but although covering some working and field trial aspects of the breed, the book was heavily loaded towards the show spaniel and the author was a life-long show breeder, although slanted towards the dual-purpose type. The work is a handy book of reference, but some of the research is inaccurate, particularly where field trials abroad are concerned. My book is intended to fill this gap.

It is sad that there have been so many great spaniel people in the past who could have left us so much, but who never put pen to paper: men like Thomas Gaunt, trainer and handler of pointers, setters, spaniels and retrievers for some of the famous early patrons of gundogs and field trials, such as Lorna, Countess Howe, and William Arkwright. John Kent, Joe Greatorex, John Forbes and Reg Hill were all famously successful trainers and handlers but left us nothing in the way of literature.

Let me now establish my credentials. I have been involved with working gundogs since the age of 16. I trained my first springer spaniel in 1955 and won my first open qualifying stake with a springer on New Year's Day 1957. Since then I have made up 20 field trial champions, 15 springers and five cockers; have won the Springer Championship twice (which goes by the rather cumbersome title of 'Any Variety Spaniel Championship But Cocker'), have won the Cocker Championship three times in succession with the same bitch, F.T.Ch. Speckle of Ardoon, a record no spaniel of any breed has ever equalled, and have won the McNeil Professional Spaniel Handlers' Award a record number of 12 times. I have also qualified dogs for the Retriever Championship and Pointer and Setter Champion Stake, gaining a third place in the latter event. I wrote my first article for the sporting press in 1950. Today I am fairly heavily engaged in sporting journalism and write on a pretty regular basis for English, Irish, French and American magazines.

In addition to my field trial activities, I have won the Game Fair Spaniel Tests twice, when this competition was an individual challenge, rather than a team event. I am a panel 'A' judge for spaniels and have judged the Irish Spaniel Championship, the equivalent to the European Championship, and hopefully, by the time these words appear in print, the Swedish Spaniel Championship.

I will nail my colours to the mast at the outset and state that I am completely opposed to the breeding of gundogs for the purposes of showing *per se*. The first dog show ever held was organized by a gamekeeper, Mr R. Brailsford, at Newcastle in 1859. The show was for pointers and setters only. All were pure working dogs, yet within a few short years, dogs of these breeds were winning at shows when they themselves had never seen a partridge or a grouse, so on 18 April 1865, the first official field trial was held for these breeds at Southill in Bedfordshire, on the estate of Sir Samuel Whitbread. It was held on paired grey partridges. There were 16 entries, and black-and-tan setters won all three places.

I have nothing against hound shows. All hounds are bred solely for hunting. There are no purpose-bred show hounds, and the judges simply pick the best conformed. So it is in Italy with the Bracco Italiano, a hunting breed which can be dated back to the fifth century BC. All the Bracchi Italiani are pure working dogs, and are shown in the same manner as we show our hounds. Other countries have similar ideas. After major pointer events, the Danes show their winning dogs on railway stations on Sunday mornings, as no trains run in Denmark on Sundays; and I have actually shown a springer in Holland, gaining a fourth prize, grade very good, after its owner handled it to its International Field Trial Champion title, in La Coupe d'Europe field trials in 1988. There is absolutely no harm in any of these procedures at all, but I find it extremely irritating when show people tell me that the arbitrary breed standards which are laid down for show dogs will actually enhance a dog's performance in the field because it is the 'right' shape. A dog can be physically sound without in any way conforming to a 'standard', but the overriding consideration is what is going on inside the dog's mind. It is not a matter of whether a dog's muzzle is large and square, or if it is narrow and snipey when we approach the question of retrieving large game like hares and cock pheasants. Such skills are entirely dependent on breeders in the past having done their homework and developed *temperaments* which enable the dog to accomplish such tasks with a combination of an intense desire to get the job done, coupled with an uncanny knack to do it.

I have shot over spaniels extensively over the entire period I have been involved with the breed and have frequently been nonplussed when persons have asked me, in all innocence, 'Do you do any shooting with your dogs, apart from running them in trials?' I have never been able to work out how one would give sufficient game experience to a trial dog without shooting over it, but clearly there are some who still believe one can have a pure competition spaniel which is completely divorced from the shooting field. I can never separate the two, and unless a trial spaniel can give a good account of itself in the shooting field, and show reasonable stamina, to me it is no spaniel at all.

Although this is an in-depth book about the working springer spaniel, it has much to commend it to owners of working cocker spaniels. Both breeds perform almost an identical function which in its purest form is hunting within comfortable shot of the gun, finding and flushing unshot game, then retrieving the shot game tenderly to hand. Granted, their respective temperaments tend to differ, as generally cockers are the more effusive of the two and, if anything, tend to be tougher and more resilient in mental attitude, but by and large the same guidelines apply to their training and handling as would be suitable for springers – although with the proviso that it is perhaps better if the cocker owner is well endowed with patience and a sense of humour!

1

Origins of the Springer

If one peruses the year book of the English Springer Spaniel Club, the claim will be noted that the English springer 'is of pure and ancient origin'. Ancient it certainly is. Pure it most definitely is not. There are records of spaniels in Wales in the year AD 900, but I do not believe these dogs figure in the ancestry of the English springer. They were red and white, and from this source I believe the Welsh springer spaniel derives, as the Welsh springer breeds true to this colouration and no other. The triangular, vine-shaped ears of the Welsh springer bear no resemblance to the wider-bottomed ears of the English springer, but there is a close resemblance to the vine-shaped appendages of the Brittany spaniel, which should also breed true to the red and white, or orange and white colour. Some French Brittanies show liver and white or black and white colours, but this is incorrect, and due to miscegenation with other local French spaniels after the 1939–45 war, when so few *sang pur* Brittanies of breeding age remained in the country. I believe some cocker spaniels probably strain back to these early Welsh spaniels, but not the English springer. As the name spaniel would seem to suggest, it is thought by some that the early specimens originated in Spain, but the evidence is flimsy – although the argument that the breed would be more numerous in Spain now if this were the case does not carry much weight, since English setters of working strain are now very scarce in their country of origin, whereas 20,000 English setters are registered annually with the Italian Kennel Club.

The name 'spaniel' appears frequently in early English literature and seems to have been a rather loose term for any type of hunting dog employed in the pursuit of small game, with either net, hawk or falcon. Some setter-like dogs were referred to as 'rough' spaniels, while those of pointer type were dubbed 'smooth' spaniels. The earliest authentic reference to a spaniel appears late in the fourteenth century, in Geoffrey Chaucer's *Prologue to the Wife of Bath's Tale*: 'For as a spaynel she wol on him lepe', which speaks volumes for the ardour of the lady in question, and for the exuberant nature of the spaniels of the period, very much as we know them today. Another reference to spaniels appears in *The Hunting Book of Gaston Phoebus*, in 1387. Gaston was Count of Foix and Viscount of Bearn; he kept a large kennel of hunting dogs and doubtless used a hack writer to write his book on hunting.

The Master of Game, by Edward, Duke of York, which was written between 1406 and 1413, is another work where spaniels are mentioned. I believe Edward was one of the few English nobles who were killed at the Battle of Agincourt. Another sporting work which contains references to spaniels is *The Boke of St Albans*, by Dame Juliana Berners, published in 1486.

It seems fairly certain that flushing spaniels and crouching setters both stemmed from the same root stock; possibly those dogs which showed a tendency to go in and flush hard were encouraged to develop along these lines, in order to get the game into the air for hawk or falcon, whilst those which showed hesitation on the scent of game were trained as net dogs, for taking partridges on the ground. It could well be that both types could emerge from the same litter.

Moving on to the early days of game shooting, the old

sporting prints, most of which seemed to be executed in the second half of the eighteenth century, show a type of spaniel very similar to the pure working dogs of today. These spaniels are portrayed in pursuit of pheasants, woodcock or waterfowl and all appear rather wild, running in to flush and fall of game with gay abandon, and contrasting sharply with the sedate pointers and setters of the same period.

I have read elsewhere that the Boughey family, of Aqualate in Shropshire, had their own strain of English springers and that in the early nineteenth century they used a standard poodle to secure extra sagacity. I can well believe this as, over 30 years ago, a friend from Northern Ireland bought a springer bitch from Ruabon in North Wales, which is only about 40 miles up the road from Aqualate. This bitch had a most distinctive poodle-like head, with a rather bare muzzle and enormous top-knot. Around this time, I also saw a gamekeeper with a couple of spaniels of almost identical appearance – large dogs but obviously not show type, with distinctive poodle heads and faces. Poodle blood, however, although possibly beneficial in terms of brain power, would hardly improve the style and movement of spaniels, the qualities that were so sought after in later years, with the advent of field trials.

An interesting and important question arises apropos the old sporting prints, regarding the retrieving ability of these middle-period spaniels. In the early days, when these gamefinders were simply used in conjunction with net or falcon, retrieving requirements would never enter the picture, as the dogs were gamefinders pure and simple. The advent of gunpowder obviously changed the scenario. In the case of water spaniels, retrieving ability would be absolutely essential. In bygone times, and even well into our own century, 'flapper shooting' of immature ducks in late July and early August was a permissible and accepted sport. Even today, the season for duck in the Loire Valley in France starts on 1 August. 'Flappers' do not spring cleanly from the water like mature ducks. They hug the waterside cover and reeds and require a dog to flush them, so these water spaniels which were employed would have had the triple role of hunter, flusher and retriever from water. How well did they retrieve? It is a well-known fact that a great many dogs will retrieve an object from water (many mongrels show this faculty), but will abandon the retrieve directly they reach dry land. So did these early water spaniels simply perform the essential function of getting the bird off the water and on to the land, where the bird could be picked by hand, or did the dogs emerge from the water and deliver nicely to hand? My guess is that some would abandon the retrieve at the water's edge and some would retrieve right to hand, both variations of technique in all probability being encountered within the same litter.

But what of the land spaniels? According to the old prints, the dogs are invariably shown well on the way to the falling birds. What happened when they arrived at the fall? Did the first dog on the scene grab the prize and have to engage in a tug-of-war with its brace mate(s), with the bird hopefully rescued by human agency, or did the other spaniels honour the dog which arrived first? Improbable though this may seem, I have heard very recently of an occasion in France, close to the Spanish border, where an English gun was shooting over four English setters. All were absolutely steady on point, and 'backing' their team mates, then when a bird was shot, all four ran in and the first dog to arrive at the fall picked the bird and retrieved it from under the noses of the other dogs without any interference whatsoever. It must be said that such decorous behaviour would seem to be decidedly un-spaniel-like, which is perhaps why, for a considerable period of time following the era of the sporting pictures, spaniels were in most cases not required to retrieve at all. This was probably after the advent of the percussion cap muzzle loader (the shooters in the old prints were all using improved flintlocks), when shooting gentlemen decided that their forays with dog and gun should be more orderly affairs, without wild spaniels dashing all over the place and, in all probability, trying to tear the game to pieces.

It seems to have been argued that the best way to keep a spaniel steady to its game was never to allow it to handle the shot bird. If its job ended with the find, and drop to flush, it would be kept in ignorance of the delights of getting out into the cover and finding the bird which it had flushed. It may seem strange to us today, as we all expect our spaniels to perform this dual function and, for the greater part, to remain perfectly steady to flush, shot and fall, that our forebears decided that the only way to keep a spaniel steady was to keep it in ignorance of the retrieve. But perhaps, after all, this is not so strange – even to this day, the purist pointer and setter people in Britain believe that if bird-dogs are allowed to retrieve, it will 'ruin' them.

I well remember a very favourite pointer which I sold to Texas as a quail dog. On our last hunt together, I had shot three grouse over him when he came on point facing a sheep fence. He roaded-in right up to the fence, where I unloaded and put the gun over the fence. I lifted the pointer over by the base of his tail and his collar, and set him down on the other side of the barbed wire, just like a cardboard cut-out dog, still rigid on point, climbed the fence and reloaded and the pointer resumed his road-in. A covey of five grouse exploded and I picked a bird which fell on top of a heathery ridge and fluttered. The dog stood absolutely steady, marking the fall, and after a decent interval, I sent him for the grouse. He went in, picked the bird and made a perfect retrieve. He had always been a natural retriever and I had exploited this trait to its full advantage. It never 'spoiled' him, because during our time together I had always built in the wait after a successful shot, so he never developed the idea that every bird down was for his immediate attention. In fact I frequently worked a spaniel or German pointer with him, the pair of them sharing the retrieving. There is a very useful negative maxim which I learned many years ago, apropos training any breed of gundog, which is: 'Make up your mind what you don't want your dog to do, and see that he doesn't do it.' The assumption is that if you channel a dog in the right direction, heredity will ensure that it will perform its essential gamefinding functions efficiently. It seems that at the stage of our forebears' progression into the new realm of steady gamefinders, before training techniques were as efficient or imaginative as they later became, the axiom was to play safe, and expose the dog to the minimum amount of temptation, doubtless on the assumption that 'what they've never had, they'll never miss'. Modern training techniques tend to be slanted towards exposing our dogs to maximum temptation and educating them to withstand it.

I believe that this caution regarding never allowing a spaniel to handle shot game during this period of the breed's history may have had a knock-on effect which occasionally can cause us problems today. Sometimes we encounter spaniels with minimal to non-existent retrieving instincts, this perhaps stemming genetically from the period when spaniels were not expected to retrieve.

Many years ago, I visited the famous Rivington Kennels in south-west Scotland, formerly owned by C. A. Phillips, one of the greatest names in the early development of both springer and cocker spaniels. His former trainer, James Thomson, was still alive, in his nineties and still very astute. The kennel rafters were plastered with award cards, many from dog shows. I was absolutely amazed and asked James what a famous working kennel had been doing to get involved with dog shows. He explained that shows for spaniels came into being before the advent of field trials, so for a number of years, showing was the only competitive activity open to spaniel owners. However, he assured me that no breeding for show *per se* took place at the Rivington Kennels. All their spaniels were bred for work, and the kennels simply showed their workers. The show cards in the kennels eventually were joined by field trial award cards, and one intriguing feature was that many of the older ones bore the legend, 'For Any Variety Retrieving Spaniel'. Regrettably, I never questioned James on this point, so am unable to say whether the 'Retrieving Spaniel' clause indicated that in some trials for spaniels, retrieving was not required, or if it was simply a way of conveying the message that spaniels were now required to retrieve in these events, so if one's dog was a non-retriever it would be pointless to enter.

Another point to be considered is that team events were held where a handler worked a team of spaniels, only one of which was required to do the retrieving. Thus a kennel could produce good hunting dogs, many of which would not retrieve, but could get by in team stakes with the odd retrieving spaniel which the strain managed to produce. We would do well to bear in mind that our present-day spaniels stem from such backgrounds, and whereas much has been done to promote good retrieving over the years, by selective breeding, such genetic material in the distant past might be responsible for some retrieving problems which spaniel trainers of the present day still occasionally encounter.

Moving on into the twentieth century, although Mr Phillips showed his spaniels as well as shooting over them and competing in trials, he never made a dual champion cocker or springer. Nor has any other trainer succeeded in this with a cocker spaniel, and only three have ever achieved this supreme accolade with an English springer. I did question James Thomson on the question of type in these early Rivington dogs, which did so well for them in shows, and he informed me that the accepted show standards before the turn of the century were completely different from those of the present day (the time being the late 1950s) – in other words, somebody had moved the goalposts!

The first dual champion springer which completed its title was William Humphrey's Dual Ch. Horsford Hetman, (whose name always intrigued me, as a Hetman was a democratically appointed leader of a Cossack community, and liable to be booted out of office if the other Cossacks considered him unsatisfactory, which may have included a too-small capacity for 140 proof vodka!) Hetman was made up in the early 1920s. The second dual champion was a son of Hetman, Colonel F. H. B. Carrell's Dual Ch. Thoughtful of Harting. The third and last springer dual champion was probably the most publicized of all, the Duke of Hamilton's Dual Ch. Flint of Avendale. Flint was trained and handled by the great Thomas Gaunt, and when the ducal kennels were disbanded in the early twentieth century Flint was sold. Most of the other Avendale springers were bought by Eudore Chevrier, of Alberta, Canada, but for some undisclosed reason he did not manage to buy Flint direct, claiming that he acquired the dog in 1925 from a third party, for a record sum of $4,000. Chevrier was an entrepreneur and made sure Flint received maximum exposure. He claimed he was the first springer stud dog in North America to stand at a fee of $150, and had to turn several bitches away, so great was the demand for him at stud. Flint was black, blue roan and tan. He had cocker blood on his dam's side and was a big dog, weighing 56 pounds and standing 20 inches at the shoulder. His ability in the field, according to his new owner, was nothing short of phenomenal, and he sired 'hundreds and hundreds of winners, which won in many lands'. Having seen an old photograph of Flint, I can testify that certainly he was an exceptional looker, although some contemporary critics considered him somewhat 'settery'. Having in all probability come from the same taproot as those animals we now call English, or Llewellin, setters, it is hardly surprising that occasionally some springers show setter characteristics, particularly as, from time to time, certain individuals have deliberately introduced fresh English or Llewellin blood. James Thomson admitted that the Rivington Kennels had done just this, explaining that he once bought an English setter bitch from Reg Hill, 'for 30 bob [£1.50] as a foster mother'. She was a good setter, and was subsequently mated to one of their springers, the progeny being absorbed into their breeding programme. James also said that setter blood was introduced again at a later date; this introduction of alien blood is known as 'stamping in the genes'. Up to about 1969 such outcrossing could be practised with Kennel Club approval, but this was in the days when we had a more far-sighted Kennel Club than we have today. Since then, similar things have been done surreptitiously, to produce certain desired characteristics, such as wide, fast running and high head carriage, so if the English Springer Spaniel Club still insists that the breed is 'of pure and ancient origin', I will just say that it's a wise dog that knows its own genes.

2

The Relationship between Dog and Man

There can be little doubt that the dog was the first animal to be domesticated by man, but just how did man set about it? Did he catch wild dog puppies and tame them, or did wild dogs voluntarily join forces with the human race? This is something upon which we can only speculate, as no conclusive proof exists either way. Taking into account the character of the canine species, I believe the dog joined man for its own ends. With creatures like the hawk or falcon, the only possibility is that man took them from the wild. We can forget about the captive breeding programmes which have become so sophisticated in recent times. There is nothing which a wild hunting hawk would ever require from man, so this bird would hold itself completely aloof from the human race, even though kites and vultures, being scavengers and useless for sport, have always exploited human refuse and kills.

The dog, however, is both hunter and scavenger, so in prehistoric times there was much for it to gain by a closer association with man. Human beings were hunters of both large and small game and, being more intelligent than dogs, could bring about the downfall of large animals such as the mammoth, woolly rhinoceros, cave bear and wild ox, all of which, when fit and healthy, would have been beyond the scope of any pack of wild dogs. There would be rich pickings to be had from such kills in the form of bones, intestines, feet and scraps of hide. The dog also enjoys the comfort of a fire, if allowed such a privilege, and dogs living in close proximity to humans will also clean up human waste. This may appear disgusting to us, with our 'civilized' outlook, but even today it is looked upon as natural and useful by some central African tribes, where the basenji dog is the local hunter/scavenger.

It seems a possible over-simplification to assume that all dogs originated from wolves which became domesticated, as recent study of primitive remains points fairly conclusively to the fact that even in very early times, there were large and small dogs, the large ones fulfilling the role of hunter/guard dogs and the smaller ones the role of scavenger/companion/warmth-providers. There is also another quaint purpose the smaller dogs may have served. Dog fleas will not live on human beings, but fleas which plague the human race are even more keen on afflicting the canine species, so it would seem that the more dogs lived in close proximity to man, the fewer flea bites the latter would suffer.

It is less easy to guess which was the next animal to join the domesticated list. It is tempting to nominate the horse, which was also an important quarry species for primitive man, but it could have been the ox, or even the reindeer, towards the end of the Ice Age, when the ancestors of the Lapps (correctly called Saami) and northern Siberians migrated north, following the reindeer herds, which they may by this time have semi-domesticated.

But whenever the domestication of the horse took place, this was to have a greater effect upon the human race than that of any other animal, and the comparison of this with the role of the dog makes an interesting study. Whole cultures became centred around the horse, which can be ridden, driven, traded or eaten. The Mongols conquered virtually all of the East, with the exception of Japan, and most of Europe and Russia to the west of their homeland, with the aid of their horse herds. A Mongol was seemingly insignificant when dismounted. Mounted and armed, he was one of the most effective and feared cavalrymen the world has ever known. By the same token, when the North American Indians stole horses from the invading Spanish conquistadores, the tribes were transformed, and a people which on foot might have had a hunting range of only about a hundred miles, would extend this for up to 1,000 miles on horseback. They became far more efficient hunters of buffalo, they developed battle tactics akin to the Mongols, to whom they are genetically connected, and the horses comprised both movable wealth and an excuse to raid the neighbouring tribe for more. Among these horse peoples, there was never any question that any individual would ever be unable to handle and ride a horse. It was second nature to all members of society, and whereas hunting and war were the provinces of the males, the females could handle horses equally well during the ordinary course of everyday living. One is always in close contact with a horse in a physical sense, either at its head, on its back or close behind, when driving. Never does one send a horse out 100 yards or more to do some specific task, neither is the horse working under temptation, whereas the dog, and in particular the gundog, very often is. So throughout the history of man, no 'Dog People' has ever arisen as a whole nation. A few Roman legionaries might have been killed in battle by the war-mastiffs of the ancient Britons, but this pales into insignificance compared to the victories of Ghengis Khan, for which the horse, and the ability of his warriors to exploit the animal to the full, were wholly responsible. With the horse, so much can be accomplished by purely physical means (although in the more sophisticated aspects of equitation, such as dressage, racing and showjumping, a good rapport with one's mount is obviously crucial). With the gundog, and in particular the gundog which is required to go out and hunt for unshot game in front of its master, with all the attendant temptations, it is absolutely essential to get well into the mind of the dog if one hopes to achieve any degree of success.

I believe there are two means whereby success in training a spaniel can be achieved: by sheer natural ability and by application. Natural ability is self-evident. A few persons have this faculty: most apparently do not. Very often the 'green fingers' variety of trainers are fairly simple people, and though anything but stupid they are often not terribly articulate and have great difficulty explaining the secrets of their success. This is perhaps the reason for the great dearth of gundog literature already mentioned, from the real masters of the competitive sphere, who could have made the most positive contribution if only they could have expressed themselves.

Nevertheless, many people can learn to train a spaniel very well through application. The most valuable asset in this case is a determination to succeed and a sufficiently strong self-discipline to stick to the job. This entails reading up on the subject as comprehensively as possible, sifting through the inevitably differing advice proffered by various authors and working out which methods seem to make the most sense, always bearing in mind that similar results can frequently be obtained by differing methods. They should get out and about among spaniel people as much as possible, attend field trials when the opportunities present themselves, and listen, rather than ask spates of questions. I have found that some of the most high-powered and academically qualified people make the worst dog handlers. I would imagine that, collectively, Members of Parliament would be the worst group of gundog trainers/handlers one could possibly find. They are too fond of the sound of their own voices and many have such monstrous egos that I think they would find it virtually impossible to relate to something as simple and potentially sensitive as a gundog. Policemen frequently seem able to apply themselves well, as do quite a few doctors and gamekeepers, if they have the interest. This is a big 'if'. A gamekeeper who says he 'never has sufficient time' is a non-starter. Any gamekeeper can make time if he so desires. A few minutes a day for ordinary basic obedience lessons is all that is required, and so much more can be built in as he takes the dog around with him. A moorkeeper obviously has the best opportunity of all, with no rearing to attend to and most likely plenty of rabbits on the margin of his moor, but still I have known very many low-ground keepers, in charge of large-scale pheasant-rearing operations, who consistently turn out first-class spaniels, frequently achieving the highest position in field trials.

3

Obtaining a Spaniel Puppy

We now reach the important point where a person decides that a springer is to be the dog of their choice, so how do they set about getting hold of one of the right sort? Nowadays the potential buyer is in a far better position than in the immediate post-war period. No field trials had been held over the war years, so gundogs of all breeds had lacked a proving ground where excellence, or the reverse, could be displayed in public. Up to now, field trials are the only medium which has been devised for the testing of working gundogs. They are imperfect, but they are all we have. Viewed in a negative sense, I would say it is not so much a question of how much good field trials have done for gundogs in the past but how infinitely worse the breeds would have been without them! All the post-war buyer had to go on was show awards, as dog showing had not been curtailed by the war years, but show awards are useless for assessing working potential.

What further confused the issue was the emergence of the now defunct Chastleton Kennels near Wolverhampton. These kennels were based on predominantly show bloodlines which would work a bit, but in no way could they measure up to really top-class stuff. The proprietrix possessed considerable entrepreneurial skills, and the means to pursue a very high-profile advertising campaign. A famous professional trainer, Ronald McDonald, was persuaded to throw in his lot with these people and he ran one of the better dogs, Squib of Chastleton, with moderate success. In the words of Captain R. W. Corbett, for whom I won the Springer Championship in 1960, 'Squib had no nose, no brains and no style, but he was an awfully good dog at frightening a rabbit out of a bush'. Another of my early mentors, Colin Thomson, son of James Thomson of the Rivington Kennels, remarked: 'Squib would gang through cover nae sensible dog would look at, wi' his tail up on end so ye could hang yer hat on it all day.' Some fearful jiggery-pokery was attempted to give Squib his field trial champion title, with 'tame' judges appointed, who on one shameful occasion awarded a *Triple* first prize, with Squib one of the dogs with his snout in the trough. Had this 'win' been ratified, Squib would have received his title by foul means, but thank goodness Joe Greatorex spoke up against the enormity of the business at the Kennel Club, and the plot, for such it undoubtedly was, failed. Nevertheless, the Chastleton blood spread far and wide throughout the shooting community and some good working bloodlines were adulterated by it in the process, but in the course of time things averaged out, as inevitably they do. This blood faded into the background and several pure working lines emerged which were unsullied by these bloodlines.

Here a word would not go amiss regarding Miss C. M. Francis's dual purpose 'Higham' bloodlines. These dogs could win at shows but lacked the exaggerations of many show dogs. They acquitted themselves well at trials without ever getting to the top. There never was a Higham field trial champion. These dogs went back to William Humphrey's Dual Ch. Horsford Hetman, and my own springers go back to the Higham dogs on several lines. Some are not bad-looking dogs either. The Higham lines in my dogs are all concentrated through F.T.Ch. Gwibernant Ashley Robb, who was a great-great-grandson of a Higham bitch. It is an awful long way back now, but as Robb has been heavily line-bred to, these genes will be well stamped-in and could still have some influence.

So as far as the present buyer goes, I can only advise him or her to avoid show blood like the plague. This should not prove too difficult as, thanks to the continual publicity given to the pure working breeds by writers like Peter Moxon (46 years Kennel Editor to *Shooting Times*), most breeders have become educated to the realities of springer breeding and only go for the pure trial blood. Even so, the business is not without its snags. Even pure working blood is not invariably 'top drawer'. Dogs of working breeding manifest themselves as good, bad and indifferent. The great Irish authority, the late John Nash, more famous for his Irish setters but with an unplumbable depth of wisdom in all gundog matters, once remarked that the bane of all gundog breeding was bad or mediocre bitches from good bloodlines being mated to good or fashionable stud dogs. The danger is that frequently it seems to work, but weaker genes get into the line which seem to produce inconsistencies in future generations. Many years ago, a Canadian authority stated that if you get a good field trial champion dog out of a poor dam, it will not make much of a stud dog itself. Through close observation of the situation, I would say he hit the nail on the head. At the time of writing there is in Britain a very fashionable dog, a winner many times over and which has been used extensively at stud. His dam was out of a well-bred non-worker which had to be given away as a pet. All this dog's progeny, while not useless, tend to be inconsistent, and the good ones seem to be very few and far between.

William Arkwright, who in 1899 hosted the first official spaniel trial ever to be held, writing the Foreword to H. W. Carlton's classic, *Spaniels: Their Breaking for Sport and Field Trials*, remarked that the ideal brood bitch was one which was the favourite shooting companion of its master. A very simple, seemingly self-evident statement, but how true. My first springer, Breckonhill Brando, born 1954, could not be bettered as a shooting dog and, when mated to Conygree Simon, produced a litter which was to have far-reaching effects within the breed, including the production of the legendary sire Hales Smut. Later, I mated the brilliant shooting bitch, Macsiccar Auchtertyre Donna, to a son of Smut, F.T.Ch. Gwibernant Ashley Robb. She produced two litters to Robb from which five became field trial champions; but not only did they get their titles, four of them became noted stud forces, with a knock-on effect right to the most recent Championship.

Theoretically, the best source of supply should be the regular field trial competitors, most of whom do a certain amount of breeding. There is of course no guarantee that a pup from such a source will be successful, but I suppose the odds are increased in favour. However, there is nowadays another point over which one should be wary, which I cannot stress strongly enough. After the initial epidemic of myxomatosis around 1953–4, the boat was rocked for spaniel owners regarding curtailed training facilities and general access to game. Generally speaking, springer owners and their dogs rapidly overcame this handicap and springers converted to being predominantly pheasant dogs, a situation most took in their stride. These curtailed facilities tended to bring to the fore very keen, courageous springers which were willing to hunt for a minimum of game, and did not require a rabbit sitting under every tuft of grass to get them going. Consequently the 1960s produced a quality of springer which is far less common today. They were excellent cover dogs and really could sort the brambles out. The situation has now turned full circle. Rabbits have returned to northern areas as never before, but the terrain tends to be 'soft' – heather, rushes, white grass and short green bracken. Many field trials are now won under such conditions, which can scarcely be claimed to be a test of courage. This means that at the moment we have field trial champions which will not go near a bramble, and also a type of springer which, as a youngster, will not get going until it has had 60 rabbits shot over it, which is all very fine if one has 60 rabbits to shoot but not so clever if one has more restricted facilities. After all, the *sine qua non* of the springer is to hunt with enthusiasm where game is scarce, not to demand large quantities of it laid on by the plateful. There are areas of the Midlands and Wales, and of the South and West Countries where the cover is pretty stiff. People in these areas do not require a 'grass dog' as hard cover has to be penetrated, and even though there are some rabbits now in most parts of the country, once away from the northern areas, they are unlikely to be queuing up to surrender. It behoves one, therefore, to go into the question of the parents' ability in cover most carefully before making a purchase. Something has to be amiss somewhere when a Welsh rabbit trial is arranged on what is normally bracken and a bit of gorse, then a few days before the event, the ground is changed to a young plantation with undercover of stiff brambles, and two of the top handlers in the country immediately withdraw their dogs.

Having made a decision on source of supply, the question now arises which pup to choose, should the breeder be prepared to offer a choice. My own inclination is to avoid the most nervous pup, but having said that, some springers which are nervous at the outset develop into confident, mature animals. I read one piece by a gundog adviser to a national magazine who recently offered the following pearl of wisdom: the litter of pups should be brought out of their kennel, then one should run towards them, with much hand clapping – but not at my kennels, if you please. Had this gentleman attempted such a method of selection, he would have found himself smartly on the road to Yorkshire again, without the customary cup of coffee and definitely minus pup. Springers are a sensitive breed, and if one deliberately looks for nervousness in them, the chances are that one will find it. I would prefer to watch them playing within the confines of their own kennel for a while, giving the thumbs down to any which skulked in the background and were unwilling to join the others. I would pick up the ones I fancied, one at a time, and carry them on to a bit of strange ground away from their kennel. I would place them gently on the ground, where the pups would spreadeagle themselves, legs out and belly on the ground. I would take note how soon they tucked their legs under them again and started to nose around, particularly looking out for any tail action. I would avoid a liver and white pup with a pale blue eye. These usually grow up to have a light or yellow eye, which need not be the end of the world, but a higher proportion of light-eyed springers turn out to be duds than do hazel or dark-eyed specimens. Avoid a pup with a large navel rupture, say the size of a large grape. At this size it will require surgery, to avoid the risk of possible gut strangulation and death. Smaller ruptures can be ignored, for as the pup grows, the hernia stays the same size and is barely noticeable, if at all, in adulthood. However, I am not certain about the hereditary aspect of these hernias. My own idea is that they do tend to be hereditary, and all other things being equal, it is better to pick a pup with no hernia. Look at the mouth to see if the muzzle is badly undershot or overshot. A slightly undershot mouth in a puppy sometimes changes for the better when it grows its permanent teeth. Avoid a pup with a noticeable gap where its teeth should meet.

Some books pay lip-service to the idea that both parents should have had their hips and eyes tested (see chapter 6, where I discuss these points in more detail). In the case of some breeds, which are predisposed to progressive retinal atrophy (PRA) and hip dysplasia, I would agree. At this time, I believe the working springer is clear of PRA, though can be affected by retinal dysplasia, which only causes minimal problems in a small number of cases. The breed is not without hip dysplasia, but clinical cases are rare (I have never seen one) and hardly anyone bothers to have their springers X-rayed. Only about 250 springers have been X-rayed and scored by the official British Veterinary Association/Kennel Club panel, of which over half are show springers. I estimate that I have had about 12–15 per cent of the total of working springers scored myself, so the chances of a potential springer puppy buyer finding a litter where both parents have been hip scored is very low indeed.

One difficulty the potential buyer is likely to encounter in the future is finding a litter which has been subjected to the essential one-third tail dock. Here I am afraid I can offer little help. There is currently such a furore over this matter within the veterinary profession, that all I can say is that some breeders will find a vet still willing to dock working dogs of recognized questing breeds, others will not. The matter merits a chapter on its own, so please read on, and the best of luck.

4

Why We Must Dock

Returning once more to the old sporting prints of shooting over spaniels, two salient features manifest themselves. Invariably, the spaniels are running in to flush and fall of game. Secondly, all are docked, with tails a sensible length. These works were executed in the late eighteenth and early nineteenth century, many years before the advent of the first dog shows or field trials.

It is, therefore, impossible to argue that the docked tails were in any way influenced by the dictates of fashion, but rather that docking served a sound, practical purpose, and prevented tail damage when a spaniel was about its everyday business. One might well ask why the removal of about one third of a spaniel's tail was sufficient to prevent damage, and why not the whole tail.

When an impecunious youth, I skinned many carnivores. The skin on the lower third of any animal's tail is thinner and more tender than the skin of the upper reaches. In addition, the length of a full tail means that the tail tip travels in a much wider arc than does the end of a docked tail, giving the full tail greater momentum and harder striking power when it encounters any object whatsoever, be it bramble, tree branch or even the dog's own flank. I keep a few pointers, a breed traditionally left undocked. Frequently, in a normal course of events, I receive a cut across the leg from a tail. The force is surprising, and I can feel the sting for about 30 seconds afterwards. Hitherto, the effect of such continuous plying of the full tail of any breed of dog whose work is done for the greater part in thick cover has never been questioned. A full tail has always been regarded as a liability in such breeds, and to prevent damage to the tail, and distress to the dog, a quick snip at three days of age, before the puppy's pain reflexes are fully developed, has been sufficient to ensure the dog's trouble-free working function for life.

About the year 1985, the Royal College of Veterinary Surgeons (RCVS) became concerned over the 'cosmetic' docking of certain show breeds, and condemned such practices as 'unnecessary mutilation'. Unfortunately, the RCVS seems unable to appreciate that certain working breeds exist in which partial docking is not only desirable but essential. Strangely, there is no objection by the RCVS over the removal of dew claws. I think it argues thus. All dogs are 'pets'. Pets live in houses. Houses contain furniture. Dew claws are likely to catch on furniture fabric and cause injury to the dog, so off with its dew claws. The RCVS seems unable, or unwilling, to grasp the essential fact that tails of some working breeds can, and do, become damaged in cover. But is the RCVS so naive as is apparent at first sight? It concedes that tails of adult dogs may be docked for 'theraputic reasons' without such surgery constituting 'unethical' operations. Thus, if a tail is caught in a car door, or even damaged whilst a dog is working, a vet would be allowed to rectify matters by docking. A good friend and colleague has already pre-empted my thoughts in a contemporary magazine, by speculating upon the not inconsiderable amounts of revenue RCVS members would be able to pull in if there was a blanket ban on all docking and, as a result, countless damaged tails of working dogs were presented for surgery. My own estimates were that such operations could cost £100–£150, but more of this anon.

Some laypersons, unfamiliar with working spaniels and Continental hunt, point and retrieve breeds, seem unable to grasp the inevitability of tail damage in undocked specimens of these breeds. One of my favourite hunting correspondents cannot see what all the fuss is about, pointing out that foxhounds seem able to draw coverts without suffering tail damage. Here he rushes in where angels fear to tread. The *modus operandi* of the foxhound drawing a covert is completely different from the breakneck hunting technique of a high-couraged spaniel. The foxhound draws at quite a leisurely pace, stern aloft and waving gently, well out of harm's way. The draw is the forerunner of the main event, which takes place in open country, unless one is hunting in big woodlands. The spaniel attacks cover with far more vigour, tail down below the level of its back, swinging its hindquarters, with furiously lashing tail. No less a person than David Maclean, MP, former junior Minister of Agriculture, and a supporter of the tail docking ban, aspired to put us all to rights on the matter. He cited the case of his own, show-bred golden retriever, which, he claims, faces cover with impunity. With respect, the progress of a show-bred golden through cover, tail held gingerly aloft, is hardly likely to cause any portion of its anatomy significant damage, but Mr Maclean has the answer to the spaniel problem. Believing that any damage is likely to be caused by the tail being torn by snagging on brambles, Mr Maclean instructs us to trim the hair on the dog's tail. Neither he, nor the RCVS, has worked it out that the damage caused to a full tail is occasioned by the beating action of the tail against the surrounding cover, and hair on the upper portion of the tail actually can protect it in that particular area. It is the last few inches which is vulnerable and which must *never* be allowed to grow through failure to dock.

All the foregoing might have been pure conjecture, had I not had it confirmed recently by bitter experience. Until 1992, the only undocked spaniel I had ever trained was a cocker which I trained purely as a driven game shooter's dog.

A single, sickly puppy, her breeders considered her too weak to stand even the minor trauma of what a normal pup would take in its stride. She was not required to hunt cover, but even she developed a bare tail tip, through normal wear and tear. Then there arrived a springer spaniel with a full tail. Five minutes in brambles and the tail would bleed. Half an hour in cover and its flanks were red, as were my trousers when I walked it to heel. In addition, an unwillingness to enter cover manifested itself, in a dog which basically was a good cover dog. The dog's owner, upon being acquainted with the problem, appreciated that something had got to be done. He contacted various London vets. Some refused to operate, even upon a damaged tail. One was willing to undertake this work, but at a cost of £155.68, including VAT. By comparison, my own vet's (unbelievably low) quote made me catch my breath, and it was confirmed in my mind just how much the more expensive members of the veterinary profession would benefit from future generations of undocked, formerly docked, breeds, if the RCVS continues to be stubborn in its refusal to consider the opinions of those grass-roots persons who are at the sharp end of the working gundog business and who know what they are about.

5

Spaniel Size and Efficiency

Quite recently, a dog writer produced a most instructive article on gundog breeding, which was required reading for any novice reader who might be contemplating breeding a litter of pups, and there was also much that the more experienced reader could learn to his advantage. However, having been closely involved with English springer spaniels for four decades, and having profited by the counsel of many who came before me, men like Talbot Radcliffe, John Kent and Joe Greatorex, I noted a flaw in the narrative which requires closer scrutiny. He wrote: 'But don't expect to put a small bitch to a big dog and come out with a litter of medium-sized dogs – very rarely do opposite characteristics seem to average out.'

I would like to quote from Robert G. Wehle's classic, *Wing and Shot*. Wehle is an American author from New York State. He is owner of the famous 'Elhew' pointers (Elhew being Wehle spelt in reverse). The Elhew Kennel is famous worldwide, and Wehle has the distinction of belonging to that very small group of authors who have themselves reached the heights of field trial competition, with an impressive score of field trial champions and Championship winners. In his chapter on breeding, Wehle has this to say regarding the question of size:

There is a phenomenon that is recognized by most successful breeders today that is constantly influencing the results
of every breeding program. This phenomenon, sometimes
referred to as 'the drag of the race' is a natural tendency
toward mediocrity – a constant leaning toward average. We
know that, in the case of humans, tall men generally seek
out tall mates and vice versa. If the resulting children were
as tall or taller than their parents and they, in turn, sought
tall mates, theoretically we would soon have a strain of
giants. We know this cannot happen – the reason being the
hereditary tendency toward average. Tall people's children
will almost always be shorter than the average height of
their parents. The same is true of short people. The children
of two unusually short people will almost always be taller.
Of course, there are exceptions to every rule.

In the foregoing, Wehle weaves two themes together, how in
gundog breeding there is an inevitable tendency to return to
mediocrity unless much thought is given to successive matings
over the generations, and how there is an equal tendency for
size to lean toward the average.

As far as my experience of English springer spaniels goes,
I have found that if one mates a large dog to a small
bitch, usually one can immediately produce large dogs,
as large as or even larger than their sire. Seldom does this
happen in the case of the bitch pups, and this is where
this theory almost, but not quite, holds water. There is a
distinct tendency for some bitches to grow no bigger than
their dam, but a proportion may grow bigger and even
make medium size, but this is far more likely to manifest
itself should their sire's dam have some size about her. If
a breeder wishes to upgrade the size of their female line,
obviously these larger specimens are the ones to retain as
breeding prospects, always supposing, of course, that they
are at least the equals, in terms of working ability, of their
smaller sisters. But here in itself lies a big temptation. Many
small bitches can, superficially at any rate, be such impressive,

stylish performers. The tendency to breed from such little 'firecrackers' is ever-present.

I have in my kennels at the moment a large dog out of a dam no bigger than a cocker. His sire is a substantial dog of about 42 pounds, but he is several pounds heavier. Interestingly, a very small bitch was brought to this dog's sire over a year ago. The bitch was very inbred, as its Scottish breeder is completely adamant about not using any of the blood from further south which currently is doing well today. It is almost an impossibility to find a complete outcross nowadays in working springers, so restricted has the gene pool become, but this mating was virtually a true outcross. The mating produced a young bitch of very pleasing size and substance, and far nicer than her dam, but I am told this can happen when one mates a very small, closely bred animal to a partner from a completely different bloodline.

One might well ask why, when there are so many nice little springer bitches about, should it be considered desirable to grade up on size. The lessons of history suggest that a little extra poundage often makes all the difference in field trial competition at its highest level. Looking back over the past 30 years and more, very few small springers have won the Spaniel Championship, and when one did so a few seasons ago, a famous trial host and brilliant shot remarked in some surprise, 'It's no bigger than a four-lettered mouse'.

Since the increase of the rabbit population in northern areas, we have witnessed the emergence of what some describe as 'grass dogs': small, stylish springers, clever gamefinders in rushes and white grass, but lacking substance, and with what a recent Irish Spaniel Championship winner describes as 'an assisted hunting method' (i.e. guiding the dog continuously, rather than letting it use its own initiative). Many people further south have to contend with heavy brambles, both in field trials and on shooting expeditions. Just as a sumo wrestler relies on his weight, as well as his speed, to propel his opponent out of the ring, so a spaniel requires weight to push the brambles aside. Some argue that a small spaniel can get into cover which a bigger dog can't penetrate. False. I'm sure we have all enjoyed Colin Willock's stories (in *Shooting Times*) of Drake, his huge springer which was like a tank in cover and which would not only shift tree trunks, but retrieve them also!

Interestingly, I recently turned up a quote on 'The Matter of Size in Spaniels', in *Spaniels in the Field* by Eudore Chevrier (1886–1982), said to be 'the Father of North American Springers', although actually domiciled on the Canadian prairies. Chevrier states:

> When breeding springers for shows, one must watch the size one is breeding. But there is no such problem when breeding for field trials and hunting. The criteria are brains, nose, hunting ability, birdiness, soft mouth, fast retrieving, quality and style. Naturally, if you can combine good looks with all other desirable quality, it is worth striving for. But first, last, and all the time, it is the fire and intensity in hunting that counts. This we always try to breed into our working springers. I have seen too many of the fine old sporting breeds of dogs deteriorate into nice statues, when bred for show purposes only. Some of the best show champions would cut a sorry story in the field. And most field trial champions would not get far in shows.
>
> I have bred sixty pound springers that were used for fetching geese from the ocean and from swift flowing rivers when the ice was running. They did as fine work as any breed of retriever could accomplish. Some of the big trial winners today are small dogs. True, they can all do good work on upland birds. No big size is needed for brush shooting. All in all, I would say that from forty to fifty-five pounds is the size one should strive to breed in the working springers.

I must confess that I find this passage something of an eye-opener, and wonder if Chevrier tended to exaggerate the weights of contemporary springers when he wrote this piece.

The largest pure-bred working springer which I have handled weighed 49 pounds in fit condition, and at the moment I have in my kennels a dog very closely related to the latter, which, at 46 pounds, I would classify as a big dog, far bigger than the average springer of today. It does seem, however, that even though Chevrier classes as an average-sized dog that which I would recognize as a big dog, his ideas coincide with mine that a bit of poundage can put a springer at an advantage. What he would have thought to some of our current small 'grass dogs' is wide open to speculation.

6

Hips and Eyes in Spaniels

Some while ago, there appeared in *Shooting Gazette* a most informative article on hip dysplasia (HD) and eye problems in retrievers. It went deeper into the subject of HD than other writers have done, and gave some indication of what the 'hip scores' actually mean. To recap, nine areas of each hip are given a score of points, with a maximum of 53 on each hip. In contrast to the Continental system, where the higher the score, the better the hips, those following the British system look for the lowest scores.

There are many gundog owners who believe that HD doesn't occur in working spaniels, simply because they have never seen or heard of a clinically lame spaniel. Having had many hundreds of spaniels through my hands, I can state that I have never seen a lame one either, but I do know that the odd case does manifest itself. As far as I can make out, the working cocker does appear to be 'clear' of HD, but the issue regarding English springers is not so clear cut. Occasionally, a springer is born which is affected by HD, to such an extent that as a potential worker it is a non-starter. But here the situation seems to differ from that of the labrador, to such a degree that there are some spaniel people who believe it is a different phase of the abnormality.

It seems common for some labradors to show no outward sign of HD until 18 months of age, or even older, from which point they become progressively more lame until they are completely non-functional as shooting dogs and experience a degree of pain during normal locomotion. In spaniels, I have only heard of one case, in America, when a dog performed normally up to the age of 5 years, then 'seized up' in obvious pain. The positive cases of HD in springers which have come to my notice in Britain have been completely different. The problem has appeared at about the age of 4–6 months, so no training time has ever been wasted on such affected animals. Those which have survived this seemingly crucial demarcation line all appear to have been sound for life. But what would have been revealed on X-ray, had every working springer ever born been subjected to this test, could well be another matter. It seems that the springer, although occasionally affected, is not predisposed to the condition, as is the labrador, Clumber spaniel and German shepherd dog, so clinical cases are rare.

However, even when fully functional, many springer hips are not so wonderful from a purely scientific angle. This has come to light through the hip scores of those springer spaniels which have already been tested. A short while ago, a total of about 279 springers had been hip scored by the British Veterinary Association (BVA). The mean score at that time worked out at about 12.5 points. The dogs tested included both show and working springers. A total score of no more than 4 points, with no more than 3 on one hip, is regarded as a pass under the old, harsh system, and a maximum total of 8 is regarded as the original 'breeder's letter', although the leading hip expert of today considers these scores to be somewhat arbitrary. Others believe that it is safe to use as breeding prospects those animals which do not exceed the mean score for the breed. This also is arbitrary, as the mean score varies from month to month, according to how many good or bad hips have shown up over a given period. An understanding of which areas of the hip have attracted points is helpful. The first mentioned on the score sheet is the Norberg angle, which is a measurement rather than part of the hip. The next is subluxation, arguably the most significant, as this relates to joint fit, how well bedded into the socket is the ball of the thigh bone, or how shallow. Then comes the cranial acetabular edge. These first three illustrate joint fit, and the last two items out of the nine, femoral head/neck exostosis and femoral head recontouring, refer to extra bone growth, a feature which may, or may not, cause arthritis later on. My own vet says, 'Let's face it, a 0/0 score is a fluke, but if a dog had one point only on each division, it would have virtually perfect hips, but a score of 18, well over the mean.' Similarly, if a dog scored 6/6 on subluxation, it would be a dysplastic, even though within the mean, so *where* a hip scores, and how heavily, is of the greatest significance.

It was put to me many years ago by a doctor, who is himself a springer breeder, that the springer doesn't have its own scoring system, but is scored exactly the same as other breeds. He felt that here there was a lack of logic, because of the unique movement of a stylish springer. When hunting, the hips swing like a pendulum, putting great strain on the lumbar vertebrae, although slipped discs are most uncommon. At the same time, the dog drives forward from the hocks, so theoretically, a two-way strain is put on the hip joint. My doctor friend said it was only logical that more laxity of the hip joint should be tolerated in the springer than in any other breed. I have discovered that a score of 2/3 subluxation in the most stylish specimens is commonplace, and carries them into old age. Neither is there any problem with their progeny.

Although the springer is listed as a possible sufferer from progressive retinal atrophy (PRA), I honestly believe that the pure working strains are completely clear, and only some show springers may be affected. There was a scare in the mid-1960s, when two or three working springers were diagnosed positive, but I believe these dogs had rare cases of retinal detachment (an extreme and uncommon phase of retinal dysplasia), before the eye examiners knew exactly what they were looking at. My theory has not been disputed by the leading eye specialist of the present day. Then, retinal dysplasia was positively diagnosed and it was panic stations. In hindsight, I believe RD has been with us since the year dot, before the springer divided into show and working types, and retinal detachment has been responsible over the decades for 'the odd blind dog' spoken of by the late John Kent, who ran his first spaniel trial in 1900. As it is a recessive condition, it can't be eliminated. This would involve wholesale test mating and destruction, in an attempt to eliminate a condition which usually causes only minimal problems, even in confirmed cases. Many clinical cases have perfect sight. Conversely, some clinically clear dogs are poor markers.

For many years I believed that the working cocker was free from all hereditary eye problems. One breeder tried to scare me many years ago over my Triple Championship winner, F.T.Ch. Speckle of Ardoon, who alleged that one of Speckle's bloodlines carried the more dangerous, recessive phase of generalized PRA, and even though Speckle proved clear on test, she should not be bred from. Fortunately I ignored this lady, who was a great theorist. Speckle has been very heavily line-bred to, with absolutely no untoward effects. However, when judging in Holland in 1991, I heard disturbing news. A very classy bitch running under me, about 6 years of age, had failing vision and had been diagnosed PRA positive. Her sire, an imported Scottish dog, also had PRA and had become blind. Nearer home, it has emerged that an excellent cocker which is still sighted at 9 years has sired a dog which is now blind. An examination of the blind dog's pedigree showed the suspect Scottish line on both sides.

To sum up, although spaniels have fewer hereditary problems than labradors, Clumber spaniels and golden retrievers, we must beware of a dangerous complacency.

7

Pre-Training Procedure

Ideally, your new puppy will have been inoculated at around 6 weeks of age against parvo virus by the breeder. Unfortunately, not all breeders are so meticulous and many are prepared to take chances to save the cost of the vaccine. In my view this is a short-sighted policy, as there is no telling when and where parvo will strike. Pups carry a certain immunity to the disease from their dam, but without a specific blood test, there is no knowing when maternal immunity will wane. A major difficulty is that if pups are injected with some brands of live vaccine, and they still contain maternal antibodies, these antibodies will override the live vaccine, thus rendering it ineffective. Bearing this in mind, I used to vaccinate with 'Kavac' dead vaccine. I never had a breakdown, then 'Nobi-vac' appeared on the market. Nobi-vac is a live vaccine, but the makers claim that in the majority of cases, it has the properties to override any residual maternal antibodies. Extensive field trials have been conducted in large breeding establishments where the virus is known to be endemic, with very convincing results. I vaccinate all my pups with Nobi-vac at 6 weeks, and, touch wood, so far it has worked for me. (As a layman in veterinary matters, it is perfectly ethical for me to discuss brand names of various vaccines, whereas vets are bound by the constraints of their profession and cannot mention brand names in print. I would also like to make it clear that I do not receive a 'cut' from the manufacturers of Nobi-vac either, more's the pity, but mention their product simply to render what I believe is the most up-to-date assistance to the reader.)

If the pup has not had its first parvo shot, it should be done immediately after purchase, then this should tide it over until the age of 12 weeks, when it should receive its initial course of injections for hardpad/distemper, hepatitis, two forms of leptospirosis and parvo again. Not less than two weeks later, and not later than four weeks after its main vaccination, the pup should have a second leptospirosis/parvo inoculation. This should see it safe for the next 12 months at least, but even so it is still not really safe to allow the pup contact with the outside world for at least 10 days after its final shot. A 'titre' must be given time to develop.

I do not believe that for the next four to six months, the springer pup should be given any formal training whatsoever. This is an important growing period for mind and body. It should be fed a good quality diet (avoid those with a lot of loose husks floating around in the bag) three times a day until it is 6 months of age, then twice a day until it reaches 12 months. I prefer gundogs to live outside, but this is a choice for the individual owner. However, particularly where a springer spaniel is concerned, they do not do well if merely fed, then dumped in a kennel and virtually forgotten until training age. A springer needs 'humanizing' and will benefit if brought into the house for limited periods. It can benefit the pup if it is played with by children, but only under supervision. Some children tend to be too rough with a pup; they must not throw things for it or indulge in a tug-of-war when the pup runs off with Teddy.

A pup should be given strictly controlled exercise, which is a valuable part of the humanizing process. A hundred yards out and back is quite sufficient for a very young pup, perhaps fifty would be safer. Excessive exercise can be damaging to the joints, particularly the hip joints. Apropos this matter, I have been told that it can be a very bad thing for a pup to live in a kennel which is designed so that a pup can spend long periods looking out, and standing on its hind legs. Further along these lines, some premium food manufacturers do not recommend that their products should be hopper-fed ad lib, as this can promote abnormal bone growth and possibly hip dysplasia.

During this period of early development, a springer pup's retrieving instincts should be stimulated, but never to the point of boredom. There is always a danger with a spaniel that if an interest in retrieving is not fostered quite early, it might decide later on that hunting is such fun that it will not be bothered about retrieving. Remember, going back to chapter 1, 'Origins of the Springer', the pup might carry the genes of non-retrieving springers from the distant past. I always use a small rabbit skin dummy. A whole dried rabbit skin, folded in three, then secured by string, and with nothing in the middle to weight it, seems ideal, but the choice is endless and even simple sock dummies can be very attractive to a pup. Two or three retrieves on any one occasion are sufficient, preferably in a fairly confined situation where it is more difficult for the pup to make rings round its handler. It can be a good idea to place oneself between the pup and its kennel, or alternatively, its bed. It is only natural for a puppy to be possessive over its retrieves. The retrieving instinct of the canine race is geared to two natural practices. One is to carry its own young from one place to another, and from this action stems the ability to retrieve tenderly *if the dog so wishes*. The other is to carry a kill, either to its own young ones, or to a more convenient location for personal consumption. With a young puppy, it is the latter instinct which comes to the fore when it retrieves, so do not expect the pup to deliver nicely to hand every time.

Similar traits can manifest themselves even among children. Some years ago, I had been shooting at a cocker trial in Suffolk. We adjourned to the keeper's house after the trial for a late lunch, and inside the house was the two-year-old daughter of the winner of the trial, who is now a very well-known professional trainer. I offered the little girl a piece of chocolate. She approached me very cautiously, then seized the chocolate and ran as fast as she could into the furthest corner of the room to eat it. This struck me as very primitive behaviour, which could have stemmed from very early times, when perhaps there was competition for food between children in primitive communities, just as there is still competition for food between puppies and wolf cubs.

During this pre-training period, I always allow a puppy to run straight in to a dummy with no attempt made to restrain it. Steadiness to the dummy should be firmly built into the pup's repertoire during training proper. An exception can sometimes be made when testing marking ability. On occasion, I will hold a puppy at chest level and throw the dummy downhill in full view. As soon as the dummy hits the ground, I set the pup down and let it go for the dummy. As it is not right on the tail of the dummy as it flies through the air, this is a better test of marking, and perseverance, should it not find the dummy right away and have to hunt for it.

If practical, introduction to water should be made during this period, avoiding very cold water, fast running water, very soft muddy margins into which the pup will sink, or steeply shelving banks.

Pups are notoriously catholic in their tastes over what they consider to be a desirable retrieve. After a spell of myxomatosis in the local rabbit population, there will be a seemingly endless supply of goodies in the form of dry, crow-picked skins and bones, corpses in varying degrees of putrefaction and live rabbits in varying stages of the disease. The spaniel owner must show considerable forbearance, accepting whatever the pup decides to retrieve, with no show of anger or disgust, otherwise the pup could be put off retrieving for life.

The owner should be very careful over livestock which the pup might chase and injure, such as sheep or poultry, or which could kill or injure the pup, like cattle or horses. It is far safer to keep pups right out of the way of potentially dangerous livestock, and always to keep them on a lead in the presence of sheep or poultry. It is also helpful if a young spaniel puppy can be exercised among sheep before it is sufficiently developed to chase them. I have a veterinary friend in Aberdeenshire who is a breeder and trainer of pointers – a breed very prone to sheep chasing unless carefully managed. As very small puppies they are taken among sheep and whenever she can see that the pups' eyes rest on a sheep, she growls at them, 'Arrrrgh! Nasty, smelly, dirty sheep!' Such admonishments seem to work if impressed upon them from an early age. It can work just as well with spaniels but as mentioned below, once a pup is steady to rabbits in the pen, it usually has minimal interest in sheep and a verbal rebuke should it look towards a sheep will be found to be sufficient. Once steadiness to game and rabbits is achieved, sheep and poultry should cause no problems later on. If, in spite of the best intentions of the owner, sheep or poultry should be encountered in a situation where such contact was not expected, the owner should chase the pup, catch it and put it on a lead with no outward show of displeasure. Pups will accept routine correction during the training course provided it is geared to the temperament and sensitivity of the pupil, but to punish in the heat of the moment, and in all probability too severely, could ruin a prospect for life.

The owner should have decided at the outset which method of introducing the pup to hunting should be used. There are basically three approaches. One is to take the pup into game-holding country where there is no farmstock and let it hunt and chase at will. This was the favoured method of Joe Greatorex, and as he made up 18 field trial champion spaniels, and won the Springer Championship six times, obviously, for Joe, the system worked. Another system is to let the pup have one or two chases, most probably within the confines of a rabbit pen, just to acquaint it with the idea that game exists, and that game means fun, then proceed right away with steadiness training. The third method is never to let the pup chase in its life, if one can help it, and make it stop to game from the first head it ever sees. The first method is to be recommended for trainers of exceptional ability, and conversely, for spaniels of very little ability and which require the maximum amount of stimulation. If they ever do get going, this sort are usually very easy to steady again when the time comes. The second method is the one most likely to suit the average trainer with the average dog, whatever this should constitute; it is the method I use for ordinary shooting dogs, which is my main concern at present, having virtually put field trials behind me. The third method would best suit the more timid handler who wishes to play safe, or the very exceptional dog which has so much inbuilt drive and quality, even before it knows what game is, that all that is required is to run it in a piece of country and curb its enthusiasm when the situations arise. However, such animals are extremely rare, perhaps being limited to one in a lifetime if one is lucky. The informed trainer can spot them when they do manifest themselves, and if they are sound in every other department, they will carry all before them in a trial career.

8

Training Equipment

Gundog training is hardly a high-tech activity, and provided one has the necessary latent aptitude for the job, the actual training equipment needed is fairly basic and the end product is unlikely to be enhanced by a plenitude of gimmicks and gadgets. A whistle is essential, or two if you favour one to turn and recall, another to stop. For years I used a stagshorn or plastic whistle with pea to turn, and an 'Acme Thunderer' metal whistle to stop; however, after some time I abandoned the pea-type whistle, as when it was blown frequently the pea would become damp and jam up, causing the whistle to emit an unfamiliar sound. I finally decided also that the mighty blast of the Thunderer was really taking a sledgehammer to crack a nut. I now use an Acme 210½ for all purposes. I use two pips to turn, several to recall, and one hard, sharp blast to stop. I care not at all for the 'silent' type of metal whistle. I believe trial handlers who use this type are trying to fool the judge into believing what quiet handlers they are. They should try this on a judge who is wearing a hearing aid. This device amplifies the sound of a silent whistle, so the judge is made aware most forcibly just how much the whistle is being used.

A respected colleague, now regrettably deceased, the late

Ron Dukes, had little time for the silent whistle either. He had some pheasants to look after down a wood, and at feeding time, as an experiment, blew various whistles at the birds. No pattern of whistle, not even the great Thunderer, upset the game, but the silent whistle had them running for their lives. It has also been brought to my attention that rats can be shifted from warehouses by continuously playing very high frequency sounds, so the disturbing influence of this device on game is a very real question.

Next on the list is a lead, preferably several, for if you are anything like me, you will lose them with some regularity, or your friends will 'borrow' them on permanent loan. I do not use a metal choke chain, as advocated by the late Barbara Woodhouse, and now apparently debunked by animal behaviourist Dr Roger Mugford. I use a soft nylon slip rope. A shoulder bag is essential in which to carry one's bits and pieces. I do not use a heavy, elaborate game bag, but one of these small things which can be picked up at any army surplus stores. I favour rabbit skin covered dummies for both young and older dogs but use canvas dummies for water work, as a skin dummy becomes soggy and unpleasant. I also use canvas dummies for routine retrieving work, provided the dog will accept them. Most will, but the odd dog refuses to have anything to do with a canvas dummy.

Various objects which will make varying degrees of noise are of course essential to all forms of gundog training. It is a complex subject and requires a chapter on its own. An excellent source of supply for all training equipment is: Messrs Turner Richards, Cardigan Street, Birmingham B4 7SA (tel. 0121–359–5577).

Never, but never, be inveigled into believing that the electric training collar has any place in the training armoury of the gundog trainer. It is a diabolical device and nobody can guess how many gundogs have been ruined by its incorrect application. Even 'correctly' used it can create its own set of problems. It can mask temperamental faults and put into the winners' circle, and thereby the breeding pool, a dog which can then pass on its own faults, most likely hard-headedness and dishonesty, to a good many of its offspring.

If you live in the United States or Canada, or in any country where there are dangerous beasties, such as poisonous snakes or porcupines, both of which can spell death to an inquisitive gundog, then the use of an electric collar for creating aversion therapy is fully justified. Better a shocked dog than a dead dog. But as a training aid, *per se*, Never, Never, Never.

9

Dogging Guns and Ammo

Unless a gundog is to be relegated purely to falconry or short-wing hawking, an absolute essential in its make-up must surely be its complete fearlessness of gunfire. All good gundog training manuals deal with this subject in greater or lesser measure, but little has been written in depth on the actual instruments with which to achieve this most necessary state. Of course we will always have the character who never reads training books or articles, who takes his new pup out and fires a 12-bore over its head 'to see if it is gun-shy'. The remarkable thing is that some of these people get away with it, and save themselves quite a lot of the training time which more circumspect trainers spend on trying to do the job right, and avoid ruining for life those dogs which would be affected adversely by such insensitive treatment.

In the latest training manual to come into my possession, the chapter dealing with introduction to gunfire jumps straight from using a starting pistol firing short blanks, to a 12-bore, enlisting the aid of an assistant to fire the pistol/shotgun at varying distances. I cannot fault the procedure outlined and I am sure it will work for the writer, who trains spaniels and retrievers only, but I train alone and also occasionally include pointers and setters, over which breeds gun technique differs from the retrieving breeds. I don't believe that under my particular circumstances I am being over-cautious to build up the gunfire training with a fairly comprehensive ascending scale of noise-producing weaponry. Several years ago, an abominable training pistol was marketed which had no barrel to contain the report. It simply exploded a .22 long rifle blank in a hand-operated revolving chamber, producing a terrible crack, which hurt even *my* eardrums. I soon abandoned this monstrosity and acquired a converted .38 ex-service revolver, which fired black powder blanks. This gun gave a loud, flat report and was useful for more advanced pupils, but the price of the ammunition increased over the years to more than shotgun cartridges, so I disposed of it. I now start all my puppies with a .22 pistol, firing the short 'extra loud' blank, which is not really loud at all. This is a most useful device but unfortunately I seem unable to find a really good quality pistol, and I get more misfires than reports.

When things are progressing satisfactorily I move on to a shotgun, but only a .410. This is a converted 7 mm Mauser, model 1907. I don't normally use it for shooting, but simply to make a bang. However, there was an occasion when I was working on a very touchy young Irish setter bitch. I was working her with an old experienced pointer, intending to fire a shot when the old dog located birds, and had done this a couple of times without producing an adverse reaction in the red bitch, when the pointer roaded out a nice covey of grouse, with the red bitch backing. The birds presented themselves just right for the .410 and I shot one, allowing the young bitch to lick the head of the bird, then nibble it off as I held the body safely in my hand. This was an old American quail hunter's ploy and it worked. It was subsequently proved to have been 'the making' of her.

So much can be done for the young spaniel or retriever by incorporating the retrieve in the gunfire training. The anticipation of the retrieve, and the flight of the dummy through the air, both help to distract the pupil from the actual shot. This is not possible with the young bird-dog. It was therefore no surprise when I stayed with the famous pointer and setter man, the late John Nash, from Co. Limerick, to find a 20-bore standing in the corner of his tack room, this bore being ideal for shooting over sensitive young bird-dogs. Years later, I found myself in possession of a promising young pointer whose initial contact with a pistol had not been brought about in the correct context before I acquired him. His was a stubborn case of gun-nervousness. I started the cure by running him hard on the mountain until he was thirsty, then stopping him, pouring him a drink, retreating rapidly a few yards, then firing a 2″ .410 cartridge, pointed away from him. It started the cure and I shot a few grouse over him with a borrowed 20-bore. Things were developing well. Then I shot over him with my 16-bore and we were back to square one. I have used this gun since I was 17 and it has never caused any problems, but this pointer took an intense dislike to its particular report. So I bought an AYA No.3 20-bore of my own. I gradually rehabilitated the pointer, then moved him on to a 12-bore.

When moving on to the shotguns, I give consideration to the type of ammunition which I use. In the old days, for my 16-bore, I used either Eley Grand Prix 15/16 oz or Gallyon's hand-loaded 1 oz loads. Latterly, a bewildering selection of foreign cartridges has appeared on the market, some extremely effective, and considered by many shooters to have proved superior to home-grown products. They tend to be of higher velocity, but this can be a disadvantage when working with sensitive young dogs. I start the young dogs either with Eley or Jones Bros. special light loads. Jones Bros., of the North Wales Shooting School, near Chester, supply their own 11/16 oz 20-bore loads and 15/16 oz 12-bore cartridges. Both are very gentle loads and ideal for a young dog's first few head of game. When I am sure the pupil is fully confident, I move on to something Continental and lively.

I have so far deliberately avoided any mention of the popular and potentially very useful dummy launcher. This is because I believe it has no place in early puppy training. It produces a peculiar report, rather like a huge cork coming out of a champagne bottle, which many dogs find disconcerting, even when fully confident with the shotgun. But individual attitudes vary. Many dogs will accept the launcher, and in these cases it can be a most useful tool for teaching advanced retrieving work, particularly in schooling for Game Fair events and the like. It is unrivalled at placing a succession of blind retrieves out in the training area, whilst the dog is still in its kennel. It saves much pedestrian activity on the part of the trainer and avoids fouling the area with human footscent, which many cunning dogs can use to their advantage.

10

Early Obedience Lessons

All authorities, from General Hutchinson, through Richard Sharpe to Peter Moxon (former Kennel Editors to *Shooting Times*), agree that the most important aspect of gundog training by far is the early obedience course. All the gamefinding ability, style and drive in the world will be as nought unless this power can be harnessed, and the end product works for its handler rather than itself. With some breeds, like pointers and setters, control can be minimal. Provided the dog does not chase farmstock and can be kept more or less on its beat by command, precise range is unimportant, as one is not working within fine limits, and the dog's pointing ability acts as a built-in brake when game is encountered. In America there is often no requirement for steadiness to wing and shot. No such latitude can be allowed in the case of the springer, if it is to be in any way effective. We are working within much finer limits, as the spaniel should flush its game immediately upon contact, which means that unless the game is flushed within shot of the gun, the operation will be unfruitful. It follows that if the game is to be flushed within shot of the gun, the dog must at all times be within range also. This is not always the easiest thing to bring about, which is why the springer must be so spot on in its obedience in order that it has the responsiveness to command which will produce instant results, absolutely every time of asking.

The training course as a whole is important, but if I were asked which facet of obedience work was of the greatest importance, unhesitatingly I would say the sit and stay. The sit prevents any further forward movement on the springer's part and, keen hunter though we require it to be, there are so many situations where the dog is required to come to a full stop: when we require a dog to sit down, simply to have a lead put on it; when it flushes a rabbit, and it is the dog's natural instinct to keep on going, but we require that it should desist; when game is shot, and forward motion should cease, while the dog marks the game and awaits the command to retrieve; when we need to cross a dangerous barbed wire fence, and require the springer to stop to command while we unload the gun, then lift the springer over the barbed wire. There are lots of other reasons why the stop to command must be so firmly embedded, and the natural follow-on, the stay, teaches patience and a willingness to wait for the next command.

To teach this lesson, I used simply to take the pup into a field and endeavour to get my hand on its hindquarters and push it down to the command, 'hup'. However, since those early days I have trained several pointers and setters, dogs which as youngsters are encouraged to get out and run, covering considerable distances in the process, and the only way to teach these dogs to drop to command is by keeping them on a lead. Nowadays, I always use this system with a spaniel. (I cannot think why I did not latch onto the idea sooner, but remember the years of discomfort which were suffered by farmers and tractor drivers before anyone thought of putting a weatherproof cab on a tractor!) The pup will be used to being on a lead, but will have been allowed to pull if it wishes, as strict lead/heel work is not dealt with at this stage. Holding the lead in one hand, I put pressure on his hindquarters with the other, push him right down and give the firm command 'hup'. This is repeated continually until he begins to get the message, and eventually will sit down to the command alone without hand pressure. This lesson can tell me an awful lot about the dog as a training prospect. Some springers dislike even simple obedience work, and resent being made to sit down and would rather one did not bother them. Their resentment will be shown by dropped tail and laid-back ears and a generally miserable demeanour. Such animals are seldom likely to make the very best, but in all probability will improve to a useful standard and gradually become more co-operative. I like a springer to look happy during these early obedience lessons, even though he may offer more resistance than the 'softer' dog. It does not worry me how many times I have to push him down provided his tail keeps going, his ears are pricked and he maintains an eager expression in his eyes. When he will sit to command on the lead, I will take some of the mental pressure off him by walking him on to a fresh bit of ground before attempting to 'hup' him again. The advantage of teaching a pup to sit to command whilst on a lead is that it enables one to circumvent a bit of mischief should it arise. Some dogs, when learning the hup, will at the first opportunity dodge past one and dart back towards their kennel. A length of cord will prevent the pup getting away with this, as one can simply restrain him by the cord and put him back where he should be.

The next move should be to incorporate the 'stay', as a natural follow-on to the hup. Once one feels the hup is firmly understood, one should commence to move away backwards, very slowly indeed, from the seated pup. It is best to move away only a few yards at first, remaining vigilant towards any attempt on the part of the pup to move, and if it should, to move forward immediately, pick up the pup and place it firmly on the original spot. If all remains well and the pup stays down whilst one retreats three or four yards, walk back to the pup and make a big fuss of him. This should be repeated several times, gradually increasing the distance between the pup and oneself until the pup is well used to the procedure and will sit there reliably until he is willing to be left for quite a distance. This is a most valuable lesson, I find, for getting the pup to focus its attention on me. When I first begin to leave the seated pup as I move away from it, the pup does not invariably keep its eyes on me. Even if it does not attempt to move from the hupped position, its eyes may wander. It may chew grass, or nibble sheep dung. It may pay attention to any passing birds, from a finch to a buzzard, and generally allow its mind to wander. The remedial action is to give a sharp hup command, even though the pup is still seated, to get its head around and concentrate on me again. I find that the further I can ease myself away, the more likely is the pup to concentrate. Curiosity takes over, and the further I recede into the distance, the more interested the pup becomes in what I am doing. The more interesting the pup finds me, to the exclusion of grass, sheep dung and buzzards, the better I find I am concentrating its mind and the rapport which is developing between us becomes stronger. As for the duration of these lessons, I would say they should not last longer than 10 minutes, with an outside limit of 15 minutes, and I would say no more lessons should be given than about five days out of every seven. It does not matter when the odd day is missed. If the pup is of the right breeding, it is not going to forget what you have taught it in a single day. A rest now and then will give you both time to recharge your mental batteries.

When it becomes apparent that the sitting and staying lessons are bearing fruit, and a reasonable rapport between dog and handler is manifesting itself, we have reached the point where these lessons can be tied in with the recall/turning whistles. During the sitting and staying lessons, it is important that after a successful sit and wait, while the handler walks away, then approaches the pup to release it from the drop again, the handler should always cast the pup *forward* again. This is to prevent the annoying habit developing during more advanced lessons, and persisting into its shooting or trial career, of moving in towards the handler after being stopped on the whistle, prior to being directed out *away* from the handler on a blind retrieve. Springers are apt to develop this frustrating habit at the least excuse, whereas retrievers are far less likely to be so affected. When the idea is well ingrained into the springer pup, that after a sit and wait it is then sent forward into the country again, the business can be done in reverse to encourage whistle response. After leaving the pup on the drop and walking away quite a distance, the handler calls the pup in towards him with the whistle. Most springers have an acute and natural response to a whistle. Additionally, although the pup has learned the sit and stay lesson well, it has been taught against his natural inclinations. He would rather not sit and stay, and would prefer to be either with his handler, or rooting about in front, showing the rudiments of natural hunting, so when the handler calls the pup in, he obeys the whistle because he is glad of the excuse to race back to his handler. A command which coincides with the pup's own wishes is seldom likely to be ignored. Response to the 'come in' whistle is therefore pleasurable. It signals release from that damnable drop and wait.

Once the 'come in' response has become ingrained, it is surprising how easily this can normally be converted to the very important turn whistle when hunting. When a springer is in motion it is surprising how very rare it is, on hearing the whistle used as a turning command, for it to come all the way in to the handler, as it did, quite correctly, when this whistle response was first taught. After the pup has turned, most respond naturally to a hand signal to left or right to continue moving across the handler's front.

Very rarely, a rebellious pupil may be encountered which, on being recalled from the drop, instead of coming in cleanly to the handler, noses around the area of the drop and refuses to come in. I would regard this as a rather bad indication regarding the trainability and co-operation of such a pup, but they cannot all be 'top drawer' and one must try to improve the responses of such a less than desirable animal. I would lay a long, light cord from the pup's neck to myself and take a pocketful of goodies, which could be either bread, bits of 'mousetrap' cheese or pieces of tripe (better carried in the training bag than in the pocket!) (Here American readers may be somewhat nonplussed. Despite EEC regulations, some of us in Great Britain can obtain a supply of raw ox tripe, but in America it seems that this commodity for feeding is completely unobtainable.) So with a stubborn case as outlined, I would back away to the end of the line I have laid; I would give the recall whistle and gently tow the pup towards me and give it a bit of something to eat, and repeat the process until it became ingrained in the pup's subconscious that a recall whistle and a return to the handler means something to eat, just as in the case of a hawk or falcon, a return to the lure means a bit of meat to eat. It is worth bearing in mind that a raptor is flown hungry, so by the same token, a pup with an empty stomach is far more likely to respond to this lesson positively than a pup with a full, or even a half-full digestive system, so be prepared to take a rather hard line in this respect. This also applies to any other situation which it is thought might be improved by the use of food.

Next on the training agenda is the stop whistle, which is relatively easy to teach provided the homework has been really well done regarding the verbal 'hup'. Usually one can dispense with a lead or cord, although this is optional. The basic principle is simply to give the chosen whistle blast to hup, immediately followed by the verbal hup command. It is not usually too long before the pup will hup to the whistle alone. The routine should be varied. The pup should be cast off in front and made to stop a few yards from the handler. It should be stopped by the whistle. The handler should walk away, then give it the recall whistle and attempt to stop it halfway in by whistle and raised hand. Some come in so fast that it is difficult for them to stop, so one must persevere on this exercise. It is most important what should be done after a successful stop. The pup must *never* then be called in the rest of the way, lest the habit of coming right in to the handler should become ingrained, to the detriment of it being sent out away from the handler in a blind retrieving situation later on in its working career. After the dog has been stopped on the way in, the handler must walk up to it and make a big fuss of it, to convey to the dog that it has done the right thing in stopping, then it *must* be cast forward again. It is important to be circumspect over just how much drill should be given to the pupil in this respect. Remember, none of these exercises are in any way pleasurable to the dog, so too much could make a soft dog 'sticky' and uncooperative, so it is up to the individual to make the correct assessment of each pupil's temperament with regard to just how much pressure would be acceptable to it.

11

Steadiness to Dummies and Retrieving

Just because, as I write, I happen to be sitting in a part of Great Britain, I will not assume that I am writing solely for a British readership. As far as the early obedience lessons outlined above are concerned, I do not think they can be bettered in any culture, but from now on we may have come to a dividing of the ways, as certain aspects of training for more advanced spaniel work can differ according to one's country.

In Britain, during formal training, it is more usual to follow the procedures designed to bring a springer somewhere near field trial or working test standard. Bearing this in mind, spaniels are commonly trained to be steady to a thrown dummy, then later on, steady to the shot and fall of game, despite the fact that most 'Saturday shooting spaniels' are not steady to shot and fall. However, lip-service is paid to the principle of the steady spaniel and all professional trainers educate their pupils towards this end, even though in the majority of cases the springer's owner quickly undoes the trainer's work in this sphere and before long the dog is running in with the best (or worst!) Few American or Italian hunters require a springer to remain steady to shot game; in fact many overseas sportsmen pour scorn on the idea of a steady springer, or indeed any other breed of gundog they may be hunting with. Many believe that the quicker the dog arrives at the fall, the less likelihood there is of the bird gaining too great an advantage if it happens to be a runner, or 'cripple' in American parlance. Up to a point this is true, but I would insert a clause that the springer must be a really good one to have this amount of latitude allowed and still remain effective. It must be an absolutely spot-on marker. Nothing 'hypes' a springer up more than being allowed to run in to its birds; therefore, in the event of a mismark, the dog will be so intent on doing its own thing and madly hunting the wrong area that it could well prove impossible to direct it to the right area of the fall. In this way, far more time could be lost on a running bird than if the dog had remained steady and gone out on command. It must be appreciated that if a springer is allowed to run in to fall, this is likely to develop a high degree of marking ability, but on the occasions when there is a mismark, the commonest happening is for the dog to overshoot the fall and carry on hunting too far out. In this situation there is a strong likelihood of the dog flushing unshot game which owing to the frame of mind it is in, it is very likely to chase, thus using energy which would have been better spent in further controlled hunting. And so for ordinary shooting I favour a springer which is steady in all departments at all times, although I respect the views of persons who, for the reasons outlined, prefer a 'hair trigger' springer.

Assuming that a person does require a steady spaniel, I will outline the steadying course, but will first examine just what our hypothetical springer's attitude is to the actual act of porterage. Quite recently, in the sporting press, this subject has caused quite a little comment, as some persons have experienced considerable difficulty in finding a truly natural retrieving springer puppy. No current 'expert' has been able to produce any coherent answer beyond a lot of uninformed waffle, but I would say the problem is symptomatic of the ups and downs of breeding. There are not all that many 'fashionable' springer sires in the country.

There may be several potentially good sires, but as they are unfashionable they are seldom used; so one only needs one or two fashionable sires with a tendency to pass on negative retrieving ability, and the sheer volume of pups by such sires considerably enhances the chances of a person finding themselves lumbered with a difficult retriever. Even some pups which are keen on the dummy can display a bewildering repertoire of variations on the theme of not quite doing the job to complete satisfaction. Some come in so far then put the dummy down and commence to pull it to bits. Others persistently circle the handler due to sheer possessiveness. Possibly the most common deviant behaviour is to drop the dummy a yard or more from the handler. The answer commonly given to overcome all these problems is to walk or run away from the pup, calling its name in the hope that it will follow and one can unobtrusively reach down and take the dummy, and practise this until the pup becomes so used to the dummy being taken from it that eventually the handler can stand his ground and the pup will come right up. For the persistent circler, a narrow retrieving alley might do the trick, followed by retrieving from an area of heavy grass, where the pup finds it is not quite so mobile; and a heavier dummy, say 2½ pounds in weight, might be conducive to keeping its mind on the job. The pup which comes so far, then lays down with the dummy, can cause the biggest problem of all. Here the Americans are ahead of us. Having fewer inhibitions than we do, they have a short answer to any such problems: force retrieving. They even use 'forcing tables' with an overhead, rigid wire, with a running choke chain which runs along the length of the wire; the dog is made to hold the dummy and walk slowly along the table with the dummy in its mouth. I suppose one purpose of the table is to spare the trainer's back. Without a table, forcing the retrieve of a springer necessitates bending over the dog for quite significant periods, which could play havoc with one's discs.

Just as the question of docking working spaniels is not understood by some vets and some gundog owners who do not own spaniels, so force retrieving is widely misunderstood in Great Britain. H. W. Carlton refers to it in his *Spaniels: Their Breaking for Sport and Field Trials* as 'the dreaded French system', which implies that it is a severe form of training. It need not be. For a start, the name is unfortunate. Secondly, some of its American exponents, more in the retriever world than among spaniel people, use severe methods, such as a pair of pliers applied to the dog's ear or a cord twisted tightly round a front toe. I have even seen a picture of a rather tough-looking young lady applying what appeared to be a form of semi-strangulation to a Chesapeake Bay retriever on a forcing table, but in her defence, I suppose one could point out that the temperament of the American-bred Chesapeakes, compared to springer spaniels, is 'something else'. One must also consider the long-term effects one form of force retrieving could have upon a breed. Some trainers ultimately can force a complete non-retriever, without a vestige of natural instinct, to pick up any object. If such animals get into the breeding pool I think it is unnecessary to spell out their potential for harm, if one should hope to keep natural retrieving to the fore in a springer bloodline. But when a young springer obviously has a keen interest in retrieving but is determined to be deliberately naughty, I believe there is a case for tidying up its retrieve.

In the past, I have passed the buck and suggested that anyone interested in the procedure should read Maurice Hopper's book *Spaniel Training for Modern Shooters*. Unfortunately Maurice is now dead and his excellent training manual is out of print, so I feel it is incumbent upon me to outline the procedure. It is best delayed until the pupil is at least 12 months of age, and the process commences with the dog on a lead. The principle involves applying a degree of discomfort to the dog, so it will open its mouth in protest, whereupon a dummy is placed in its mouth. The principle underlying the process is one of simple psychology. No dummy in its mouth equals discomfort. Holding a dummy without spitting it out means a cessation of discomfort. Arguably the best way to apply discomfort is to pinch its ear between thumbnail and first finger, working on the same spot every time. This is, after all, what a boss dog is very likely to do to a recalcitrant young kennel or pack member, using its teeth of course, to show it who is the leader. An alternative is to press the dog's upper lips against its teeth, or a foot, not clad in a rubber boot, can be pressed with minimum force on either a front or hind foot. Immediately the dog opens its mouth, a command should be given: 'take it', 'hold it', or what you will, but it must be consistent. Jim DeVoll, arguably the top American spaniel trainer of the present day, if faced with an extremely sensitive springer whose retrieve requires schooling, does not even pinch the ear. He continually rubs the ear on the same spot until the pupil opens its mouth to demand what the hell he is doing! The whole process should be deliberate, as gentle as possible and completely uncompromising. Every time it spits the dummy out, the process must be repeated without fail until the command alone suffices for the dog to take the dummy from the trainer's hand.

As the process advances, the dog should be made to sit up in front of its trainer, holding the dummy in the polished sitting delivery position, for up to thirty seconds at a time, then the dummy should be gently disengaged and much praise given for holding it. There are some dogs which, having reached this stage, would, if a dummy was thrown for them, run out, pick up the dummy and present it with a sitting delivery, but the majority require further schooling to consolidate the process. I walk them alongside me with the dummy in their mouths, then every now and then I hup them, make them face me and present me with a sitting delivery. Not all will take this in their stride. Immediately one tries to walk them, they will drop the dummy, which must be put back in their mouths again with a little 'reminder' from earlier on in the process. Some can be quite stubborn and strain on the lead in the hup position and be reluctant to walk, but one must persevere, as gently as possible, replacing the dummy every time they drop it until the desired object is achieved and the pupil will walk on the lead holding the dummy. A follow-on from this exercise is to leave the dog sitting with the dummy in its mouth, then back away several yards, the object then being to call the dog in and accept a sitting delivery. Often the dummy will be dropped on the point of delivery, then it must be replaced and the process repeated until the dog will come in, sit and retain the dummy.

The next step is to throw, or place the dummy in full view. I use a narrow tarmac road for this exercise, so there is no danger of the pupil striking a fresh rabbit scent which might distract it from the dummy. I also use a nice fresh rabbit skin dummy, not the one I have been carrying out the exercises with. Usually, this is the point where light appears at the end of the tunnel, but if the dog still refuses to get it all together, do not despair. This whole business is, in my book, only partial forcing. It differs from the technique which some use to force the complete non-retriever to pick up off the floor. This is far more intense and involves an element of fear. The dog just *dare not* refuse to pick up the dummy, whereas my system of coercing a natural but untidy retriever attempts to mould its natural retrieving instincts into what I want. In the rare case where the exercise seems to break down and apparent stalemate is reached, it is surprising what usually happens when lessons are suspended for several days and the dog is tried on a retrieve again. Often it will be found that what has not been achieved directly from the previous instruction will have worked in retrospect, and the dog goes out, returns, sits up and delivers. An interesting facet of part force retrieving is that sometimes a dog which has perhaps been less than co-operative in other directions becomes a changed animal and far easier to get on with, and an animal which has been rather cold-natured can become far more affectionate, quite the reverse effect to what those who would oppose this system through ignorance might expect. I suppose it puts the trainer, once and for all, in the position of 'Boss Dog', or as some grandly say, without really knowing what they mean, 'it establishes my leadership', when in actual fact they couldn't lead a pack of Brownies!

I am sometimes asked about the value of rewards in retrieval training. These are really only useful should a pup appear cold and aloof and unwilling to make a fuss of its trainer's hand. An edible reward can establish a pleasant connection with a human hand. Rewards can be valuable in overcoming gun nervousness, as will be explained in chapter 12, but the mental process of the dog is not sufficiently advanced to associate a reward with a job well done and if, say, coupled with retrieving exercises, could cause the pup to drop the retrieve prematurely in anticipation of the edible reward.

So having got the matter of retrieving out of the way, whether it has been there naturally without a hitch, or whether modified force has been used (which can take from about three to ten days, on an almost daily basis, assuming that the training is going to follow conventional lines), we reach the point of steadiness to the dummy. If I had my choice, this exercise would be conducted on completely flat, bare ground. There are some who state that retrieves should always be thrown into cover, in order that the dog is encouraged to use its nose. Fair enough, but if heredity dictates that a dog has it about it to use its nose, use the wind, or get its nose down on a line, a few completely seen retrieves used for a specific purpose are not going to kill its natural instincts overnight. I want the pupil to see the dummy fall on bare ground to be exposed to maximum temptation, and when I do send it for the retrieve, I want the dog to reach it in minimum time, so I can proceed with the lesson. Difficult retrieves in thick cover can come later in the curriculum. Just as the Sioux Indians have a different way of skinning a grey squirrel from the method I would use, so is there more than one way of steadying a springer to a dummy. One can find a V-shaped corner in a field, hup the dog in the apex of the V, stand several yards away and throw the dummy out into the field over one's shoulder, keeping one's eyes firmly on the dog. If it tries to make a break for the dummy, as the dog has to pass the handler, this maximizes one's chances of stopping the dog by voice or stop whistle. If the dog is too quick and beats the handler to the dummy, it must be accepted with good grace and no show of irritation, then one must try again. If the dog manages a partial run-in, it must be carried back to its starting point and the dummy must be picked by hand. It must never be given a retrieve until it remains steady, then it is better to count to twenty or thirty before sending the dog for the dummy. Repetition over a few days will drive this lesson home, with a maximum of four retrieves per session.

All these early steadiness lessons have taken place with the springer sitting on the drop. Now the regime must be varied. The pup should be cast off to hunt and when it is to the right of the handler, the dummy should be thrown to the left, or if the dog is to the left, vice versa. It is almost certain to forget its steadiness lessons and attempt to run in, but if the handler has positioned everything properly, he will be in an excellent position to stop the dog as it attempts to cross his front. The dog should be carried back to its starting point. The handler should thank providence he is not training a Newfoundland, and the dummy should be picked by hand. The process should be repeated until the dog will actually drop at the sight of the dummy sailing through the air, no matter at what angle the springer is in relation to the handler. It is worth bearing in mind that when training in hill country, as I am perpetually, a springer is far more likely to run in on a retrieve if the dummy is thrown downhill, and on account of its momentum, is virtually impossible to stop. I daresay some will remember a Spaniel Championship winner which ran in on a downhill rabbit in a February rabbit trial at Vivod, not five miles from where I write. Conversely, an uphill retrieve will offer less temptation and these are very useful for consolidating the steadiness exercises. The whole purpose of all steadiness exercises is to demonstrate to the dog what you would like him to do, rather than bully him into not doing what his instincts tell him to do. There are many contradictions in the training of a spaniel, more so than in the case of any other group of gundog. This is where good temperament is such a tremendous asset. It means that he will accept such contradictions with a good grace and at all times will demonstrate that very desirable will to please.

An alternative method of teaching steadiness to the thrown dummy might commend itself where there is a combination of a quick spaniel and a slow handler (and let's face it, we all slow down sooner or later): that is, to put a cord on the springer and tie the opposite end to something immovable. There should be sufficient slack on the cord so the pup feels no tension and does not know it is restrained but there should not be such a large amount of slack that when the pupil dashes forward, it is able to gain sufficient momentum to break its own neck or slip a disc. The dummy is thrown, the pup attempts to dash in and the command 'hup' or the stop whistle is applied just as the cord brings it up short. It should be picked up and moved back to its original starting point, given another hup command and the cord should be surreptitiously removed, so the pup does not realize it is free, and so does not dash off after the dummy without command. After a wait of several seconds, it should be sent for the retrieve. Having been brought up short by the cord, the chances are it will have lost its mark on the dummy so this is where it is a big advantage to conduct this exercise on a bare field, so it can soon spot the dummy lying there. There should be repetition of this exercise until the pup makes no attempt to run in when the dummy is thrown, which usually comes about surprisingly quickly, then one can proceed along the lines outlined in the first method, where the trainer stands in front of the dog and throws the dummy over his shoulder. Another alternative is to use a shorter cord and hold the loop in one's hand (a stout leather glove might be advisable to prevent rope burn in the case of a person who has soft hands); as before, the pup is restrained by the cord as it rushes off for the dummy. The rest of the procedure is exactly the same as the method where the loop of the cord is fixed to something solid.

12

Introducing the Gun

I have already discussed in some depth the noise-making equipment which I use during gundog training. I will now explain the most important matter of application.

Some trainers think it is a good idea to fire the first shot over a puppy when it seems to be enjoying itself and having a good rummage round. I am not keen on this idea, as I believe the shot may catch it unawares and startle it. I should explain that true gun-shyness, which manifests itself in the dog bolting for home and trying to hide, is all but unknown in the springer spaniel and I have not seen a case for over 30 years. This condition is thought to be incurable and hereditary, but gun-nervousness can be quite common, is frequently man-made and usually can be cured by an informed trainer, but if clumsily handled, can become so ingrained that the end result turns out virtually as bad as gun-shyness.

My own system of introduction to the gun begins with the springer being seated while I walk about 50 yards away. After his earlier sitting and staying exercises, his attention obviously is fully upon me. I fire the pistol which takes the very short 'extra loud' blank, and note his reaction. He should remain absolutely immobile, with ears well pricked forward; if he shows no adverse reaction, and few will at that distance and with that particular weapon, I call him in and make a fuss of him. I repeat the procedure at about 30 yards and if he still appears happy enough, I position him about 15 yards away – but this time, immediately after the shot and ensuring that he is looking in the right direction, I throw a dummy in full view. After a much shorter wait than I have imposed during steadiness to the dummy exercises, say three seconds, I send him for the retrieve. This is sufficient for a first lesson and the process is then repeated on subsequent days, then something heavier is substituted for the pistol in the shape of the .410. Initially, I use 2 ½ " cartridges but with the shot removed. These produce a flat, hollow report and are an excellent follow-on to the small pistol. I work the .410 in exactly the same way as the pistol, then give a couple of lessons with the cartridges containing shot. If everything is progressing smoothly, I move on to the 20-bore, but for some obscure reason, if I remove the shot from the 20-bore cartridges, I can get no sort of report at all, so I have to move straight on to shotted cartridges. As mentioned in my earlier chapter on training weaponry, I use the lightest loads possible and particularly avoid Winchesters, which are an excellent shooting cartridge but are too sharp for this exercise. (I use Jones Bros. or Eley.) If everything goes well with the 20-bore I do not progress for the time being to the 12-bore, as the springer's first rabbits will be shot over him with the 20-bore and, once he develops a taste for real shooting, the changeover to 12-bore will be taken in his stride.

In all exercises involving early gun work, care must be exercised at all times over the location one chooses. The outside of a wood, the inside of a wood, or anywhere near farm buildings are to be avoided, as such places can produce a frightening echo. I am always most meticulous over wind direction and make sure that in all training exercises, the wind is blowing from the pupil to me and never vice versa.

Unfortunately things do not progress as straightforwardly

as we would hope for in a minority of cases. Some pups are more sensitive to a shot than others. On hearing a shot, the pup may flinch and turn its ears back. Even if it simply ducks its head this signifies that all is not well. If one were simply to continue with the exercises regardless, the situation would get worse and worse. The idea that if the pup hears more and more shots, he will get used to gunfire, is a completely false one. He will become more and more introverted until his case is as hopeless as that of the dog which is truly gun-shy. At the first sign of gun-nervousness, one must be prepared to back-pedal and take a completely different tack. One course of action is to take the pup into a pen full of rabbits and let him chase them to kingdom come. When it is obvious that he is really steamed up, a shot should be fired when he is in hot pursuit and well away from his handler. Initially, one should use the calibre of gun below that to which he has reacted adversely, unless of course he has shown a reaction even to the small pistol, in which case there is no alternative but to use the pistol for the start of the cure. There are few springers whose confidence cannot be built up in this manner, gradually moving up a weapon as his confidence increases. However, this form of therapy can prove to be a two-edged sword. I am never worried about letting a springer pup have a few chases and will actively encourage it in some circumstances, but when operating such a therapeutic regime, for a time the rabbit chase becomes the centre of the pup's whole existence. It encourages him not only to chase but also to run in to shot. An experienced trainer can combat both conditions but the novice could well find him/herself in grave difficulty.

It is possible to play safe and use another less drastic method, which plays on the pup's natural greed. It must be kept on short rations for three days. The American writer Charles (Chuck) Goodhall advocated complete starvation for this period. The pup should then be taken onto familiar training ground, with the proviso that it must not be training ground where previously it has reacted unfavourably to shot. The pup should be left with an assistant while the trainer walks away about 100 yards. The trainer fires a shot and at this signal, the assistant slips the pup and the trainer blows the recall whistle. As the pup comes up to him, he holds out a piece of tripe, cheese or bread. I prefer tripe or bread, as if the pup is partially unnerved, it might not be prepared to put the effort into chewing a piece of cheese, whereas tripe or bread slip down its throat quite easily. Most pups respond well to this system, which then progresses to diminishing distances and louder weaponry. When progress appears to have been made, the trainer can take the pup out alone, using nothing more potent than the small pistol, and can toss bits of food for the pup to the accompaniment of a pistol shot.

I had such a case to deal with recently. We had some tremendous thunderstorms which may have exacerbated the problem. I used a combined cure, letting the bitch hunt rabbits in thick bracken. When she was hot on the line of a moving rabbit, I would fire a shot, call her in and feed her a piece of bread. When she seemed fully confident, I would get her hunting, fire a shot and give her a simple marked retrieve. The cure worked only too well. When I started to shoot rabbits for her, her attitude was more that of a 'Saturday shooting spaniel' than the usually polished young springer straight out of training, and I had to work quite hard on her to pull her back under control again.

13

Retrieving Real Game

There comes a time in the young springer's training when one has to make the transition from artificial dummies to real game. In this context 'game' is a somewhat loose term. It simply means some creature which has once drawn breath, but a fairly obvious qualification is that the creature we class as game should be of a species which we could reasonably expect a springer to handle with little effort, so whereas a starling could be game to the pupil, a road victim badger would be beyond this remit. If one has bred the pup oneself, or acquired it at an early age, providing one has had access to various quarry species, it will have been possible to have practised the pup on various kinds of cold game since before it changed its milk teeth. Very small rabbits, starlings, golden plover, moorhen, teal and feral pigeons all can be utilized. I believe this is a good upbringing and far preferable to attempting to switch it directly from dummies to dead game at about 14 months of age or even older.

As I mentioned in an earlier chapter, I am not writing this book solely for a British readership and some methods of training which may not be applicable in Britain may be perfectly acceptable elsewhere. American trainers tend to take a very direct approach. It seems that from about five months of age, they start working their springer pups on clip-winged feral pigeons. This is a multi-purpose exercise. The clip-wings are scattered about the training ground and the pup is encouraged to hunt them up. This induces it to hunt ground, as it quickly latches onto the idea that if it searches a piece of ground, it will soon find a pigeon. Secondly, it gains practice in handling live game. This is particularly valuable at this stage. The springer becomes familiar with handling live birds before it is steadied to flush, so the situation is pre-empted which frequently arises in Britain, when a dog is first steadied on game before it has handled live retrieves, which it frequently refuses to do through fear of wrongdoing. Thirdly, hunting up clip-wing pigeons encourages a springer to go in and grab the bird and so develop the 'hard flush' which is so important in American field trials. I could see the logic in the American system if the puppies were not started so young. The idea is to get the pups 'birdy', by which they mean bird-conscious. I am told by some American trial people that their springers tend to be 'cold' and nowhere near as friendly as those in Britain. I wonder if this is because they get their springer pups so intent on pigeons at such an impressionable age that this diverts their attention from their human handlers. Perhaps American trainers should heed Peter Moxon's well-tried axiom regarding gundog training: 'Make haste slowly.' And maybe history plays a part here. Although there was European settlement in America in the 1600s, the real development of the country has taken place over the past 150 years, and as the Americans have developed their nation so swiftly into one of the greatest the world has ever known, they must have acquired the habit of doing things yesterday, rather than tomorrow! Perhaps this is why they push their springer pups on at such a speed, but it does not always produce the best results.

Apropos the use of feral pigeons for springer training in North America, an amusing story has come to my notice regarding a Canadian springer trainer, Jamie Armour, who in 1969 was not as experienced as he is now. He had a

somewhat garbled idea of how he thought he might steady
a couple of rather unruly springers he had at that time, and
set about finding some pigeons so he could proceed with his
plan. Vancouver has a population of feral pigeons second only
to Venice. A great many roosted in the belfry of a Catholic
church in North Vancouver, where the incumbent priest, the
late Father Reedy, gave ready permission for a raid to be
carried out. Father Reedy had a liking for good labradors
and single malt whisky. He insisted on rendering assistance
and arrived after dark wearing his black cassock with a quart
of single malt in his right rear pocket. From Father Reedy's
demeanour, it came as no great surprise that most of the
whisky was missing. The ascent to the belfry was hairy, but
after the trapdoor was closed it was only a matter of thirty
minutes before they had caught 150 pigeons by torch-light.
The descent was extremely difficult, encumbered as they were
by sackfuls of pigeons. Doubtless due to the effects of the
missing single malt, Father Reedy dropped a sackful of birds,
about 20 of which distributed themselves around the body of
the church. The two men set about recapturing the pigeons
until only one remained, perched on the left shoulder of the
statue of the Virgin Mary. The Father approached the Virgin
Mary, bowed his head in ostensible prayer and incanted
'Hail Mary, full of grace, etc.', then grabbed the bird with
a triumphant 'Got you, you bugger!'

All North American springers are trained for field trials on
'planted' pigeons and pheasants. Pigeons are the mainstay of
training. Pheasants hot the dogs up in preparation for the
events. One can query the morality of using live, captive
game for training and trialling purpose, but in North America
it is the accepted system and nobody seemingly gives the
procedure a second thought. Pigeons are complaisant birds
and have no objection to being shipped around in crates.
An old cock pigeon can be used for retrieving practice and,
provided he is handled by a springer with a perfect gentle
mouth, upon being returned to the pigeon-house, he will
immediately duck his head and coo to the hens. I am not

so happy regarding pheasants. This species is very highly strung and I am sure pheasants suffer severe mental stress when crated and handled. Some die in the crates. Personally, I would not care to either train or trial under such a system or to witness American trials. However, the system I have outlined explains why the Americans do not have the trouble over their springers handling wounded game after being steadied which sometimes occurs under the British training system, which is normally steadiness first, then shooting experience. Not everyone has the opportunity to do this, but if it is possible for a trainer to walk around and disturb a few woodpigeons, at that stage in their springer's training when it is fully conversant with the gun and steady on its retrieving, but has not yet been steadied to flushed game, then if a few pigeons are shot, it might be possible to shoot one or two which in the natural course of events happened to be winged birds. If the young springer picks these wounded birds, this will stand him in good stead when he is asked to deal with shot game which has some life in it after he has received his steadiness training in the rabbit pen or on wild game.

I have deliberately not suggested that a springer trainer should utilize the surest method of all of shooting some pigeon, which is by decoying. The young springer might appear to be fully confident with the gun, but put him in the confines of a pigeon hide and it might be another story. Being settled down in the hide, he will see no birds fall to stimulate his interest but will have several shots fired right over his head. He might well not like it one little bit and valuable work could be undone, which would require a long and tedious rehabilitation process to rectify.

To put the introduction to the real thing in a nutshell, in the case of a young springer which has not had the advantage of a few head of cold game since puppyhood, the golden rule is cold game only to start with, never badly shot or blood-covered. Half- to three-quarter-grown rabbits are ideal. Avoid smelly old bucks or milky does. The scent and weight can put some young springers off. Feral pigeons are ideal. They are close-feathered and have a musty, bitter scent. Gundogs started on these birds will seldom refuse snipe, woodcock or duck. The same applies to starlings and jackdaws.

The next stage is to try the springer with freshly killed specimens of the varieties of 'game' which it has already handled cold. Sometimes a hitch can arise over the transition from cold retrieves to warm. Occasionally the pup can be rough with the warm specimen. Sometimes they will refuse it altogether. In the case of a rabbit, the pup sometimes licks the ears and tail of the creature and refuses to lift it. I pick the retrieve up myself and tease him with it around his muzzle. Usually he reacts by opening his mouth to get hold of it, then I throw it a few yards and let him run in to it. Usually he will make an effort to pick the retrieve up, even though he may handle it clumsily and maybe drop it halfway in. If he has had a course of partial force retrieving the problem can be simplified. One simply takes hold of the pup gently by the scruff, presents the retrieve to him with the familiar command to take hold, then one should back away a yard and call him in. He will remember his early lessons and bring the retrieve up, then the next time it is thrown he will more than likely bring it in and deliver nicely. Any difficulties experienced at this stage are likely to stem from lack of confidence and unfamiliarity, so continued exposure to the situation should increase his confidence, and retrieving any species under any circumstances should become second nature.

More difficulties seem to arise over hares than any other type of game, even snipe and woodcock. Some springers react adversely to the strong scent, then there is the sheer weight and flaccidity to contend with. Thirty years ago this was more of a problem than it is likely to be today. Then, hares very frequently figured in the bag at field trials, particularly in Scotland. Since those days, there has been a nationwide decline in the hare population, except perhaps on the established hare-coursing grounds like Six Mile Bottom and Altcar. On top of this decline, there has been a vast increase in the rabbit population. The two species do not always get on together. The rabbit nibbles the herbage right down to ground level, whereas the hare needs longer growth to sustain it. On a large agricultural estate the two species can co-exist, as the hares have a greater choice of habitat, but on marginal ground, the hares are less able to compete with the rabbits. However, Murphy's Law being as it is, if a certain springer was a complete non-retriever of hares, that would be the dog which would be asked to retrieve the only hare shot in a trial, so all trial springers should be hare-proof. I have noticed a curious syndrome regarding hares and spaniels. Because a spaniel can retrieve a hare well does not automatically guarantee that a spaniel will be first class, but viewed in reverse, virtually every first-class spaniel is a good hare retriever, should the occasion arise.

Next to a rabbit pen, I think one of the most useful things a springer trainer can possess is a loft full of free-flying homing pigeons. Pigeons are invaluable for teaching a young dog that not every bird fired at is to be retrieved. If one carries two or three in a bag, along with a couple of dummies or cold birds, a pigeon can be released and a shot fired over it and the command 'gone away' given. Then a retrieve could be given, then another pigeon fired over and so on. It is perfectly legal to shoot one's own loft pigeons as and when required, provided they are flying free, but to let a pigeon out of a box, or throw one into the air and shoot it contravenes the Captive Birds Act, which was originally instituted to outlaw live trap shooting competitions. Oddly enough, such a practice contravenes the Criminal Code of Canada, so only dead birds can be used in their field trial water tests, although 'planted' game may legally be shot during the land series. Birds are thrown and shot in American spaniel water tests, although many people now find this repugnant and are pushing for only dead birds to be used in future.

14

Hunting and Steadiness to Game

It is universally recognized that the primary function of a spaniel is to hunt its ground well and find game for the gun. The novice reader might well enquire why I have therefore left this most important aspect of its work until so late in the narrative. It is all a matter of correct sequence of events. We have already gone over the ground covering the early history of the spaniel, when it was used for hunting and flushing game only and was not required to retrieve. Even closer to our own era, in the 1950s and 1960s, one of the greatest amateur trainers of all time, the late Major Hugh Peacock, who used to shoot the Milton Park Estate near Peterborough, would use a pack of six cockers when rough shooting and keep a labrador walking at heel to do the retrieving. None of these cockers were non-retrievers, but the terrain the Major worked at that time was largely felled woodland, with undercover of low bramble, dead sticks and heavy white grass. The idea of not allowing the cockers to retrieve from such tight cover was so the little dogs did not have any hard struggles while extracting birds from cover, which could have encouraged hard mouth. The taller labrador could reach down from above the shot game and its height would allow it to carry birds back over the top of the cover without snagging, whereas the cockers would have to push the birds through the cover. However, this procedure would be exceptional according to present-day requirements, when to a shooting person, retrieving ability in a springer is essential, and to the field trialler, mandatory. I have therefore dealt with retrieving in depth in an earlier chapter, firstly because retrieving is important, albeit secondary, and secondly because of the danger that a potentially super-keen hunter, if given too much latitude in the area of hunting too early in its career, might develop these skills at the expense of its retrieving function.

Then there is the question of obedience and control, which I have already dealt with. Unless a springer has had a thorough grounding in obedience from about the age of 8 months onwards, the more natural drive and quality it has, the bigger menace it will be on a shooting day unless these qualities are properly harnessed; so to quote one of the doyens of the past, the late Richard Sharpe: 'The primary obedience course is the most important.' I would point out that in one training regime we are faced with a paradox. If a trainer decides to develop a young springer's hunting skills by allowing the pup to free hunt and chase, this rigorous obedience course actually takes place parallel to its free hunting period. One simply proceeds with the obedience course in the normal manner and on ground free of all temptation and distraction, and on other occasions, on game-holding ground, the pup is allowed to free hunt. When it is decided to steady to game a springer which has had such a start in life, the grounding in obedience is there to build into its steadiness course. This is a contradiction which a well-bred springer should have the temperament to accept, so that it should not be upset by the seeming illogicality of being allowed to chase a rabbit one day, then being prevented from chasing the next and never being allowed to have another chase ever again.

Just as Talbot Radcliffe once remarked, 'A hundred different dogs, a hundred different temperaments', there are variations in attitudes to hunting. I would say there are about four distinct categories. There is the natural hunter and almost instinctive quarterer which will hunt any ground regardless of whether there is any scent of game thereon. These spaniels are very rare – perhaps one might have one in a lifetime, with luck. Often such dogs are not natural gamefinders. They are basically not looking for scent. They just love traversing ground and diving into cover for its own sake. Usually, they learn their gamefinding skills as they mature and frequently become dogs of a lifetime. The second category lacks the instinctive natural quartering of the former group. It will get out and hunt a bit in more ragged fashion, using its nose to find what bits of game scent there are about and showing considerable animation and style when fresh scent is encountered. These spaniels generally develop their gamefinding as they go along and have to develop their drive and class through exposure to game as they mature. For this type of springer, I would advocate limited free hunting, until one can see its keenness developing, whereas the former group requires no free hunting at all. There is a third group of spaniels which initially has no desire to hunt at all. They simply accompany one without showing any interest in their surrounding. These are among the most difficult and frustrating animals of all and a minority never does make any sort of grade. All one can do with a springer from this group is to give it free hunting and chasing, absolutely ad lib, day after day, in the hope that eventually the penny might drop. They are heartbreaking animals to deal with but I have made up three field trial champions which all made such an inauspicious start, so there is no need to despair completely.

The fourth group is quite the most difficult of all. A springer of this persuasion, upon being let off the lead, bolts off in a straight line until it reaches the far boundary of the field, then proceeds to self-hunt up and down the boundary fence. I cannot say if any springers are born with this trait. Certainly I never seem troubled by this behaviour with anything I have bred myself, but as a public professional trainer, I have to deal with springers from all kinds of pre-training backgrounds. I have noticed a consistency in this type of behaviour in pups from the same source which have come to me at intervals. I am inclined therefore to believe that this problematic behaviour is more than likely to be man-induced and it is my idea that, quite probably, pheasants are the likely culprits. When a pup is taken into a field where rabbits feed, any rabbits which are not actually tucked into seats will more than likely run sideways to the nearest hedge or covert side. The scent is there to stimulate the young springer, and it will work the scent with pleasing tail action; but as the scent trails cross one's front, rather than lying in straight lines straight ahead, the pup is not tempted to go away on these rabbit lines, but rather to keep doubling on them as he hunts without attempting to get too far ahead. With pheasants it is a different matter. Many pheasants on grassland or spring corn will run ahead in straight lines. The same also applies to hares when present on the ground. The footscent of running pheasants or hares is far stronger and more compelling than that of rabbits and nothing is calculated to pull a springer out in straight lines more. This can be a difficult problem to solve and it can be misleading when the client swears the pup has never had game contact, when the trainer knows perfectly well that it has.

I have already described how the transatlantic triallers induce their pups to hunt by scattering wing-clipped pigeons around the training area. This is obviously successful for what they require except that I believe they do too much, far too young. I understand that some people in Britain hide tennis balls at intervals in the same manner, but the idea does not appeal to me as it does not appear sufficiently stimulating. One dog I have judged in trials which had such a grounding was a terrible false pointer and looked for its handler's encouragement continually. Needless to say, it received no award.

As far as I am aware, all steadiness training which is done in America is done on 'planted' pigeons which are flushed by the dog and then shot. Often the pup will hitherto have flushed and chased pigeons and had them killed in front of it when the pup is in full flight. The Americans place the utmost importance on good marking and their whole training system is geared to the springer avidly keeping its eyes on the bird at all times.

Those Americans who live in good wild pheasant country and whose interest lies in 'hunting' rather than field trials could, I think, take a leaf out of the British book. A correspondent, Lionel Andalo, formerly of London, England, lives in New York State but so vast is the country that he lives 376 miles from New York City. This is wild pheasant country. Thirty years or so ago, Mr Andalo could flush about 100 pheasants in an afternoon's walk with a springer. Owing to the development of 'clean' farming, wild birds are not so prolific now but are still to be found by a good springer. In the flat lands of Nebraska, wild pheasants are even more plentiful but I have never heard of anyone who uses these wild birds for flushing and steadiness practice. The reasoning behind the neglect of this facility is that if game is flushed and not shot, springers will avert their eyes from the birds, which will be detrimental to their marking ability. There is some truth in this idea. Too much driving in or beating on driven shoots can cause a springer to disregard a bird once it has flushed, but an intelligent dog soon begins to mark when it realizes it is in a rough shooting or field trialling situation. As I see it, the Americans, to avoid the former situation, attempt to teach two lessons in one exercise: steadiness to the flush and steadiness to the shot bird. This is contrary to the way things are done in Britain; all our steadiness is completely divorced from any shooting situation and we steady our charges either in a rabbit pen or on wild game. A rabbit pen is the best starting point, as it gives one greater command of the situation.

Here I must digress regarding the actual construction of a rabbit pen. Joe Greatorex told me to build as big a rabbit pen as I could afford. In 1967 I decided I would build a proper one. I simply fenced a hillside in, 300 yards by 40 yards close to home, narrowing to a point at the far end. At that time, the materials cost me a total of £160 plus a great deal of my own labour. It was an excellent pen, although it was so vast that I really needed an experienced dog to find the rabbits in it. It turned out to be on a par with a stately home: easily constructable when labour and materials were cheap in the eighteenth and nineteenth centuries but beyond the reach of most present-day owners to keep in a good state of repair unless the National Trust renders assistance. So when my pen required extensive repairs after 20 years' good service, prices of materials had risen so high, that, like many present-day estate owners, I found renovation costs prohibitive; and the National Trust was singularly uninterested in rendering any financial assistance, so I abandoned the original structure and built a smaller pen about 70 by 20 yards.

A rectangular pen is more useful than a square one. The lower 3 feet should be constructed of 1-inch mesh but ordinary chicken wire will suffice for the upper 3 feet. A cross-piece should be nailed to the top of each fence post, so it protrudes a minimum of 12 inches both inside the pen and out. A roll of wire netting should be run around the top of the pen and secured to the cross-pieces, so there is an overlap to prevent rabbits scaling the wire and getting out or foxes getting in from the outside. It is not really necessary to bury the wire netting around the bottom of the pen. If about 12 inches are turned inwards and laid flat along the ground and weighted with bricks and stones, this will normally suffice to keep the rabbits at home.

In an ideal world, the best type of rabbits with which to stock the pen are Dutch crossed with wild. Pure Dutch are quite good, being alert and fast, but pure wild rabbits can be somewhat complicated. I am told that the best system to work using wild rabbits is to stock the pen with bucks only. It is said that they neither fight nor try to dig their way out. One problem with wild rabbits is that until they become really acclimatized, they are very prone to clap down, refuse to move and allow themselves to be caught by the spaniel. This is not good. Nothing succeeds like success, and if a young spaniel manages to catch a rabbit, then it will know that they can be caught and the habit can be difficult to eradicate.

The advantages of a rabbit pen for steadying a young springer are manifold. For a start, there is the guaranteed find. A problem which can arise if one attempts to steady the dog on wild rabbits alone is that, on account of the type of cover rabbits use, particularly in southern, Welsh and Midland areas, so many rabbits can be found which the dog never views away. In the rabbit pen the trainer can see rabbits sitting in their seats and can stage-manage the situation so the dog is certain to see the rabbits. When I first did this I would simply turn the pup loose in the pen, attempt to stop him by whistle and run him down and catch him if the whistle did not suffice, which it seldom did on the first time of asking unless the pupil was exceptionally soft and submissive. Thirty-odd years later, I am not quite as fast as I was so I use less strenuous methods. Now I always take the pup into the pen on several feet of lead. I work him towards a rabbit and when he darts after it I pull him up sharp and give him the stop whistle. I repeat this procedure until he begins to get the idea that I am going to stop him whenever a rabbit moves, then I call it a day. The next time I take him into the pen I repeat the procedure, give him three or four drops on the lead, then drop the lead and let him hunt with a trailing lead. This is simply so he is easier to apprehend should he decide to take the law into his own hands, which he most likely will if he is an animal of any quality.

The steadiness course in the pen can last over a period of several days, or it can even run into a matter of weeks should he prove stubborn. Usually after a few visits to the pen, the trailing lead can be dispensed with. By the time this stage has been reached he should have learned that he must not grab the rabbits in their seats, even though he may still need the stop whistle to restrain him on the flush. A difficult situation can arise should a springer prove particularly persistent in its refusal to accept that it must desist from chasing. Here there might be a temptation to take a short cut and be too hard on the dog. This could be fraught with danger. Some dogs have what I term a 'cast iron temperament'. They can be very hard on the outside but will break if subjected to undue pressure, and can permanently lose their drive through harsh treatment. This is a far from ideal temperament and the only answer is to wear them down through constant repetition. Whatever the dog's temperament, the best way of inducing complete steadiness is to wear it down gradually, so by constant repetition it will eventually drop on its own directly a rabbit flushes with no need for any command. The rabbit pen is no panacea but is only a means to an end. It teaches the pup the difference between right and wrong. However, under more exciting field conditions when wild rabbits are the quarry, the young springer sometimes will throw caution to the winds and pretend he has forgotten his pen lessons. He hasn't, and is just trying it on. One must get after him immediately, pounce upon him and drag him back to his starting point where he should have dropped to flush, giving him a rough ride and blowing the stop whistle in his ear.

On such excursions we must also be aware of the continuing presence of myxomatosis in the rabbit population that an eager young dog might encounter. 'Myxy' rabbits are a hazard of our times and sometimes unavoidable. The rabbit should be taken from the dog without any fuss or histrionics, killed and thrown away. The dog should be put on the lead and walked away from the scene then hunted on again when clear of the area.

Most American springer people have a misguided conception of the rabbit pen as they believe any contact with rabbits will induce a springer to work with too low a head for their planted game requirements. However, I have already explained that this is more a matter of an individual dog's adaptability to the various situations it encounters rather than this or that 'making' a springer adopt certain characteristics. Injudicious use of a rabbit pen can cause a springer to hesitate on game or soft-flush, which is definitely 'out' as far as American trial conditions go, but it is by no means inevitable that pen training will have this effect. My first two successful American trial springers, F.T.Ch. Rivington Joe and Double American National Champion Winner (1964/65) Gwibernant Ganol, both had a thorough grounding in the rabbit pen and there was never any doubt about the hardness of their flushing.

Rabbit pens are now expensive to construct and it is virtually impossible to purchase the stout gauge wire netting which was available 30 years ago and would last for 20 years. I have known of groups of enthusiasts in South Wales and Durham who have collectively built rabbit pens; it is also possible to hire them from the many trainers all over the country who will allow use of their pens for a fee. Another way out involves a friendly gamekeeper. Far more gamekeepers nowadays are more interested in the better trained type of gundog, even if they do not compete in trials themselves, although a good number do. Certainly they appreciate well-trained springers in their beating lines and efficient spaniels and retrievers with excellent mouths as picking-up dogs. I have known of some keepers who would allow an enthusiastic amateur spaniel trainer to stock one of their pheasant release pens with rabbits when the pen was not in use for its intended purpose. This gives a fair amount of scope. A pen could be stocked with rabbits after the shooting season and the spaniel trainer would have the use of this enclosure all spring and part of the summer until July, when the new batch of poults would arrive. The pen would then be free for use in early autumn again. A bonus would be the odd flush of a pheasant that worked its way back to the pen, or even several flushes according to the mood of the birds.

One of the most exciting pens I ever saw was a pheasant release pen on the Clandeboye Estate in Northern Ireland. The headkeeper in those days was Bob Garvin, himself an experienced trial competitor, judge and deadly trial gun. Bob had stocked the pen with Irish hares in addition to wild rabbits. Irish hares are interesting animals in captivity. They are far more adaptable than the brown hare which is very difficult to keep alive in a pen and very prone to panic. Obviously, the larger the pen, the better the Irish hare will enjoy life. I well remember an Irish hare called Ben, which shared a 15-yard square pen in Co. Monaghan with a cock pheasant named Isaac. They were owned by Ruth Tenison, doyenne of Irish labrador people and founder of the 'Ballyfrema' strain of labradors. Their function was to live quietly in the pen, and occasionally Ruth would walk a labrador puppy around their pen on a lead, to acquaint the pup with the sight and scent of game. Altogether a more civilized existence than being rousted around by an ill-mannered springer pup!

15

A Breakdown on Game Scent

Throughout the history of man, numerous technologies have emerged. Rarely, they have stayed with us from earliest times to the present day, a prime example being the smoking of meat fish and game. More often, they have been abandoned in the face of new developments, although sometimes retained in a minor role as anachronisms of the past.

To digress for a moment, a very good example is that of sail on the high seas. For a considerable period, all warships, merchantmen and fishing vessels were sail rigged, and sailing masters and crewmen developed great skills in handling them. Then came steam. The old skills were lost, and in the Western world, all sailing is now for pleasure or competition. Again, the swordsmiths of medieval Japan were once famed and revered throughout the land. My guess is that only a handful will remain, for the sake of tradition.

Such has proved the case in the realm of game shooting and gundogs. From the days of the improved flintlock, through the era of the percussion, muzzle-loading shotgun, to the earlier days of the breechloader, all game which inhabits open country rather than woodland cover or marshes was shot over pointers and setters. Walking up as we know it was frowned upon. 'Tramping partridges up out of turnips' was considered unrefined, and sportsmen of the calibre of Thomas Coke, Sir Fowell Buxton, Captain Horatio Ross, Squire Osbaldeston, Charles St John and George, the Prince Regent, considered that the only true sport was to shoot one's birds which had first been located and pointed by a 'well broken' dog, which might be pointer, English setter or black-and-tan setter. The Irish gentry would do their own thing with their native setter, more likely to be white and red than solid red, in bygone times.

But just as steam superseded sail, the breechloader, with its more rapid rate of fire, plus the growing appetite among sportsmen for larger bags of driven game, sounded the virtual death-knell for the old ways of shooting over pointing dogs, and with their drastically reduced employment, so died in sportsmen's minds an understanding of these dogs and how they perform their function. All native pointing breeds are air scenters, but so few people nowadays know exactly what air scent is. Actual scenting conditions, that is whether it is good, bad, or indifferent, are never fully understood by the human brain. There are rules of thumb which can be applied. On frosty ground runners will be difficult to collect, apart from in the last half hour of daylight. Scent will be good in a fine drizzle and light breeze. Pointing dogs will be disadvantaged under muggy conditions, and if a pack of beagles is let out of the trailer and commence to roll around on their backs, scent will be virtually nil.

Going back to the elusive matter of air scent, we must consider that game gives off scent, which is carried on the wind. Some believe that scent, though invisible, is dispersed like smoke. The American spaniel triallers liken it to a charge of shot, dense close in and dispersing with distance, and their sometimes lyrical field trial reports often state that the dog, coming at full speed, 'hit the scent-cone, turned in and made a hard driving flush'. Having worked both spaniels and pointing dogs, I think their reasoning holds water. Like a charge of shot which has travelled quite a distance, so that the pattern has dispersed and is ceasing to be effective, well-dispersed scent particles, having started off at close quarters as 'body scent', now become 'air scent' and usually can only be acted on by the specialist, high-headed, air-scenting breeds. An exception to this rule was the 1952 Retriever Championship winner, the golden retriever Treunair Carla, who would hunt high-headed and hold a steady point on grouse. I always have suspected that the Irish setter figures in the ancestry of many working goldens, and the heavily line-bred goldens of today frequently exhibit strong Irish setter traits in their appearance.

Quite recently, I wrote an article on Continental hunt, point and retrieve dogs, aimed largely at the German shorthaired pointer, but mentioned the large Münsterlander in passing, a breed I have trained and shot over. I mentioned that the HPR group would never be my *first choice* as grouse dogs, the reason being that although many can prove reasonably competent in such a situation, few can compare with native British specialist bird-dogs. One gentleman who has two large Münsterlanders seemed rather upset by my comment and wrote in to assure us how well his older bitch had done on grouse and how it would work far wider than a spaniel. These comments spoke volumes as to how so many shooting people and gundog owners of the present day know so little about the function of the different breeds in all the various facets of game shooting. One cannot blame them for their shortcomings. None of us are born with an inbuilt knowledge. We all require education. The gentleman was anxious that we should appreciate that his older Münsterlander would range wider than a springer. I should hope it would, but if we consider the matter in reverse, a spaniel that would range as far as a good HPR would be virtually useless. A spaniel is not an air-scenter. It works with a lower head carriage than a true bird-dog or *good* HPR and seeks a combination of footscent and body scent, hopefully with the accent on the latter. Distant air scent from its quarry is not registered. It will register a touch of footscent to warn it of the presence of its quarry, although in Britain we don't allow a spaniel to bore

1. 'Policies of informed line breeding are the ones most likely to produce the goods . . .' A litter of English springers bred in the 1960s by the late Cyril Price of Cadoxton Kennels, South Wales. (*Author*)

2. A viking carries off his loot at the Swedish Spaniel Championship, 1993. Jörgen Sandberg, whose Welsh-bred cocker, Skenchall Mark, won the championship, was presented with his trophy by the author (left). (*Author*)

3.   Garth Tower Cottage, near the Ruabon Moor in North Wales. It was here that the late Joe Greatorex began his dog-training career, before moving to Shropshire to manage Selwyn Jones's O'Vara Kennels. 'It would be seemly if those who are winning today acknowledge the debt of gratitude they owe to those who came before them.' (*Author*)

4.   A black cocker makes a classic retrieve of a rabbit from bracken, to win a novice cocker stake which the author judged. (*Author*)

5. With frost still lying, the top hunting springer F.T.Ch. Cortman Lane retrieves a rabbit to the author. This dog won the 1986 Spaniel Championship, and became a very important international sire. (*Graham Cox*)

6. A fine delivery of a mallard by a young springer, Gwibernant Bat. (*Author*)

7. The great cocker brood bitch, F.T.Ch. Wernffrwd Pawn, with a good bag of Welsh grouse shot over pointers. Wernffrwd Pawn was the dam of the 1992 Cocker Championship winner, F.T.Ch. Jasper of Parkbreck. (*Author*)

8. 'The noblest Roman of them all'– the 1986 Championship winner, F.T.Ch. Cortman Lane. A dog of enormous quality and honesty, he is also a prepotent sire, with seven British Field Trial Champions to his credit already – perhaps more important, he has 'sired a whole generation of good, trainable shooting dogs.' (*Author*)

9. Swedish F.T.Ch. Ebony Slice, a cocker bitch owned by Hans-Erik Sjöblom, retrieves a rabbit from productive game cover during the 1993 Swedish Spaniel Championship. In Sweden, there is now a movement concerned 'with promoting the superior hunting-type spaniel (to which the show spaniels cannot hold a candle) . . .' (*Author*)

10. A perfect sitting delivery of a hen pheasant by Felltrecker Sawllowlaw, a son of F.T.Ch. Cortman Lane. The delivery is entirely natural in this particular springer and no forced retrieving was ever required. (*Author*)

11. 'It's over there, 25 yards out, stone dead.' A spaniel trial at Chirk Castle, North Wales – the judge points out the position of a shot rabbit to the handler, while the gun, Jonathan Bailey, looks on. (*Author*)

12. 'Spaniels should be judged as shooting dogs with just that bit more dash, style and polish'– a springer trial scene in hill country at Vivod, North Wales. (*Author*)

13.   A cocker field trial meet in Norfolk – 'The working cocker is in an enviable position ... Working ability is excellent and there are now many gifted cocker trainers.' (*Author*)

14.   Ci of Gwibernant, an International Field Trial Champion springer exported to Holland by the author and owned by Joep van der Vlasakker. This dog was also placed fourth in the 1988 Coupe d'Europe. 'I cannot speak highly enough of the sportsmanship, camaraderie and decorum of the Dutch handlers.' (*Joep van der Vlasakker*)

ahead on a running pheasant, unlike the Americans who set great store on a dog's ability 'to take a runner'; but to me, the classic spaniel find is where the dog winds the body scent of its squatting quarry, with no lead-in of footscent, drives in hard and flushes its quarry. Such a technique is only effective if at all times the dog hunts within comfortable gun range. A spaniel will flush tight-sitting grouse on its restricted line of advance. Many grouse don't sit tight. An air-scenting dog is required to locate them at a distance, standing well back from the quarry, and remaining on point until the guns walk to the dog, which could be a distance of 200 yards or even more, if the dog is a really good one. So although we can argue *ad infinitum* on the respective merits of native bird-dog versus HPR as a grouse dog, hopefully with good humour, the spaniel can never enter such a debate. His is a different ball game. Because a spaniel cannot take his game as far out as an air-scenting specialist or competent all-rounder, this should not imply that the spaniel's nose is in any way inferior, but that his function is completely different. A good pointer which can take its birds 50 yards out with ease, if allowed to retrieve, can look positively comical trying to locate a shot bird in thick heather at its feet!

Those all-round masters of their craft of bygone times, men like Thomas Gaunt, Reg Hill and John Forbes, who trained and handled pointers and setters in addition to spaniels, had an enormous advantage over their counterparts of today, who handle either spaniels exclusively, or no other breeds but pointers and setters. There is so much one can learn about spaniels from handling bird-dogs and a working knowledge of spaniels cannot but help the pointer and setter person. Very early in my career I was running two good spaniels in a trial in Yorkshire. The cover consisted entirely of rushes, so if a dog could quarter well, it could be shown to maximum advantage. Reg Hill was one of the judges and after both dogs had run under him he remarked, 'I like those dogs of yours. They both turn into the wind instead of away from the wind.' This was a point which someone experienced in pointers and setters could appreciate. The majority of novices in the pointer and setter lobby would appreciate it too, simply because it would have been taught to them by more experienced persons – but try that one on some of the 'A' panel spaniel judges of the present day and as likely as not, all one would receive would be a blank stare! This is a case in point of what I see as deteriorating standards of judging. There is an excellent reason why a spaniel should turn into the wind on an upwind beat. Turning forward 'bites off' a new piece of ground to traverse. Turning inwards means that some of the ground will be hunted which has already been done. A further point is that if game just happens to be lying on the extremity of the spaniel's beat and just forward of the cast it is about to complete, a turn into the wind will bring the dog within the scent spread of the game. The dog that turns away from the wind will not find the game. It will go to the opposite side of its beat, turn and come back again, then it is a toss-up whether it bumps into the game from the flank, finds it, or casts in front of it and so misses the game.

This point can best be appreciated by watching a good pointer or setter working a beat on either heather, stubble or spring corn. Although bird-dogs are faster than spaniels, it is like watching a quartering and gamefinding sequence in slow motion. The bird-dog casts almost flat to left or right of the handler. When it reaches the extremity of its beat, it will either turn on its own or the handler will use the turn whistle. It will sweep around in a smooth U-turn, biting off a piece of ground which is consistent with scenting conditions and the power of the individual dog's nose. It will make forward progress, then upon encountering the most minute particle of air scent, it will check and cautiously draw forward, head held very high, then when it is confident that it has the birds, will come on rigid point. Alternatively, and particularly if work has been in progress for some time and some birds have already been located and moved, the dog might interrupt its gallop in a split second and establish an immediate and very intense point, nose just below the level of its withers. A pound to a penny, there will be a single bird recently flown and dropped in and whose scent spread has not had time to travel far, so is strictly localized. A very easy bird to miss. Owing to the bird-dog's *modus operandi*, one is in a position to take in the entire spectacle. To quote an Italian client of mine, who formerly had only shot over pointing breeds, 'It takes time to get used to a different style of hunting with a spaniel, so active, rapid and rushed.' This hunting style is not always observed in such open country as bird-dogs normally operate in, so exactly what the spaniels are doing is not invariably as self-evident as it is in the case of the bird-dog. Thus, as the majority of present-day spaniel judges have not benefited from an education in pointers and setters, perhaps this is why some finer hunting points are not always appreciated.

One man who had enjoyed the advantages of both worlds was William Arkwright (who died in 1925), author of *The Pointer and His Predecessors*. Writing the Foreword in H. W. Carlton's *Spaniels: Their Breaking For Sport and Field Trials* (1915), Arkwright remarked: 'Style, which is chiefly merry bustle, with flashing, quivering tail – and head ever alert, now high to reach a body scent, now low to investigate a track.' These words were written by a man who knew exactly how spaniels worked in relation to game scent. Arkwright's spaniel would drop its head occasionally to acquaint it with what species of game used the ground and whether game had used the ground the previous night, or just a few minutes ago. It would get the message in a flash, never stopping to dwell upon stale scent so it could be deemed to be pottering. It would be sufficiently educated to realize that dropping its nose for more than a split second would be profitless, hence its lifting its head high to reach a body scent. Here Arkwright was ahead of some spaniel judges of today. His many years as an owner of pointers had taught him that to take a body scent, a dog's head must come up, although in the case of a spaniel, not so high as a bird-dog, as body scent is at a lower level than the bird-dog's air scent but is certainly never right at ground level.

In some quarters, particularly in Scotland, there is an unreasonable and unreasoned prejudice against a spaniel if it ever lifts its head when hunting. A case in point is a very good springer called Pel-Tan Roly. This dog ran an excellent trial under a novice judge in a young plantation and the judge gave it a top grade. It ran under the senior judge in a wet muddy field of rape where no self-respecting rabbit would have been found dead. This judge did not grade this dog highly as he told his co-judge, 'Its head is too high to find rabbits.' The dog scraped a third place. A year or two later I bought the dog for a young vet, in Washington, USA. Before the dog went to the States, I had it in my kennels for a time. A few rabbits use my morning exercise ground. Immediately Roly set foot on this ground, he hunted with his head a few inches above the ground, at exactly the right height to be consistent with rabbit finding, had any been squatting there. Over in America and Canada, working on 'planted' pheasants which apparently give off a rising scent, he got his head up and won in a big way.

It should be plain to see that an intelligent springer works according to which game its nose tells it inhabits the terrain. I subscribe to Arkwright's view that a spaniel should not hunt with its head consistently at the same level but should vary its head carriage during the course of the hunt in a manner that is fitting to deal with any game and any eventuality. If certain people wish to pursue a high-headed witch hunt, that is up to them, but they should at least make sure they have good grounds for their opinions.

16

Perfecting the Hunting Method

Taking the breed worldwide, the springer is required to hunt a great diversity of game-holding cover. Despite this diversity, the cover roughly can be divided into two groups: cover where the dog cannot be seen and more open cover where the springer can be seen all or most of the time. In the former category are large clumps of high brambles, rhododendron and laurel thickets and massive gorse clumps (whins if you live north of Hadrian's Wall). In the latter type of spaniel ground there are fields of turnips, sugar beet and rape. There is heather, white grass and flattened bracken. There are carpets of lower woodland brambles and for a time, until it is ploughed, there is corn stubble with the combined straw in swathes and potentially game-holding. Much of the cover which is investigated by American 'bird hunters' is very thick and punishing, the complete opposite in fact to the open 'courses' used by American springer field triallers to 'plant' their birds in. This is sometimes a bone of contention between those American sportsmen who view the springer more as a hunting dog which is required to put wild birds in the bag, and those persons who are more inclined to competitive work than 'hunting'. A considerable number use their springers for both purposes, but the more competitively minded have a natural bias towards field trial work. The frequently heard gripe of the 'hunter' is that field trials are often held where no wild bird would be found in a natural hunting situation. Thin weeds and grass would hardly be indicative of the security that any sensible wild pheasant would seek, and thick green grass or alfalfa would extend little charm to the wild bird either, and apparently these crops can provide very bad scenting conditions for the trial springers competing on planted pheasants.

When a springer is required to hunt in the type of cover where it cannot be seen, little human assistance can be given to help it develop the most effective hunting technique. It must crash into the cover and work it out as best it can entirely on its own. The wonder is that so many learn to do it so thoroughly. In large isolated clumps, handling the springer is not difficult as one can hear its progress as it tackles the cover and often see the tops of the rough stuff move. Usually the dog can be brought back within the handler's vision when the bush is done, without it slipping off unbidden into the next clump. The most difficult cover to hunt 'blind', although tall kale can be just as bad, are large stands of rhododendrons and laurels in woodland. Here, one either has the dog for the job or one hasn't. A minority of springers will hunt such cover hard but will never get lost. They have an uncanny knack of breaking cover every so often, just in the right position to catch the handler's eye, then having ascertained that they are still on the right course in relation to the handler's position, will dive back in again and continue their work. Few seem to have this faculty. In most cases one has to listen to the crashing of the dog and hope it responds to the turn/recall whistle when it becomes obvious that the dog is getting too far away. There is, however, a third type of spaniel which I would imagine that few of us would want. This is the very soft, slow type of springer which lacks the confidence to move more than a few yards from its handler's feet, and this type is seldom effective. Pheasants tend to creep around in rhododendrons and one really requires a bold springer which will take in a fair bit of ground, at a good pace, to get them on the move and into the air.

When dealing with the second category of cover previously mentioned, when one can see all or most of a springer's work, this situation lends itself to the perfection of hunting techniques. It is possible to guide the dog in the direction we want it to go. In these more open situations the wind has a more significant influence on the proceedings and it is under these circumstances that the finest and most polished hunting performances are witnessed. If one sees a top class pointer or setter hunting with the wind in its face, this is when precision quartering will be seen at its finest. It will move across its handler's front, left to right and vice versa, turning at the extremities of its beat and taking approximately the same amount of ground on either side of its handler's advance. A good springer should work in like manner but with one essential difference. It matters little at what range the bird-dog locates its game. It will wait there for as long as it takes its handler and/or guns to walk to the point. The springer does not, or at least should not, point. It is essentially a flushing dog. If you want a pointing dog, get one.

On the question of the pointing spaniel, here I believe some persons' ideas are dated. H. W. Carlton in *Spaniels: Their Breaking for Sport and Field Trials*, was somewhat ambiguous on the matter but I have the impression that he rather favoured a spaniel that would indicate its game. I believe Joe Greatorex was a disciple of Carlton. When Greatorex formulated the Kennel Club's 'Guide to Field Trial Judges' *circa* the early 1960s he propagated an enormous amount of spaniel wisdom, and his assertion that 'pointing is an added refinement' could have held water at the time. But not any more. Every time this Guide is re-issued, Greatorex's dictum on pointing is slavishly reaffirmed, I am certain, without those in high places who could amend the Guide giving the question serious thought. Greatorex was living in the past times of the pre-myxomatosis rabbit trial era. Many rabbits, particularly those 'stunk out' before a field trial, lay out in open 'seats' in very light cover. If a spaniel pointed one of these seated rabbits, that rabbit went nowhere until flushed on command. Although, once again, many rabbit trials are staged and a similar situation prevails, we have to consider that many more southern trials are held on pheasants and we must consider the largely degenerated behavioural patterns of this once great game bird. There are in Great Britain today just a few shoots where wild pheasants may be encountered in spaniel trials. The birds sit tight and flush freely before the intrusive spaniels' noses. Most trials which are held on pheasants have to rely on reared birds which are unlikely to prove so co-operative as their wild counterparts. Many run on ahead, and those that do stay put will, if pointed by a spaniel, take to their legs and do not provide a shot; but if a spaniel flushes boldly they have little choice but to take wing.

From a purely personal standpoint, there is also an aesthetic question. Few sights in the shooting calendar can compare with a setter, high-headed on dramatic point, the breeze ruffling the feathering on tail and ears, or a statuesque pointer, seemingly carved from marble; but in my view a pointing spaniel, low-headed and within a foot or so of its game, looks ugly. So as far as I am concerned, a spaniel always has been, and always will be, a hunting dog that flushes its game immediately its nose tells its brain that the game is there. Of course this means that the gun must be close enough to the game to stand a good chance of making a reasonable, killing shot. It automatically follows that when the game is found, the spaniel must be within comfortable shot of the gun. What does this constitute? For years we have been told by one popular gundog writer that 25 yards is the maximum distance a spaniel should go from the gun. I don't know if the writer has ever worked out the logistics of this statement but in reality 25 yards is too far. If a springer extended its cast to a distance of 25 yards to either side of its gun, every time it crossed his front, that spaniel would cover a front of 50 yards, which seems highly unrealistic. It, also allows no margin for error. A spaniel which consistently covers that width of ground would be a wide-ranging animal and on occasion doubtless would take in a few yards extra, virtually putting the dog out of shot. A pointer, doing a rhythmic 150 yards either side of its handler, is not going to cause a calamity if it extends its range to 170 yards occasionally, but a spaniel must work at all times to far finer limits. Just a yard or two too far in the case of a spaniel and the game is out of shot. It follows therefore that a maximum range of 20 yards will allow for a margin of error, but in reality few well-trained British spaniels range more than 15 yards from the Gun.

This is even more important when rabbit shooting. In many types of rabbit-inhabited cover, a rabbit flushed at 20 to 25 yards would be lost from view whereas a rabbit produced at 15 yards could be shootable. This is a point which American springer people find difficult to grasp unless they actually have had the opportunity to witness the British type of rabbit shooting. They are single minded regarding wide running in their trial springers, where the guns are mobile enough to adjust to the range of the dogs when the occasion demands, and that the tidy, close-quartering British type of spaniel work is so much at variance from what they expect from their own springers that they don't quite understand what we are doing and why.

When quartering technique is being perfected, it is essential that the same procedure is adopted with a young springer as one would employ with a pointer or setter puppy, namely that initially the springer should only be worked into the wind. Most well-bred springers have an element of natural quartering about them which one should exploit. The pup has had its rabbit pen training, and will have been hunted in natural cover and had a few finds on wild rabbits or other game, so it is learning that ground is worth searching, and it is willing to 'go'. All that is required is that it should flow smoothly in the right direction. This is accomplished by turning whistle and hand signal plus some mobility on the trainer's part should this be deemed helpful. It is largely a matter of common sense. The trainer must decide what

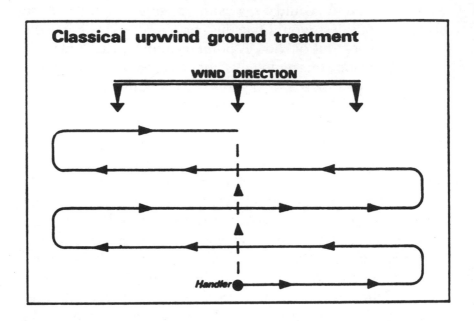

Classical upwind ground treatment

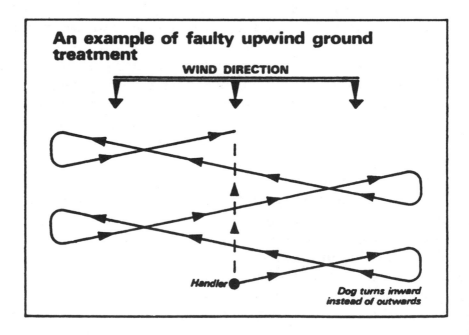

An example of faulty upwind ground treatment

constitutes a symmetrical quartering pattern and make sure that he gets the springer into the areas of the ground in front of them where the dog should be. I was once asked by a charming French lady, an 'A' judge in France, no less, for my advice on how she should treat an area of rough sand dune cover in North Holland, as she was just about due to run under the judges with her French F.T.Ch. Va Tout des Vorgines. I told her to cast her eyes ahead and decide exactly where she wanted her dog to go on the beat and see to it that the dog went there. I would offer the same advice to any person with a 'green' pup. Take a good look at the ground and decide where the pup should be turned and where it should be pushed to. Ideally, the ground being utilized should not be too bare. A closely grazed sheep pasture would offer little incentive and would simply get the pup's nose down – and remember, no game is ever found when the spaniel's nose is rubbing the turf, although many a head of game frequently is 'bumped up' under such circumstances.

An important lesson can be instilled during the course of quartering practice, which is turning instantly to the whistle in the face of possible counter-attractions, which could include the fresh footscent of recently departed game, or a patch of stale scent on which the springer drops its nose and potters. Any deviation short of an instant turn to whistle must be dealt with immediately. How it should be dealt with, of course, depends upon the temperament of the pupil. If it is a very soft springer (and there are a lot of them about), it should be dropped on the stop whistle, then rapidly approached and the loose skin under the chin taken hold of and the turn whistle pipped a couple of times in its ear. Use these tactics on a tougher pupil and it will laugh at you and hold you in contempt. Such an animal should be stopped, then seized roughly round the muzzle and dragged for a couple of yards in the direction it should have turned in, to the accompaniment of the turn whistle. If the dog appears to be of super quality and likely to become 'stallion of the breed' material, it could be issuing a determined challenge to one's authority. This is a

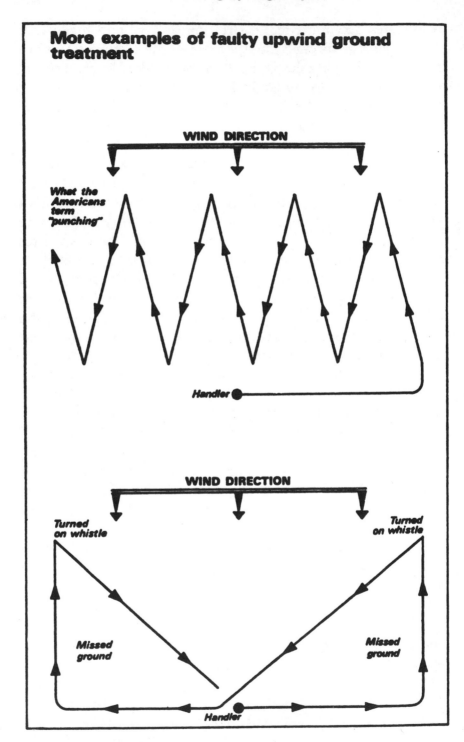

More examples of faulty upwind ground treatment

WIND DIRECTION

What the Americans term "punching"

Handler

WIND DIRECTION

Turned on whistle

Turned on whistle

Missed ground

Missed ground

Handler

battle the trainer must win. In addition to the hand clamped round the muzzle, the other hand should give an ear a few hard tugs. This should be sufficient to convince a really tough springer that the handler is the master. If it does not, I think the question should be asked whether or not the dog has the temperament to become a first rate performer.

I have heard of another method, which I have never needed to try, advocated by a top trainer, Steve Studnicki, of the immediate post-war American trial era. We must bear in mind that at this time, pure working springer breeding had hardly got under way and many working and trial springers were heavily tainted with show blood. The first (1947) National Championship winner, Russet of Middle Field, appeared to be more show-bred than working and had a hard, bleak eye. It is reasonable to suppose that on this account, some springers of this era were harder headed and less co-operative than is the case today. If all else failed to turn a springer, Steve Studnicki would walk the dog tightly to heel. Every now and then, he would make a smart about-turn on his heel, blow the turn whistle and give the dog a sharp cut down the ribs with a switch. The dog would shy away from the blow, moving in the direction Steve had taken and thus completing an effective turn. I dislike the idea of this 'forcing to turn' method, and Steve only used it apparently as a last resort, but it is only fair to concede that for a time, he swept all before him in top flight trial competition.

To illustrate what can happen when the instant turn is not instilled properly, I can quote the example of one who is quite a good amateur handler but who is nervous and jumpy in competition. His dogs are well trained and I can't remember one of his dogs ever running in, but instead of insisting on a double-pip turn, he allows them to get away with laxity in this department and relies on three or four more pips to do the job, which makes the performance a mite untidy. I once judged one of this handler's dogs with a top class Irish judge. He liked the dog this handler was running on this occasion but remarked that when the turn

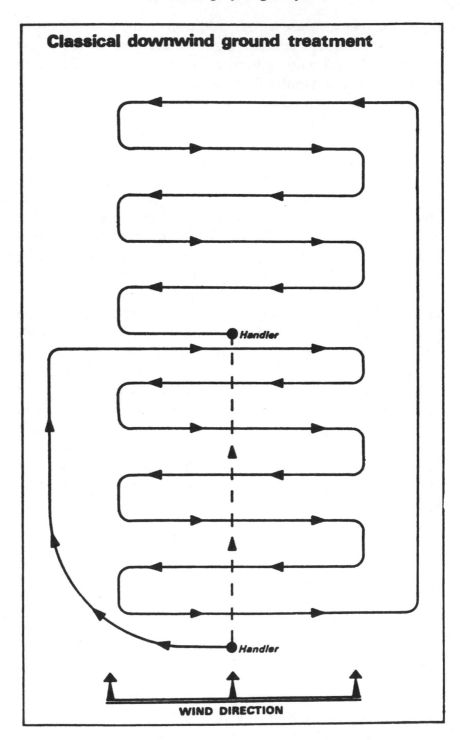

Classical downwind ground treatment

WIND DIRECTION

whistle was applied, instead of turning instantly, the dog said, 'I'll consider it'.

After quartering on an upwind beat has been perfected, it is time to master the downwind beat. This is not understood as fully as it might be, despite the fact that Joe Greatorex explained precisely how a spaniel should handle a downwind beat in the aforementioned 'Guide to Field Trial Judges'. I sometimes wonder if some persons who are alleged to be experienced in spaniel matters ever bother to read rule books, guides, etc., or even apply ordinary common sense. It was once said of a certain handler who has done his fair share, or better, of winning: 'Peter wants his dog to hunt flat across his boots at all times, whether the wind is upwind, downwind, crosswind, or coming straight up out of a hole in the ground.' Dark stories are told across the Atlantic of one top class lady handler who is so terrified of running a downwind beat that if she can foresee that her run will be on a downwind course, she always needs to go to the loo until the course is taken into the wind again. In Britain this wouldn't wash. If you are not there when your number is called, you are on your bike. No

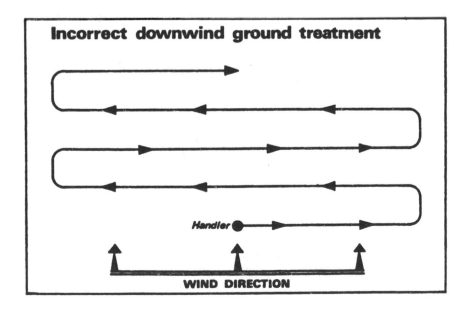

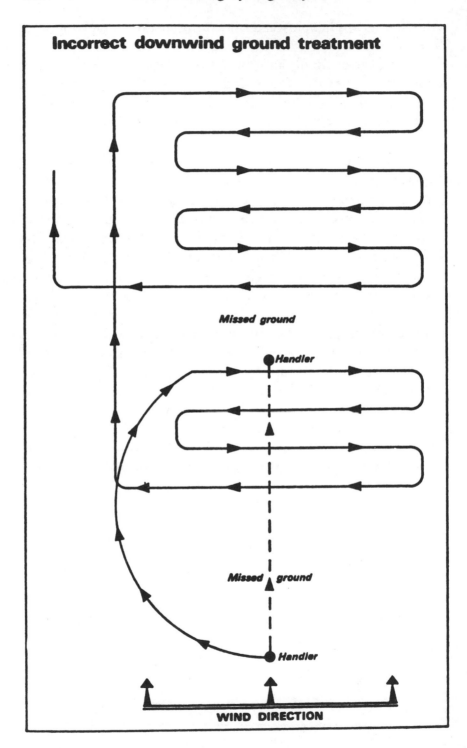

Incorrect downwind ground treatment

running out of order is allowed unless the circumstances are extraordinary, such as if one is handling two spaniels and one has not finished its run when the other dog's number is called on the opposite side. I don't know what all the fuss is about. I find very few spaniels unable to master a downwind beat. Most are willing to circle out in front in an arc and quarter in reverse, right back to the handler's feet. Those who understand downwind ground treatment are agreed that it is permissible for a spaniel to arc out further on its initial cast than would be acceptable on an upwind beat, but some handlers try to bluff their way out of a situation downwind when their spaniel really is not quite under control. It doesn't run amok but reaches out downwind much further than it should, almost out of shot, and never works the ground right back to its handler before taking another forward downwind cast. This is the surest way to miss game as there are gaps in the pattern. Of course the handler will complain that the line was moving forward too rapidly to allow him to make good his ground!

An injustice can occur on a downwind beat if a judge should be inexperienced, negative or both, in the following circumstances. The spaniel has positioned itself correctly downwind and is just about to commence quartering back towards its handler when touchy game, which happens to be positioned between dog and handler, departs of its own volition before the spaniel can make contact. Some judges will put a dog out under such circumstances for 'passing game'. Of course the dog has passed game, but it hasn't *missed* game. Can't these persons of restricted knowledge see that on a following wind, the spaniel must first pass the game to put itself in a position to wind it if the game is sufficiently obliging to stay put? (One night ask who chose such judges in the first place . . .)

Trickiest of all for a spaniel to master is the sidewind, if it is to do a classic job. It must handle the wind in the same manner as a following wind but must do it across the front of the handler from right to left or vice versa. Its initial cast should be across the toes of its handler, down the sidewind, then it should turn into the wind, when it has bitten off a chunk of ground, and should work sort of corskcrew fashion across its handler's front. It is surprising how few can demonstrate this classic pattern. Most handle a sidewind almost like an upwind, which can be effective if the game happens to lie on the spaniel's line of advance as it crosses against the wind, but this method can hardly be considered classic.

In an earlier chapter, when discussing the four types of attitudes to hunting which might be encountered in young

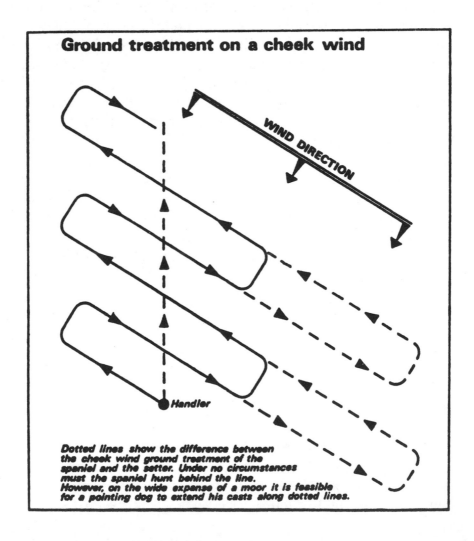

Ground treatment on a cheek wind

WIND DIRECTION

Handler

Dotted lines show the difference between the cheek wind ground treatment of the spaniel and the setter. Under no circumstances must the spaniel hunt behind the line. However, on the wide expanse of a moor it is feasible for a pointing dog to extend his casts along dotted lines.

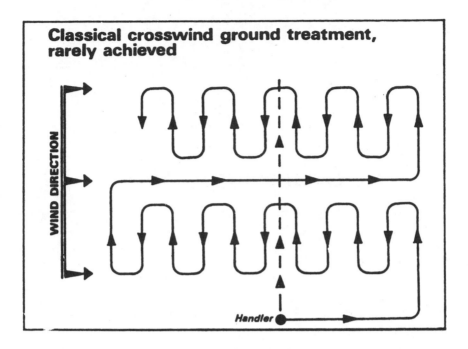

Classical crosswind ground treatment, rarely achieved

WIND DIRECTION

Handler

spaniels, I mentioned the maddening animal which, when turned loose, makes a beeline for the horizon and commences to self-hunt when it reaches a fence. This is the most difficult spaniel of all to get on terms with. My method is to teach it to walk strictly to heel, before I normally would teach this lesson to a more amenable spaniel; and I would give it very short hunts, say no more than 20 yards, in specific pieces of fairly heavy cover, then call it to heel again before it could start 'reaching for country'. Fine in the case of the young bird-dog but definitely not on for a spaniel. By repetition of these short hunts and periods of heeling, hopefully the miscreant will become conditioned to keeping somewhere near me and a steadiness course within the confines of the rabbit pen will with luck consolidate the business. I can only hope that eventually the penny will drop, by which time I will be about ready to thumb the Yellow Pages in search of a good psychiatrist!

17

Dropping to Shot

It is an advantage if a spaniel will drop to shot with no prompting by either command or whistle. A dog which automatically drops to shot has its own built-in steadiness mechanism as the action of dropping to shot is the antithesis of running in to shot. Another advantage is that not every head of game shot over a spaniel under rough shooting conditions will actually have been flushed by the dog. Game can flush wild, either beyond the flanks of the spaniel's beat, or ahead of the questing dog, before nose contact can be made. Under such circumstances, often a dog will drop to shot and get its head up just in time to see the bird hit the ground, so it is able to make a marked retrieve.

I never teach a spaniel, or for that matter a bird-dog, to drop to shot *per se*, but build this lesson in gradually. Theoretically it could be taught in the same manner as a spaniel is taught to drop to whistle, i.e., a blast on the stop whistle followed by the command 'hup'. I do not believe in firing meaningless shots. It is possible for a gundog of any breed not to show any adverse reaction to a shot, yet to be incipiently gun-nervous. This is best illustrated by an experienced trainer's verdict on a cocker spaniel which he was training, whose progress I had enquired about. My colleague replied, 'She's a silly little thing.

She's not gun-nervous, but fire 20 shots over her in a grouse butt and she would be.' To elaborate, a spaniel sitting in the bottom of a butt or hide sees nothing but hears a great deal. It hears every shot that is fired but sees no game fall, nor is the dog ever allowed to retrieve until the drive is over. Unless a dog is 100 per cent confident with the gun and has no hidden reservations about a shot, a succession of shots fired very close to it with no stimulus of falling game to divert its attention could well cause a rot to set in which could set the clock back several weeks, or months – or even, in unskilled hands, ultimately render the pupil non-operative.

It is for this reason that I do not teach dropping to shot by taking the spaniel onto its obedience training area, firing a succession of shots, each followed by the command 'hup'. Some would tolerate such a regime, others would not. My method is to build in dropping to shot in conjunction with marked retrieving. The spaniel by this time is conditioned to drop to the fall of a dummy when it is hunting in front of the trainer. When a shot is introduced, this simply follows the drop to the dummy, so is built in gradually over a period. However, a word of warning which can be applied to any exercise when marked retrieves are given in conjunction with hunting. It is so easy to condition a spaniel to anticipate the dummy to the extent that its hunting can be inhibited through looking at the handler and waiting for the dummy to be thrown. I believe the answer is never to allow the spaniel to see one's arm go back and the dummy to leave the hand. I think the exercise should be stage-managed carefully so the dummy is only thrown when the spaniel is positioned so it is looking *away* from the handler; then, when it catches sight of the dummy in the air, it is not actually aware that the handler has thrown it. Here a dummy launcher can be useful provided the spaniel is fully confident with this somewhat tricky to use device. It can be fired far more surreptitiously than a dummy can be thrown. There is no fumbling in the trainer's bag for a dummy. The spaniel does not see the dummy dangling from the trainer's hand and there is no arm movement as the dummy is thrown. The launcher can be held in front of the handler's body. At the opportune moment, when the spaniel in the course of its hunt is positioned so it cannot see what the handler is doing, the dummy can be launched. But for the actual dropping to shot lessons, I don't think the .22 pistol and the thrown dummy can be bettered.

Once a spaniel will drop to shot smartly, some effort must be made on the part of the handler to ensure that this faculty is not lost. It was brought home to me quite recently how working a spaniel in a beating line can cause it to become lax in this department. The dog will check to every bird it flushes but can hardly be expected to drop to every shot it hears in front, as at times, during a heavy drive, shots can develop into a continuous cannonade. A spaniel under such circumstances would remain permanently seated if it attempted to honour every shot. However, if the handler who works his dog in the beating line aspires to field trial competition he must make an effort to ensure that his charge appreciates the difference between a day's beating and a field trial. Recently, as it happened, I was judging a spaniel field trial and one of the better dogs entered a large area of very tough cover whereupon a rabbit departed unseen by handler, spaniel or myself but had two shots fired at it by the gun on the far side of the cover. The springer didn't check to the shots. Neither did it show any signs of bad behaviour, like leaping out of the cover with bulging eyes, saying 'What was that? Where did he go? Let's have him quick!' The handler was not as quick with his stop whistle as he might have been, but the rabbit was hit and when I told the handler to send his dog, it went through the hedge, struck the rabbit line and collected the legged rabbit unaided. According to the rule book, the dog committed a 'major fault' in 'not stopping to shot and game'. My interpretation of this rule is that after a flush or shot, the dog continues in the direction of the game and is then forcibly stopped by whistle or loud command. This did not apply in this incident and, in any case, the writers of the rule book were not peering over my shoulder. I simply assessed it as rather untidy and the kind of happening which could be used to divide two dogs of equal merit, or during a close finish in a run-off.

However, I did mention it to the handler after the trial. The dog was already a field trial champion and took second place on this occasion, and the handler was experienced and in my opinion is a capable judge himself. His reply was rather surprising. He said: 'He hasn't had a shot fired over him since last January.' I felt the handler had been rather lax. It was obvious that the dog had developed a rough edge or two through beating the previous season and should have been well drilled again in preparation for the following field trial season. All that would have been required would have been for the dog to have been given a few sessions with a dummy and a shotgun, with an insistence on the handler's part, reinforced by verbal command or whistle if necessary, that the dog dropped instantly to every shot fired. Field trials are won by pre-trial training, not just by what happens on the day, as so often the latter is heavily influenced by the former.

18

Working on Blind Retrieves

Good marking ability in a spaniel is a most important attribute. It saves time and eliminates the need for whistles and vocal commands. A spaniel going out in virtually a straight line is far less likely to disturb unshot game which might well lie ahead than if it hunted the ground towards the fall. Nevertheless, there can be instances when a spaniel is unable to mark. Theoretically, when a spaniel flushes winged game, it should immediately drop to flush and never take its eye off the bird until it is killed or missed. In the open situations which one associates with American field trials, this is normally possible and accurate marking can be developed to a fine art, but in the more natural shooting or field trial situations in varying types of cover which one would associate with Great Britain, Europe and the Scandinavian countries, situations will arise when a spaniel is unable to mark. The eye level of a spaniel is limited by its relatively small stature. In large bramble bushes the spaniel often will be completely buried in cover when a bird flushes. In a lower carpet of brambles or bracken, commonly encountered on a woodland floor, even when one can keep the dog in view at all times, an extra six inches of cover above the spaniel's head when a bird flushes could make all the difference between a marked or a blind retrieve. Also bear in mind that a spaniel should vary its head carriage when hunting, sometimes high, sometimes low, so when its head is well down, it is further disadvantaged.

We would live in an ideal world if each and every spaniel possessed the brain power of the great cocker stud force F.T.Ch. Jade of Livermere. When competing in the 1987 Cocker Championship which was held at Vaynor in Powys, Jade had his first run in fairly strong bracken. On locating a pheasant, he struck hard with his nose then immediately lifted his head above the bracken to view the bird away. He did this with every bird so had a perfect mark on every one.

So bearing in mind that there will be many situations when a spaniel will be unable to mark, we must consider how important it is for a spaniel to take direction on a blind retrieve. In many, even the majority, of situations in the shooting field when a spaniel is unable to mark, the shooter will simply mark the bird himself, walk the dog to within a few yards of the bird and hunt it onto the retrieve. Usually this will prove quite effective and few shooting men will demand more, but a difficulty can arise should the bird fall in or over water. A recent example occurred in Sweden. I shot 16 birds in a short afternoon. One fell over a deep drain in arable country in a field where the rich black soil had been ridged for some purpose unknown to myself. The dog I was shooting over, Sheena's Major, crossed the drain and handled out across the furrowed ground, and after quite a bit of handling, located the pheasant. A little later, having worked around a rectangular duck pond, he flushed a hen which fell out into the pond onto a small island. The spaniel was blinded by a screen of willow bushes but worked to command and soon had my bird back. A non-handling dog would have been at a distinct disadvantage.

In British and Irish field trials, handling onto unseen retrieves is an absolute 'must' as so many situations can arise when a dog is faced with a blind retrieve; apart from difficulties which can be encountered when the dog is actually hunting and flushing its own game, it sometimes happens that its brace mate under the other judge fails on a retrieve and the dog which has not flushed the game is expected to attempt the retrieve. British judges do not walk the second dog down right up to the fall. They expect the dog to make a reasonable effort on the retrieve no closer than the gun who shot the game. Another situation can occur when a judge on one side of the line encounters more game than his opposite number, who might be starved for game, and offers a retrieve to his counterpart. The chances are that the dog which is offered the retrieve will have had no opportunity to mark, so must get out and handle blind.

The first step to teaching a dog to get out and search for a blind retrieve is to start it on double-marked retrieves, thrown a few yards apart in easy cover and not too far out. The pup is sent out for what is a marked retrieve and has the option of collecting whichever it first encounters. By the time it has delivered the first dummy, it may have partially forgotten the remaining retrieve and need encouragement to get out and collect. Now the retrieving command should be varied to the one which the trainer decides upon to be the blind retrieving command for the rest of the dog's working life. It could be 'get back', 'get out', or simply 'back' or 'out'. When the pup will go out with confidence and search for the second dummy in response to the new command, it is well on the way to making the mental adjustment from hunting ground in front of its handler to going out in a straight line and hunting for something at a greater distance from the handler than would be consistent with a spaniel's normal hunting pattern.

For a dog to become fully competent on blind retrieves, it must eventually learn to stop to the whistle at a distance, look at its handler and cast either further back, or left or right. To introduce the stop whistle, the pup should be cast ahead, then the stop whistle blown and the dummy thrown right over its head to lie beyond it. A hand signal should be made towards the dummy accompanied by the chosen command. The psychology of this exercise is that the dog stops to the whistle, then can see a dummy lying beyond it in full view, then turns its back on the dummy to face its handler. The blind retrieving command then follows to get out beyond where the handler has stopped it to pick up a dummy, the site of which it is perfectly aware of. After some repetition, the pup should begin to grasp the idea that even when a dummy is not lying in full view beyond it, the specific command following a stop to whistle should be a signal to extend its cast from where it has been stopped, away from, and never back towards, the handler.

The follow-on from this exercise is the 'going back retrieve'. A dummy should be thrown in full view of the pup, then it should be walked away from the retrieve for increasing distances and sent back on the chosen command. When it has demonstrated its willingness to go back for the retrieve with confidence, the pup can be allowed to go back about 20 yards and then be stopped on the whistle. A hand signal and the going back command is then given and the pup completes the retrieve. The follow-on is to allow the pup to get out further and further towards the dummy before being stopped, so eventually one has sufficient control over the pup to stop it within 10 yards of the dummy. The follow-on to this is to put two dummies out for the going back exercise. I would not advocate that the pup is stopped on the first dummy. The last thing one requires is that the pup should anticipate the stop whistle and stop before the whistle is blown. American retriever trainers call this 'popping' and it is a true symptom of overtraining.

Great care must be exercised at all times during directional training. Many springers are rather sensitive and too much intensive work of this nature can cause a loss of initiative and the aforementioned anticipation of the stop whistle and other commands. An amusing situation in reverse can occur in the case of a tough, keen, bold spaniel. I have known a few which, upon being stopped by the whistle, anticipate the next command before it is given and cast themselves back unbidden! – which I suppose is far better than moving back *towards* the handler when told to get back in the opposite direction.

The next step is to teach the left and right hand signal. Most spaniels adapt more readily to this exercise than going straight back, as to cross the front of the handler in either direction is simply an extension of a spaniel's natural quartering. I start this lesson by sitting the pupil down on a completely bare field, throwing a dummy to left or right then backing away about 25 yards. I give a clear hand signal towards the dummy followed by a verbal command to fetch. This is normally learned fairly rapidly, so I make things a little more complicated. I throw one dummy a short distance to one side and a second dummy further out on the opposite side. I want the pup to ignore the last dummy thrown and take my hand signal to pick the first dummy, whereas the last one thrown is uppermost in his mind. This is simplified for him as the first dummy thrown, which I require, lies closer to him in full view. As the last one thrown lies at a greater distance from him, there is a greater margin for error should he elect to go for the wrong one. He can be stopped by whistle before he has gone more than a yard and the hand signal and command for the correct dummy should be repeated. Then, leaving the last dummy thrown on the ground after he has retrieved the correct one, the next step is to walk him back to his sitting position and throw a dummy in the opposite direction to the one already lying there. He is then required to take the hand signal to pick the dummy already on the ground and which he may partially or even wholly have forgotten. Various permutations can be arranged as he becomes more competent, and among the left/right exercises the odd dummy can be placed behind him for a going back retrieve.

Having built into the pupil the idea of taking a hand signal to pick a dummy the whereabouts of which he is fully or at least partially aware of, the next stage is to handle him out to dummies which he has not actually seen thrown. A simple starting exercise is to hup him, cover up his eyes with one hand, throw the dummy behind him and back away several yards. The hand signal and going back command is given and you are well on course if he turns around, takes a step in the right direction, sees the dummy lying there and retrieves it.

If you live in stone wall country, a useful exercise involves sitting the pup down tight under a wall, standing back and throwing a dummy or two over the wall. He sees the dummy leave the trainer's hand but cannot mark the fall, yet has confidence that it lies out there somewhere, so should be in a receptive frame of mind to accept directions from his handler. An advanced directional exercise can be to place two or three dummies out on the ground whilst the pup is still in its kennel, or alternatively, they can be fired out there with a dummy launcher, which saves the trainer's legs and prevents laying human scent trails in the vicinity of the retrieves, which some cunning pupils can learn to profit by.

Some years ago, very many years in fact, I advocated that occasionally it might be a good idea to fire a shotgun in the direction of the retrieves, then make the pupil wait about a minute, then commence the blind retrieving exercise. I believe this can inspire 'gun-sense' and I think a loaded cartridge is so much more effective than a blank shot. Gundogs are extremely highly tuned creatures, far more perceptive than ever we can imagine. After the report, can a dog detect the hiss of the shot charge through the air and does burnt gunpowder scent mean anything to the canine species? We mere humans can never know, but I believe there may be quite a lot in this matter which we don't understand. I was extremely gratified a year or two ago to read something which was quoted as having been said by one of our top labrador handlers, Alan Thornton. Alan stated that sometimes he would fire a shotgun in the direction of blind retrieves. As my career in gundogs preceded Alan's by several years, I wondered if Alan had picked this tip up from my earlier work, or if he had worked it out for himself. Whatever the answer, it seems that with this idea, I am in good company!

Spaniels vary considerably in their attitude to blind retrieving and some quality hunting dogs never really master the art. Others only grasp the point when they are shot over, and in such cases picking up at a few driven shoots can prove extremely beneficial.

19

Jumping Fences

In the locality where I live, there is little scope for spaniel athletics over fences. North Wales is sheep country and sheep mean fences, nasty, dangerous fences of pig netting and barbed wire. Added to this most of the fields are sloping which can be an advantage to a jumping dog when it is on the higher side of the fence, but the uphill approach to the fence when the dog returns with its retrieve can be impossibly dangerous. Some spaniels learn to jump very well but unlike many sheepdogs and retrievers that can jump a fence 'clean', never touching the top strand, a spaniel normally makes for the top strand, balances there for a split second then propels itself forward by a powerful thrust of its hind feet. Here lies the danger. The spaniel can miscalculate or slip, and a trapped or torn leg or abdomen can result. We know that to foxhounds and sheepdogs barbed wire is a natural hazard, but these animals, apart from being better conformed for jumping, are not encumbered by retrieves when negotiating wire.

Some fences are perfectly safe. Modern forestry plantations are often not surrounded by dangerous fences, just strand wire fences to keep cattle out, and a dog can slip through these. However, in sheep country the hazard can remain, and of course many rabbit-fenced plantations still exist and will do so for many years to come.

Jumping really is more of a cosmetic exercise. It looks nice and can save a certain amount of time. I well remember a nice retrieve my triple championship-winning cocker made on hill pastures adjacent to the once famous Ruabon grouse moor. Speckle flushed a woodcock which I shot over a rare sheep fence with no barbed wire topping. The bird fell blind to her and she handled over the fence and out into the adjoining field beautifully and returned with the woodcock, barely touching the top of the fence. Well maintained dry stone walls are perfectly jumpable if of reasonable height, but crumbling walls can present a hazard as a loose top stone can follow the dog down and might catch it as it lands. Some spaniels love jumping fences for no good reason and completely unbidden, and on occasion can become hung up by a hind leg threaded round the top strand then entrapped in the first mesh below. Prompt action on the part of the handler then is required. He must dash forward and seize the spaniel by the scruff of the neck with one hand with the other under the rib-cage, the object being initially to take the weight of the dog's body off the ensnared limb. This can be extremely tricky. Some dogs in such a situation panic and will bite their rescuer, and it can be a big advantage if another person is present who can render assistance.

Specially constructed jumps can be useful. Rabbit wire has the advantage over pig netting as the spaniel can push its head through the latter and try to get through, rather than over. A rail of 4" × 1" timber fixed at the top of the jump serves a dual purpose of keeping the top rigid and giving the spaniel a tangible objective to jump for. It is best to have a series of jumps of varying height on a graduated scale, starting very low to give raw novices confidence, then increasing in height. Many years ago I saw a most sophisticated jumping alley at the Harpersbrook Kennels of Keith and Jack Chudley in Northamptonshire. One side of their rabbit pen formed a side of the alley and another length of wire formed the opposite side. Running the length of the alley were about six jumps of varying construction, including a five-barred gate.

I am rather wary over allowing pupils to jump when very young. After all, out of consideration for its joints, no right-minded person would school a young horse over jumps, so by the same token, I would say that in the case of a spaniel 12 months should be the absolute minimum age for the commencement of jumping lessons.

Very often, if you stride over a jump yourself, the pup will make quite a good attempt to follow, and once he has got the hang of negotiating a low jump, there is nothing like a simple marked dummy thrown over the jump for encouraging him to get over without the example of his trainer climbing over the jump in front of him. Some pupils seem to be completely lacking in confidence when it comes to jumping and will need a lot of gentle persuasion. Here the lead comes in useful. After getting over the fence yourself, the lead proves invaluable in preventing the pup rushing up and down in a panic on his side of the obstacle. He can be lifted so his front paws hook over the top and a hand can be placed at the back of his neck. Usually he will begin to kick against the wire netting of the jump and should scramble over. Beware of trying to tow him over with a slip lead or choke chain. This could panic him and, rather than encouraging him to jump, could implant a fear of obstacles which might be very difficult to overcome. Another encouraging move is to press your knee into the wire netting from your side, thus creating a bulge on his side which could prove more attractive to scramble over than a sheer wall of wire netting. It goes without saying that during all these jumping exercises, a jumping command should be used which will remain constant for the rest of his career.

20

Water Work

Ability in water where a spaniel is concerned amounts to far more than a cosmetic exercise, and its importance will be governed to a large extent by the type of shooting activity the dog is required for. Under many shooting conditions a spaniel need never wet its feet. Under others a spaniel that would not swim would be virtually useless. Many shooters flight duck on fed ponds. Short swims are the norm but occasionally a duck will fall well out and require a greater effort. Some wildfowlers use spaniels, although I feel they might be better served by one of the retriever breeds; but if a wildfowler is also a rough shooter, as many are, and is restricted by circumstances to one dog, then the obvious choice would be to opt for a spaniel unless he preferred one of the Continental hunt, point and retrieve breeds.

A most important point to consider is that under severe wildfowling conditions, a spaniel is less suited than a retriever to frequent immersions followed by waiting under freezing conditions. Coat and body size are important factors. A labrador with a good undercoat is ideally equipped for such a job but spaniel coats vary enormously in type. Some are very thin-coated; they soak up water like blotting paper and emerge from water with their coats plastered flat to their bodies. Then there are rougher-coated springers with almost double coats. I once had such a bitch who possessed quite an oily coat, giving her a distinct off-white colour. Then there is the question of sheer bodily size. A larger animal will lose heat less rapidly than a smaller specimen of the same species, so by this token a large springer is better suited to severe water work than a small springer or cocker spaniel. Although I take with a pinch of salt the claims made by the late Eudore Chevrier (whom I mentioned in chapter 5, 'Spaniel Size and Efficiency') that some of his springers weighed over 60 pounds and could equal any retriever at retrieving wild geese from the ocean, I go along with Chevrier that a big springer is better suited for such a task.

Many shoots have rivers or drains running through them. Where there is good cover on the banks (more likely to be found in agricultural country where there is less likelihood of the banks being grazed right down to the water's edge by hungry sheep), such banks are very favourite places for pheasants to tuck up. Under such circumstances, more birds will attempt to cross the water than will simply fly straight ahead so it is an absolute 'must' that under those shooting conditions a spaniel will retrieve from, and from over, water.

Great care must be exercised when a puppy is introduced to water for the first time. Nothing must happen to alarm it or it might be put off water for the rest of its life. Optimum conditions are a gently shelving entry point preferably with a gravel, rather than a soft muddy bottom, and it is better if the day chosen is rather warm. It is important not to throw a dummy too far out into deep water. A timid pup will not have the confidence to attempt such a swim and an over-bold pup might throw himself in, receive an unfamiliar ducking and require a great deal of time spent on him to persuade him to enter water again. I throw the first few retrieves where he can recover them simply by wading, then gradually place the dummies further out so he has to swim a stroke or two to retrieve. The usual progression is that the pup rapidly increases in confidence and before too long will mark and swim for a dummy as far as it is possible to throw one. However, occasionally a spaniel is encountered which steadfastly refuses to enter water out of its depth. Here a pair of waders will prove their worth. One can then wade across shallow rivers with the pup on a lead, gently towing it behind. One can also wade in and support the pup's body with a hand under its chin and the other under its belly and launch it like a toy boat, to induce it to swim a stroke or two. Usually this will work. A variation is to take the pup swimming – but be warned, you can finish up being horribly scratched when the pup attempts to use you as a landing stage!

Once a pup will retrieve with confidence, the next step is to induce it to retrieve from *over* water. This is sometimes easier said than done. If the opposite bank is at all steep, many young dogs seem to have an aversion to coming down the bank at an angle, head first and with a dummy in their mouths. They will enter with confidence for the initial swim, possibly because the presence of their handler gives them confidence, but once on the other side, having located the retrieve and returned to the river bank, the close proximity of the handler is lacking, despite the spate of encouraging noises which the handler is directing at the reluctant pup. One method which I have used to overcome such a problem is to put a long cord on the pup, keeping hold of the end of the cord and gently towing it down the canal bank when it has located the dummy. Great care must be taken not to jerk the cord, which is likely to cause the pup to drop the dummy and build up an even stronger aversion to entering water from an opposite bank.

21

Walking to Heel

This lesson is the first exercise which normally is taught to a young retriever at the commencement of its obedience course. In the case of the spaniel, however, most authorities would appear to agree that walking to heel should be left till last, otherwise its essential hunting desire might well be blunted. Nevertheless, when a young spaniel is well on in its training and hunting well, it is most essential that it should be taught this valuable lesson for convenience in the shooting field.

A shooting spaniel is not required to hunt all the time. It is expected to deal with specific pieces of cover, then having finished a hunt, walk quietly to heel across pasture, plough or bare stubble until its services are required again. Another instance of where heel keeping is required occurs when the shooter creeps up to a pond or flash, hoping to surprise a wild duck or two, and the same applies when 'duck jumping' along a river, drain or canal. Walking up a snipe bog is another shooting activity where a spaniel is better at heel than hunting. Occasionally snipe will sit tight enough to be flushed by a spaniel. More often they don't and tend to rise of their own volition fairly well in front. When hunters are walking up grouse in line, as opposed to the art form of shooting over pointers and setters, grouse often will sit tight on a warmish afternoon and may well require the services of a spaniel to flush them, but in wet or windy weather grouse are inclined to be jumpy, so under these conditions, it is better to use a spaniel walking to heel as a pure retriever.

Some trainers seem to favour the choke chain to teach heeling, and advocate jerking the pupil back with the choke lead if it pulls in front or jerking it forward if it drags behind. I manage perfectly well with a soft slip lead and a green hazel switch cut from the nearest hedge. The majority of spaniels pull like blazes and I hold the lead in my left hand and fan the switch in front of his nose, using the command 'heel'. He soon learns to respect the switch but will keep trying it on and boring forward if he thinks my vigilance is relaxing, then he receives a gentle tap on the snout accompanied by the command 'heel'. From here on, it is simply a matter of repetition. I use a narrow lane for this purpose and always keep a bank or hedge to the left-hand side of him so the only direction he can try to deviate in is behind me to the right, whereupon he receives a tap and is pulled round behind me into the correct position on my left.

The next step is to teach him to heel free, once walking comfortably on the lead has been mastered. I simply drop the lead and let it drag. During all heeling exercises, either on the lead, with lead dragging or ultimately off the lead, I incorporate a series of sharp turns into the exercises and ensure that the dog turns tightly in his own length when I do. The follow-on to walking to heel with a dragging lead, which offers some slight restraint, is to place the lead in a couple of loops like an 'S' along his back. There is no drag from the lead, so he may believe he is free, and may attempt to break heel. Here the lead is a handy commodity to grab and to drag him back to his correct position, accompanied by the verbal command and a tap on the nose. It is but a short step to walking to heel minus the lead. To ensure that the exercise really is ingrained, after walking him for a distance I will cast him off to hunt for a few yards then call him back to heel. This breaks his concentration and at this point he is unlikely to come cleanly in to heel. I hup him by voice, walk to him and press the switch diagonally across his chest, restraining him until I place myself in the correct heeling position, then, I give the heeling command and we walk on. With repetition of this exercise he will soon learn that not only must he walk to heel, he must *come in* to heel on command when he would rather be doing something else.

Even in a field trial, where dogs are always kept on leads until required to perform, it is important to have a dog which can be called in to heel. If a beat has been dealt with and it is quite a long walk to fresh ground, normally a judge will tell the handler to put the spaniel on a lead. If, however, the distance should only be about 50 yards or so to the next piece of huntable ground, the judge will expect the handler to keep the dog in until required to hunt. He won't attach the same importance to the spaniel's keeping rigidly to heel as would a retriever judge, but he would expect the spaniel to be capable of being kept somewhere in the vicinity of handler and judge and not pulling off unbidden to the next piece of cover. On a recent trip to France, I was most unimpressed with the manners of the French trial spaniels which, when we were changing ground, would rake about all over the place, frequently ranging 100 yards up a woodland ride to no good purpose. Such antics would hardly impress a British judge, so even though it is not so important in a spaniel trial as in a retriever event, most definitely all trialling and shooting spaniels *must* be taught to walk to heel.

22

Artificial Lines

One of the most desirable attributes in any gundog, whatever the breed, is the ability to collect wounded game. Running pheasants, partridges and 'legged' rabbits frequently move a considerable distance beyond the point of impact, grouse less so, but even these can move quite a way from the fall if the ground is fairly open. There are various ploys which can be utilized during the initial training course to encourage a young spaniel to take the line of shot game which it may encounter later on in its shooting career. Having said that, it must be admitted that some dogs never do become proficient on runners no matter how much encouragement is given during the training course or how many runners they are exposed to in a shooting situation. Some just do not seem to develop that essential co-ordination between nose and brain which, let's face it, is the cornerstone of all nose work in a gundog. On top of all other factors, we humans do not really know which scent a dog follows in the case of a wounded bird or animal. Is it blood scent, which some authorities state is a very weak scent indeed, or is it a stronger scent occasioned by shock? Whatever it is, I am convinced the scent from a wounded creature is more difficult to detect than scent given off from an unwounded bird or beast. Did you ever see a wild

'Saturday shooting spaniel' that was incapable of unerringly taking the line of a running pheasant and flushing it ahead well out of shot? The same dog may not necessarily be as good on a shot runner which one desperately needs to put in the bag.

One scent which all dogs seem to acknowlege with absolutely no trouble at all is human footscent, so much so that some transatlantic field trial spaniels become adept at trailing the 'bird planter' who works ahead of the advancing line, 'planting' live pheasants for the competing spaniels to locate and flush. It therefore follows that in any venture involving the laying of artificial lines, it is important that the ground used for the exercise must not be contaminated by human scent. A somewhat laborious method involving the employment of two persons is to tie a dead bird or rabbit to the centre point of a long cord. Each person takes hold of a cord end and the two people proceed forward, holding the cord like a skipping rope with the retrieve dangling in the middle. It is dragged along the ground between the two operatives then, at the end of the trail, it is disengaged and left on the ground. The human participants roll up the cord then make a wide berth to the starting point. The dog is released from its kennel (or travelling box in the car, if ground away from home is to be utilized, which often will be the case where an amateur trainer is involved), and the dog is put on the line.

A simpler method which only requires one person to put into operation requires a length of cord and a hammer. The cord is attached to the hammer and the retrieve is tied to the other end. The operator then throws the hammer as far as he can, which pays out the cord as far as the fall of the hammer. The trainer then runs round in a wide semi-circle to the hammer's location and drags the retrieve in towards him. He unties the cord, which experience tells me he should roll up and take, along with the hammer, back to the starting point – I once had a young golden retriever make a magnificent retrieve of the hammer with miles of cord streaming along behind the dog! So there we have a good uncontaminated line which the pup can be tried on.

A very useful ally when laying lines can be a captive wild duck. In Britain this method requires the services of two persons. One secretes himself some distance ahead of the starting point. There the trainer releases a pinioned wild duck – well, 'wild' simply denotes species, as wild mallard in captivity soon become very tame indeed. They can be quite maddening. Usually when released they will stand with their heads up and quack, going nowhere, but if one is patient, sooner or later the duck will drop its head and snake away, particularly if there is a fair bit of rushy cover on the training area. The accomplice who is carrying out a watching brief picks his moment when the duck has moved a fair distance, runs out and catches the duck in a landing net. Right on the spot where he has arrested the duck, he puts down a dead bird then makes himself scarce. Now there is a lovely natural, though contrived, line to follow. A duck normally leaves a very good scent, whether a bit of blood from a dead retrieve is smeared on the live duck or not. A running duck drags its breast along the ground and the line usually will lay well for several minutes, so you do not need to be in too much of a hurry to lay the dog on.

Of course in some cultures there would be no need to substitute a dead bird for the duck: the dog could simply be allowed to retrieve the duck. Certainly I know for a fact that no legislation in America exists which would proscribe the use of a live duck for retrieving practice. In Britain such a practice could be risky. The duck in nearly all cases would be completely undamaged – ducks have fantastic body armour, but a case brought by the RSPCA for causing the duck unnecessary suffering would be messy and the resulting publicity would not do the cause of field sports a great deal of good. In Britain we must be careful to watch our backs and not to give our opponents any grounds for complaint against us.

23

Punishment

This is an emotive subject in gundog circles, and is a
ready vehicle for mystique, tongue-in-cheek, ambiguity and
sometimes downright hypocrisy, few writers seemingly being
willing to take the bull by the horns and face the issue
squarely. It is well documented, and not infrequently clichéd,
that dogs are pack animals and instinctively look for a leader,
and that to succeed in any form of dog management a human
being must assume the role of pack leader. This seems logical
but we would do well to consider exactly what does happen
within a group of wild dogs or wolves. Not every animal
aspires to be a pack leader, which is just as well, otherwise
there would be mayhem. Among human males, it is said that
the dominant male averages out at about one in twenty. This
is the conclusion the North Koreans came to in the Korean
War, claiming that by careful observation of Allied prisoners,
they could identify the dominants and isolate them. Any
group of prisoners lacking the presence of such a dominant
was much easier to control.

Applying the same logic to the canine race, it would appear
that perhaps a similar proportion of dominants would arise,
both male and female. In a wild situation it is the job of the
dominant male to keep order. In most cases, a growl, raised

hackles and a stiff-legged walk would be sufficient to warn off a potential transgressor. Another, more determined, might have to be rolled over onto its back and menaced with open mouth. Yet another might make a serious attempt on the leadership and receive slashes across the muzzle, ears and forelegs. But if an adversary more evenly matched in size, weight and confidence threw down a challenge, the matter could only end with one of the contestants receiving a severe hiding, which would result in either the challenger being driven off or the original leader being deposed. When we consider punishment during the course of gundog training, these are factors which need to be taken into account. We must also appreciate that a mild punishment, such as a growl or a shaking, which is perfectly adequate for a submissive animal, just would not work on a tough character, and if we give a sensitive animal a really good 'sorting out', we could ruin it for life. My own policy, therefore, is one of 'minimum force'.

In a recent issue of a shooting magazine, three people all registered their strong disapproval of beating a dog, sentiments with which I totally concur. But what is the precise definition of 'beating'? I was privileged to know the late Frank Bell, of the 'Adee' affix. Frank had keepered the Pentrevoelas Moor, in North Wales, prior to the 1914–18 war. He did not consider himself a 'hard' man with a dog and deplored his own father's attitude, which had always been 'give 'em plenty of stick'. Frank further gave the lie to the commonly held belief that gundogs of yesteryear were tougher than are their counterparts of the present day, remarking how nervous many were, and despite regular libations of ash-plant, 'continually broke in through being on edge'. We frequently shot together on a nice piece of arable land near Shrewsbury. Frank brought out a young black labrador one day, his 20-bore and a green hazel stick. The labrador had a penchant for hares. During the course of the morning, Frank's labrador chased four or five hares and received a severe thrashing from Frank each time he caught up with the dog. The punishment seemed excessive but the dog was obviously very tough and finally got the message.

Peter Moxon, for over 40 years Kennel Editor of *Shooting Times*, always promoted the soft approach, but qualified this policy with the observation that occasionally a tougher specimen would be encountered which would require 'three or four strokes with a leather lead'. Would this qualify as a beating? I would say not, in the case of a dog which really had been 'trying it on'.

One authority on the subject quite correctly points out that, in relation to the pain barrier of a dog, physical correction may make a dog dislike you. There are, however, individual cases when a dog is of particularly tough mental resilience, so one is unable to hurt its feelings through vocal displeasure or shaking. Its physical pain barrier must be touched in order to get the message across and, to quote the inimitable Joe Irving, 'give him a glimpse of hell'. But I have always held the view that a prolonged beating is likely to cause a dog so much pain and distress that it will most likely forget what it is being beaten for, and will end up either permanently cowed or completely case-hardened. I also associate this type of punishment with loss of temper, which is a sure recipe for failure in the gundog training stakes.

The question of degree of punishment assumes its most significant proportions when top class field trial dogs are concerned – and I mean the real ones, capable of becoming pillars of their breeds, not the also-ran, occasional novice stake award dogs. They have to be absolutely spot on regarding behaviour, but must not have their dash and flair blunted. Remember, too, that many top-producing sires can be 'almost too much dog', and require firm and talented handling. I know. I've been there. Some top trial handlers acquire unenviable reputations for being too hard on their dogs, on what foundations I know not, although one knowledgeable shooting proprietor and field trial host of my acquaintance was rather upset by the harsh treatment meted out to their charges, on one of his grouse moors, by a couple of top flight labrador handlers.

However, in the light of recent developments, I think it is all too easy to forget that gundogs are now suffering from insidious punishment more than ever before. I refer, of course, to the electric training collar. It is a source of amazement to thinking North Americans, that just when they are beginning to register the undesirability of some of their worst inventions, these seem to catch on in Great Britain. There has been a sustained advertising campaign for these contraptions. Advertising doesn't come cheap. To justify such a high profile promotion, a great many must have been sold. To illustrate the barbarity of these devices, I can do no better than quote from some top American spaniel triallers who are completely opposed to electricity as a training/correction medium, and who have won everything worth winning. They are also keen 'hunters', and on an expedition to shoot chukor (partridge), they rode up a rough mountain track in a 4 × 4. The vehicle hit a pothole and lurched violently. An English setter in the back began to scream in agony. They thought it was in the throes of a fit. It wasn't. It was wearing an electric collar. Its owner carried the transmitter in his shooting vest. The jolt had activated the button, so at close quarters my friends were able to appreciate the horrendous effects of the device.

Man and hunting dog have formed a mutually beneficial partnership for thousands of years. Who wants a push-button partner?

During a fairly long association with field trials (37 years as I write), one of the less salubrious features of these events which has come to my frequent notice over the years is the tendency of some people to kick their dogs for the 'crime' of pulling on the lead. I have never observed this reprehensible behaviour at retriever trials but occasionally have done so at pointer and setter trials and more often at spaniel events. It gives the sport a poor image and is a form of behaviour never indulged in by the top people, and by definition, 'top people' are not invariably those who seem to do the most winning. The matter goes much deeper than that. Kicking a dog is never a fit punishment and, in fact, can be downright life-threatening. Going back in time a great many years, Captain Horatio Ross, a famous shot in his day, made a wager with one of his contemporaries as to who could shoot the most partridges over dogs during a given period. To reach his shooting grounds, Ross journeyed on foot through the East End of London, his team of pointers and setters walking more or less to heel. One must have strayed somewhat from the straight and narrow and seemingly incurred the wrath of a costermonger who gave the dog a kick, whereupon the unfortunate animal died of a ruptured spleen. This must have been an unlucky blow, as the spleen of a dog is a relatively small target, about an inch wide and four or five inches long. My own local vet has informed me of two cases of farm collies which have died from ruptured spleens through being kicked by cows. Apparently they showed no immediate ill-effects but died within two or three hours. I also have a friend who had a rugby-playing friend many years ago who received a kick in the spleen during a match and died as a result. All these fatalities were the result of a kick, not a slap nor a blow from whip or stick, so even though a large measure of ill-luck must have manifested itself in all four cases, these cases prove beyond all shadow of doubt that the toe of a boot is a completely unfit medium for canine correction.

24

His Raison d'Être

Once a young spaniel is through its initial training course it is ready to embark on the voyage of its true vocation. A spaniel is capable of accomplishing a multiplicity of tasks; in fact I would say without fear of contradiction that the only task a spaniel is unable to do is to range far and wide across a grouse moor, take air scent and hold a steady point until the gun can walk up to it. In other words a spaniel can be every dog but a bird-dog. Its true vocation, and the one which my whole training course is specifically intended to cover, is to hunt ground at all times within comfortable gun range of its handler, to find any game thereon and flush it without any attempt to seize the game. This regime applies to British, European and Scandinavian shooting. It must be modified in the case of North America where 'planted' pigeons and pheasants are used for training and trialling. Often these birds are too stupefied to flush so tolerance must be exercised in the case of a pick-up, or 'a trap' as the American triallers call it; and of course, as the American trialler is at all times working towards the hardest possible flush, to try to steady a dog down as it goes in to a hard flush, or to attempt to make the spaniel release the trapped bird, could well end up with softening the dog's flush which is the worst possible thing that could happen. (I don't think we in Britain can afford to adopt a holier-than-thou attitude towards our American counterparts over this, but must appreciate that their facilities and conditions are so different from ours. I poke a bit of fun at action pictures of their spaniels, so proudly displayed in American magazines, going in on birds with their mouths open like crocodiles and with the obvious intention of grabbing the bird before it can take flight, so a flush is simply the result of the bird being quicker than the dog; but I think my American friends are used to me by now and don't take offence. At least they still seem willing to read what I write!)

After the flush, the dog must immediately sit down and watch the game away. It must do so for its own safety, particularly where a rabbit or low-flying woodcock is involved. Although many shooters allow, or even encourage, a dog to run in to the fall of shot game, it is my own belief that a steady dog marks more accurately than its counterpart that begins to move directly the shot hits the game. So many running-in dogs overshoot the fall through excitement and can be the very devil to pull back onto the retrieve, and they run the risk of flushing unshot game that lies ahead. A good marker saves time and avoids disturbing ground. It should be borne in mind that very frequently, when working rough, broken country which can typify much rough shooting terrain in both Britain and America, the spaniel frequently is not in a position at the point of flush to mark the fall; it is in such a situation that a little rudimentary handling ability on what may be a blind, or semi-blind, retrieve can be of considerable use. In a trial spaniel on my side of the Atlantic such a faculty is essential. There are far more rabbits about in many parts of Britain and southern Ireland than was the case a few years ago and, when rabbit shooting, the ability to take the line of a shot rabbit from the flush to the kill saves time and looks good, particularly to a field trial judge, and is valuable in the case of a 'legged' rabbit.

It is of paramount importance to appreciate that when one

starts to shoot game over a spaniel it does not remain the same animal that it was at the end of its training course. The dog begins to develop and the handler, whether he is the original trainer or a new owner, must develop at the same rate as the dog and preferably keep one jump ahead. Once the spaniel finds his true vocation, a rise in his excitement will manifest itself which would never be present to the same extent when working on dummies or cold game, or even when hunting rabbits under pen conditions.

Under shooting conditions the two problems most likely to manifest themselves are pulling too far out away from the handler and running in to shot game. In the first case the handler has a whistle to keep the dog within required range. If it goes beyond that range it can only mean that the dog has disobeyed the whistle. This will be the beginning of the end unless this behaviour is firmly nipped in the bud. If the dog refuses to turn *immediately* the whistle is blown, one should never 'play a tune' on the whistle hoping that the dog eventually will turn. Sometimes it will, but the situation then arises whereby the handler plays the tune continually to keep the dog within shot, which would be annoying for fellow guns and potentially disturbing to game. The time to act is the very first time the dog disobeys the turn whistle. The whistle should never be blown a second, third or fourth time. The gun should quickly be emptied and placed on the ground. The stop whistle should be blown and the handler must cover the intervening yards between himself and the dog with all possible haste. (This is far easier than when a young pointer or setter transgresses in like manner when it is well out into the country and gullies and peat hags intervene to impede the handler's progress and possibly break his legs.) If my instructions have been followed meticulously in the section on stopping to whistle and the spaniel never has transgressed before, it will stop to the stop whistle and allow the handler to catch it. He must then catch hold of the dog by the skin of the throat and tug the errant animal towards him for a few yards, pipping the turn whistle close to its ear. The dog should then be hupped and the handler should count to 20 or 30 to allow the lesson to sink in before it is recast. The retribution should be quite sufficient for any reasonably sensitive young spaniel of 15 to 18 months, but occasionally a dog might be encountered which would laugh at such correction. Such a tougher specimen should be seized roughly around the muzzle and an ear grabbed by the other hand and tugged hard a few times as the dog is dragged towards the handler, to the accompaniment of the turning whistle. Forget the electric collar before you have even thought about it. Hell's own invention has no part in spaniel training unless you live in poisonous snake or porcupine country, but that's another story.

It has been remarked upon by another author that when one shoots over a young spaniel it is most likely to attempt to run in on about its sixth head of game. According to my own experience this would seem to be about right. Its level of interest increases with each head of game it is sent for, and very frequently, by about the sixth retrieve on the ground, it will anticipate the command and attempt the retrieve unbidden, even though hitherto the handler has been most circumspect, always giving a reinforcing 'hup' command before sending, reloading the weapon and making the dog wait about 20 seconds. Usually a vigilant handler can stop the spaniel in its tracks before it has moved more than a yard or two. The culprit should be roughly seized and put back on the exact spot it has moved from and a cuff under the chin should be given. The handler should then pick the retrieve himself and show it to the pup, and the whole incident should be discussed in a growling tone. Dogs do not understand English, French or Dutch, nor the accent of Brooklyn or the West Coast, but they do seem to understand tone of voice with all its implications. One American writer has gone so far as to point out that if one says to a dog 'We're going hunting' in a very unpleasant manner, the dog will look abashed, but should it be said 'We're going to the vet to have you neutered' in a pleasant tone, the dog will wag its tail and give every indication that it thinks the suggestion is an excellent idea!

If the dog refuses to stop to command after its first attempted run in, which, although rare, is always possible, the dog must be pursued with all haste and much vocal displeasure. The object is to distract it and get its head up so one can either grab the dog before it reaches the game, or frighten it away from the fall area. It must be dragged back to the starting point, leaving the game where it fell, and appropriate punishment meted out. Here one must be circumspect. If punishment is too severe it can cause almost insurmountable problems. If it is too light a tough, crafty animal could hold its handler in contempt and try it on again at the first possible opportunity.

Going back to near-basics can reap positive dividends in the case of both the dog which attempts to abandon its correct hunting method and whistle response and the animal which shows signs of unsteadiness to shot game. In the first instance much can be accomplished by simply hunting the dog, gunless, on ground which holds game and therefore scent. It is not the tucked-in game which causes problems but the game that runs ahead and is likely to pull the dog out of its correct pattern. With no intention of shooting, the handler can concentrate entirely on the dog and iron out any rough edges by use of the methods described earlier. (In Britain, expectations differ from those of the Americans; British triallers expect their spaniels to maintain a flowing pattern at all times and be capable of being pulled off moving game instantly, whereas the Americans follow any moving birds, which they term 'runners'. Indeed, in their field trials the Americans have built up a whole major judging scenario where running birds are of the greatest possible importance and can have an enormous bearing on the final placements according to how the contestants deal with 'runners'. A similar scenario exists in reverse between British and American bird-dog trials. In the latter, where no retrieving is required, as in the National Quail Championship, once the point has been established, the dog's work is done. The handler moves ahead of the dog and attempts to flush the game himself. In British trials, once the point has been made the dog must work it out and actually produce the birds for the judge – and woe betide if it is 'sticky' and won't road-in freely and engage its birds! (Particularly if the judge happens to be an Irishman!)

Much can be done in a contrived situation to steady a dog to shot game if it is showing signs of running in. Here again natural ground with some game scent is the most useful as the dog can soon be encouraged to get a move on, then when it is really enjoying itself and its head is looking away from the handler, a cold bird can be thrown and a live cartridge fired. This should be carefully stage-managed so that if the dog is, say, to the left of the handler, then the bird should be thrown to the right. If the dog is in motion when it hears the shot fired, spins round and sees the bird falling, it is virtually guaranteed to run in, but as it has to cross the front of the handler to get to the bird, the handler is in the best possible position to intercept the dog. A moving dog is far more likely to run in to something that, out of the corner of its eye, it sees falling, than if it had actually found game and hupped to it, then seen it shot, even though on a shooting expedition it may have run in to game which it had found and flushed. The object is to create a situation of maximum temptation so the dog can fully commit itself, and corrective measures can then be taken.

Occasionally I have been asked for advice on such a steadiness problem, which I have given as above. The questioner has then informed me that he 'took her shooting and just managed to hold her'. Result: the bitch ran in at her very next trial. It is no use being able 'to just hold her' in a shooting situation. To a potentially unsteady dog tensions inevitably are much higher in a trial than out shooting, so away she goes! One must be able to not merely 'just hold' a spaniel in a shooting situation. In such a scenario it is most essential to be able to hold it by a very substantial margin so that in the more rarefied atmosphere of a trial, it is sufficiently stable that *it does not want to run in*. It is quite possible to achieve such a happy state of affairs without taking any of the fire out of the spaniel. My last notable spaniel only once ever ran in on me in a shooting situation, and I stopped him within four yards and convinced him it just wasn't on. He learned the lesson very well and never ran in at a trial, nor ever needed restraining. Whilst hunting it was impossible to whistle him down on a flush. His reaction to game was so fast that he could put his behind down quicker than I could blow a whistle. Had he been other than 100 per cent honest he could have been after the game just as quickly!

The foregoing has covered the main function of the spaniel but is only applicable if the handler has access to good rough shooting. Not every spaniel owner is so blessed, which is reflected in the fact that nearly all the major stakes nowadays are won by those persons who do have access to plenty of shooting, even though some may have to travel quite a long way to find it, maybe over 500 miles in some cases. Many persons without such facilities have to rely on work in the beating line of driven pheasant shoots to subject their spaniels to any game contact at all. At one time, dogging in pheasants for a friendly gamekeeper could provide game contact, but owing to changing habits in the modern reared pheasant, it is now far more difficult to get useful flushes. So many reared pheasants refuse to tuck in and simply run ahead of the approaching spaniel and handler in a bunch and seldom flush at all. I am not too keen on working a potential trial spaniel in a beating line but I have done it, and in the absence of shooting facilities, such work is better than no work at all. A major problem is that as the flushed birds are not shot over the spaniels in the beating line, there is no encouragement to mark the many flushed birds and the tendency is for the spaniel to turn its head away after a bird has departed. I must admit that at times when I have worked spaniels in the line, I have also had access to adequate rough shooting so my spaniels may not have been so disadvantaged as some.

Another avenue to be explored for finding work for spaniels is by picking up at driven game shoots. This can be useful for giving a dog experience in retrieving, particularly in developing its confidence and ability on runners and tucked-in wounded game. It can also serve to teach a dog scent discrimination, so when searching for wounded game, it learns to distinguish between the scent of a bird which may only have one pellet in it and the completely untouched bird which the spaniel should honour by simply flushing it with no attempt to grab it then watching it away and continuing its search for legitimate quarry. Over 30 years ago when most shooting parties were happy to shoot between 100 and 150 birds on a shooting day, some excellent picking up could be enjoyed by standing well back behind the guns and marking down individual hit birds. One could walk to within sensible handling distance then send the dog out for useful blind retrieves. Nowadays the tendency is for larger bags and pickers-up frequently are expected to pick up large quantities of birds which fall directly behind the guns (many of them come from overseas and are by this token, dogless). A colleague describes this type of picking up as 'browsing on birds'. There are so many down that picking a designated bird is difficult, if not impossible. It does nothing for a dog's handling ability and if a trial spaniel is subjected to this type of work, really it should have one lesson at home to brush it up on its handling technique after every day's heavy picking up – difficult perhaps when a picker-up works on commercial shoots when frequently many consecutive days' shooting take place. Leaving aside the pros and cons of picking up as just described, one positive aspect is that picking up can teach patience and stability under heavy shooting conditions, although it might send a minority of spaniels right over the top! Personally I have never had any such problems. Spaniels on the whole may appear to be restless, highly charged dogs when about their traditional business of hunting for and flushing game, but I have discovered that nearly all spaniels 'switch off' during a heavy drive and never squeak or attempt to run in. Nor do they seem to require specific training. Many years ago I had a lovely, class springer that was not quite right in his head. He had a light but soft-expressioned eye (in itself something of a rarity). He was very steady under normal conditions but would boil over on the second day of a Championship. I first took him picking up when he was over 5 years of age and he adapted to it like a duck to water, quiet, dead easy and deadly efficient. Not surprisingly, he was a disappointment at stud, siring only three novice stake winners, although a grandson won the Spaniel Championship.

It seems most unusual for a light-eyed springer to make a good stud dog. This is one of the imponderables of the spaniel world and the reason for it cannot properly be pinned down. There is no guarantee that a dark-eyed springer will make a good stud but it is an inescapable fact that most successful studs have been dark-eyed. In this category I would place Wakefares Sprig, Pinehawk Sark, Hales Smut, Markdown Muffin, Gwibernant Ashley Robb, Saighton's Stinger (in America only), Rytex Rex, Badgercourt Druid, Cortman Lane, Badgercourt Moss, Skipper of Arford, Robbson of Gwibernant and Conygree Simon. Conversely, Willie of Barnacre and Robbie of Barnacre were disappointing studs and left no good recessive qualities as some poor studs seem capable of, usually through sound but non-competitive daughters. Willie and Robbie were both dark-eyed.

Springers can make excellent dogs for evening flighting at fed flight ponds and also for flighting on marshes and 'washes'. Some have used them for coastal wildfowling, although my first choice for this would be any of the retriever breeds. It is worth repeating that spaniels, being smaller than retrievers, lose body heat quicker, so for frequent immersions, a large springer is at a distinct advantage.

I have used springers quite successfully for walking up grouse, walking them to heel retriever-fashion, and sometimes hunting up with them on a warm afternoon when grouse were lying tight; but not all springers are the best dogs for working in conjunction with pointers and setters when handling one's own bird-dogs. Not many persons in Britain would attempt such an activity but I have done, and discovered that a really fiery springer resents being walked to heel. When roading-out birds, the springer, although not designed by nature to be an air-scenting dog, can get the air scent of the grouse as the bird-dog roads in and needs constant reminding not to go in and flush. Some softer springers register their jealousy by laying down in the heather and refusing to move. I would imagine that if a person were to take a springer picking up to assist when shooting over dogs, such problems might not arise. Dog handling is such a personal business between dog and handler that a springer most likely would not mind walking to heel with its master while another handler worked the bird-dogs; but for myself, the system has not worked too well.

Another burning question is whether or not a spaniel is a suitable dog for the average shot to use as a driven game dog. Here I believe the answer lies more with the individual gun than the choice of gundog. A good working-bred spaniel can make a perfectly adequate driven game dog but really the handler should be a committed spaniel handler. I have always used spaniels on the rare occasions when I shoot driven pheasants and it has worked perfectly well, our above-average performance giving the lie to those pundits who insist that if a spaniel is used at a drive it will fidget, give tongue and run in. I have shot with as many as three trial spaniels sitting in front of me together on a 300-bird day. However, this is not to say that it would work for everyone. A great deal depends on the handler. I am afraid that in the shooting field I am not very good company. I tend to avoid groups when walking to my peg and concentrate on keeping my dog(s) walking tidily to heel. I do not indulge in loud banter and leg-pulling but prefer to keep that until luncheon or the end of the day. So many driven game shooters work hard all week then use their Saturday shooting days to relax and have fun, and who am I to blame them? But it is not conducive to disciplined spaniel work. Unless getting well on in years, no dog is quicker to take advantage of laxity on the part of its handler than a spaniel. One has to be really serious-minded or else behaviour is likely to lapse irrevocably.

Two cases in point of serious shooting men were the late Colonel Sir Watkin Williams–Wynn, MFH, and the late Sir Joseph Nickerson. Sir Watkin always shot over spaniels, usually black-and-white. Although, admittedly, they did not possess the fire of trial spaniels, his dogs were perfectly behaved in grouse butt or at covert side and methodically picked his birds after each drive. Sir Watkin, although by no means humourless, always conducted himself with the utmost decorum characteristic of a bygone age and it seemed to rub off on his canine charges. Sir Joseph Nickerson was something of a martinet on shooting days. Everything had to be just right and his dogs were always spot on. Usually he shot over labradors, although in his latter years he had a black cocker spaniel. Such was his command of man or beast that whether he had used a cocker or a capuchin monkey, either would have behaved impeccably!

The rot seems to set in with a spaniel if it needs to be tethered. If it needs pegging down this means that it wants to be in after the birds directly they hit the ground. If it is then restrained, most spaniels will resent this and give tongue, much to the annoyance of the fellow guns. If a driven game shot decides on a spaniel, it is probably better if he keeps it on a lead between drives then takes the lead off when he reaches his peg. The spaniel should be seated in front of him where he can keep an eye on it continually, and as a bird approaches which is clearly his, should give a sharp command 'hup' as he mounts his gun, to impress upon his spaniel that it is still under surveillance. If the bird is killed, the gun should deliver another 'hup' as he breaks his gun to reload, just to remind the spaniel that it has not been forgotten in the excitement of the shot.

25

The Importance of a Good Mouth

That a gundog should possess a 'soft' mouth is understood by many, even those who do not shoot. Read any book written on dogs by a non-shooting pundit and the chances are that under some gundog breed heading, the statement 'This breed is noted for its soft mouth' will most assuredly appear. Those of us who shoot and who handle gundogs realize full well that this is a sweeping generalization and in reality the position is subject to a great many variables.

Some time ago I read a letter in a contemporary country magazine where the writer denigrated the modern field trial type labrador as regards its physical conformation and eulogized the 'old-fashioned type', with its 'soft square muzzle designed for handling game tenderly'. I replied to this letter and pointed out that this 'soft square muzzle' was armed with a set of sharp teeth and awesome jaw power, and that what a given dog, whatever its conformation, did or did not do to its game was completely dependent on what was going on inside the dog's brain. In simple terms, the *intention* of the dog towards its game is far more important than mouth structure. The bottom line is that any dog of any breed can retrieve tenderly should it wish so to do. Every carnivore, large and small, has the inherent ability to carry its own young should danger threaten or if it simply decides to use another earth or den. The stoat has a mouth full of needle-like teeth but can transport its own kits, and at considerable speed too. A stoat nearly always seems to be in a hurry. That notorious killer, the domestic cat, which proportionately has a much smaller mouth than a dog, can also carry its live prey considerable distances when transporting mice or young rabbits home for its kittens to play with, to further their education in the predatory game. Once I saw one of my own cats approaching me with a bird in its mouth about the size of a quail. It had one wing free, which it stretched out at intervals. I identified the bird as a greater spotted woodpecker, a species far too rare and desirable to be converted into cat food, so I threw a plastic measure at the cat. Fortunately my aim was true and upon being hit by the measuring jug, the cat released the woodpecker which flew out of the cat's mouth with no encumbrance and perfectly normal flight.

Shot game ultimately is destined for human consumption and either will grace the table of the shooter responsible for its downfall or, if a by-product of larger shoots, will enter the game market and could well be exported to those Continental and Scandinavian countries where game is more esteemed at the present time than it seems to be in Britain. When a deer or moose is killed by a high velocity bullet there will be a limited amount of meat spoilage around the area where the bullet exits, but in larger game, even a roe deer, such spoilage is sustainable whereas in the case of small game, dog damage is intolerable. From a personal point of view, I like game to be hung as long as possible, with the exception of wild duck, snipe and woodcock, and of course one must be circumspect over grouse in warm weather. The more cleanly shot game is, the better it will age when hanging and the same applies regarding lack of dog damage. Should a gundog crush the ribs of game, the meat of the breast and legs will not be damaged, but should one attempt to hang the bird, it will commence to putrefy around the site of the bruising and crushing. If the game is eaten fresh this factor could be avoided, but I for one have no taste for too fresh game. I also believe a hereditary factor can enter the picture and if one breeds from a dog which is inclined to damage the ribs of its game, subsequent generations could turn out to be far worse and a strain of manglers could arise where the meat would be chewed up in addition to the ribs being crushed.

This factor, although I have always subscribed to this theory, recently was brought home to me by an article I read in an American gundog magazine, written by one of its regular columnists, on hard mouth and its 'cure'. I am not about to fall into the trap of saying 'all American gundogs are hard-mouthed'. I certainly do not believe this is the case, but taking into account the large number of articles I have read by American writers it seems that the incidence of hard mouth experienced on that continent is greater than we would expect to find *in our top working and field trial lines in Britain*. In giving his personal assessment of hard mouth, this writer spoke volumes. He stated that if a dog retrieved a bird and that bird was 'fit to eat', then as far as he was concerned he was happy with that dog's mouth and presumably would consider it to be a suitable breeding prospect. In Britain our greatest gundog authorities always have considered hard mouth to be incurable. I well remember the late Joe Greatorex giving the shortest answers to a two-part question at a gundog forum which I attended as a panellist alongside Joe. A questioner asked, 'Is hard mouth hereditary and can it be cured?' Joe stood up and said 'Yes, and No.' There you have it in a nutshell. However, other schools of thought exist in America. The writer of the article referred to went on to describe how he cured a German shorthaired pointer which positively mangled its birds. He started by giving it a complete course of force retrieving with a dummy so he could walk the dog around on a lead for up to half an hour at a time until the dog was absolutely fed up with carting the dummy around. He then substituted the dummy for a deep frozen pigeon which the dog was unable to bite even if it had wished, and again repeated the exercise to the point of boredom. He claimed that this effected a cure for the dog's hard mouth, but I wonder what his attitude would be towards the dog as a future breeding prospect? Informed breeders in Britain certainly would never dream of using such a dog for breeding, and as we have no tradition of attempting to cure hard mouth, the dog would have most likely been relegated to the status of a falconer's dog where retrieving does not enter the curriculum.

One of the most important aspects of field trials for all breeds which are required to retrieve is that, provided the judges are up to their job, trials discriminate against hard mouth and (theoretically at any rate) provide a *cordon sanitaire* to guard against the perpetuation of this fault. This is where a judge's shooting and gundog handling experience is of such enormous significance as it will prevent those doubtful animals slipping through the net which a lesser judge might allow, either through inexperience or through lack of guts and fear for his own popularity. The judge who knows what he is about will also be more understanding in relation to game which may have been damaged by shot, fall or tree strike. Shot birds can fall with amazing velocity, even the comparatively low, going away birds one encounters most commonly when shooting over spaniels. Birds which are shot dead close in can be particularly hard to judge on when presented in a damaged condition. Often one can observe the bird crumple into a ball and be driven a yard or so through the air at the impact of the shot, and on a still day a haze of cut feather fronds can be seen to hang in the air above the fallen bird, signifying a hard body strike. A dog should never have its mouth queried in such a situation but when a bird is killed with a really nice 35- to 40-yard shot, probably in the head and neck, I would expect that bird to be delivered intact; if damaged, I would require to be made aware of other extraneous circumstances which could have caused the damage before I exonerated the dog.

Live birds are far easier to judge on than those which are killed stone dead. If a bird is hit so hard by shot that its ribs are damaged there is no way that bird is ever going to run.

Shot which breaks ribs is going to carry on into the body cavity and do serious internal damage, accompanied by heavy shock. A bird which hits the ground running needs to come back alive and undamaged but one must bear in mind that a single pellet in the edge of the lung, which delivers minimal shock, can allow a bird to run a considerable distance before it collapses. I have found through experience that such birds are delivered limp and stone dead, with no reflexive fluttering. I don't like it when a dog picks a lively runner then presents the bird in a dying condition accompanied by heavy wing beating. Usually this proves to be the hallmark of a killed runner. The dog catches the bird, bites it and the bird dies on the way in, fluttering and closing its eyelids. The lung-hit bird which runs away strongly dies before the dog catches up with it in the majority of cases, and as death is due to haemorrhage, dies quietly and without the violent reflex actions of a bitten bird. It will of course be found to have all its ribs intact and in such a case there should be no doubt whatsoever in the judge's mind as to what has happened. It seems that in American spaniel trials there is frequently controversy over birds which are picked up in a dead or dying condition from where they have been 'planted'. Really there should be no problem. Weak birds sometimes die after being planted. A minority can die of shock just through being handled, so the criteria should simply be: a dead undamaged bird and the dog is still in, a squashed dead or dying bird and the dog is out.

An additional factor which can govern whether game is damaged or not is related to the kind of cover a bird falls into. Some dogs have perfect mouths when retrieving from open ground, even when they have to contend with lively runners, but seem all at sea when a bird has to be pulled out of cover. Some never seem to acquire the knack of extracting a bird from cover without causing the game damage. It seems that when they encounter resistance from cover which holds onto the bird, they meet such resistance with force and take too tight a hold on the bird rather than extracting it carefully. I think such skills or lack of them can run in families. I had one famous springer stud dog which could take a live bird out of the thickest brambles intact and so could all the six field trial champions he sired, yet there is another fashionable stud dog that always seemed to have problems in this department and some of whose progeny seem similarly affected. I think this is where a brainy dog is at a distinct advantage.

26

The Principles of Breeding Good Spaniels

Livestock breeding is relatively easy: getting it right is a far more difficult proposition. The gundog breeder is somewhat at a disadvantage over, say, the bloodstock breeder. The breeding of thoroughbred racehorses is arguably the most sophisticated animal breeding industry known to man. An enormous amount of money, worldwide, has been thrown into this enterprise, often by individuals who comfortably can afford to lose millions when things go wrong but for whom the rewards can be very great when their breeding (or buying) ventures prove successful. By contrast, a minuscule amount of finance is poured into gundog breeding and, as far as Great Britain is concerned, less money is put into gundog breeding than in former times, before the breakup of the great estates, many of which bred their own strains of gundogs and employed private trainers and handlers. Those of us today who are in possession of shallower purses than many of our predecessors owe a great debt of gratitude to those who came before, from the fifteenth-century developers of the 'Land spaniels' on the Continent, from which both the English setter and English springer spaniel derive, to the early field triallers of our own century, people such as Mr C. A. Phillips, C. C. Eversfield, Lorna, Countess Howe,

Captain Traherne, Mr Trotter and Mr Selwyn Jones. To us they bequeathed a legacy of good sound stock which some of us have been able to convert into good working and winning stock in our own era.

The financial returns from any ventures into gundogs, be they breeding, trialling or both, are very meagre compared to what a successful racehorse can win in prize money or, if allowed to remain entire, to earn at stud. Nevertheless, despite the wealth and sophistication of the industry, the racehorse breeders still cannot always get it right. If only winners were bred, how could there be any losers? The gundog breeder, on far more limited resources, has to produce far more in his hunting or trialling spaniels than does the racehorse breeder or, it could be argued, any other form of livestock. A racehorse needs the speed to win and the competitive will to race. The track greyhound simply requires the speed to chase an artificial hare around a racetrack faster than the other dogs. A coursing greyhound requires the speed to overhaul a hare and the ability to turn sharply after its quarry, which nature has provided with the ability to turn far tighter than its pursuer. The fighting bull, whether it fulfils its destiny in the gory bullrings of Spain or the bloodless arenas of Portugal or the Camargue, must be willing to charge any human being that confronts it. The spaniel must pursue its natural predatory instinct to hunt game but must desist from catching the game on close contact. It must learn to forgo its natural desire to pursue the game, whether it is the game it finds and flushes or any game it accidentally bumps into during its search for shot game. All this is a very tall order and full of contradictions. Consider how much more simple is the training and function of a bird-dog. Granted, it should be steady to rabbits and hares but as these creatures are not the traditional quarry of pointers and setters, it should be simpler to persuade the dog to ignore them through not stimulating its interest in them, whereas the spaniel must hunt them diligently and so possess a keen interest in ground game. As for the rest of the bird-dog's function, it has its brakes on when game is encountered and the situation under a traditional British regime precludes its bumping into game when out on a retrieve, as purists do not expect their bird-dogs to retrieve. There is also the important question of range. A spaniel must have the temperament whereby it can be kept within comfortable gun range at all times with minimal effort, whereas if a bird-dog covers an extra 30 yards more to its flank, nothing is spoiled. The spaniel must work within far more precise limits and not allow its keenness to be blunted on account of such fine limits being imposed upon it.

The English springer spaniel of the present time is largely descended from three strains, being in terms of seniority the Rivington, the Bryngarw and the O'Vara. The Rivington strain was founded by Mr C. A. Phillips and his spaniels were handled by James Thomson and later his son Colin. The Bryngarw dogs were owned by Captain Traherne and handled by Mr Church, and the O'Vara dogs, arguably the most famous and influential of them all, were owned by Mr Selwyn Jones and handled by Joe Greatorex. The most famous Rivington dog of the post-war period was F.T.Ch. Rivington Glensaugh Glean, who won the Any Variety Spaniel Championship but Cocker in 1950 at Blenheim Park in Oxfordshire. Glean was an outcross, having been sired by John Kent's F.T.Ch. Silverstar of Chrishall out of Kingsham Keepsake. Glean was a fantastically stylish mover with a built-in hunting pattern, but, although deadly on the line of a wounded rabbit, was not renowned as the greatest finder of unshot game. His career at stud was somewhat strange. Altogether Glean sired nine field trial champions, including two Championship winners, but a concentration of his blood on two or more lines could produce either brilliance or insanity.

The Bryngarw bloodlines have come down to us via the late Tom Evans, who managed to scrounge one or two bitches from Captain Traherne. Joe Greatorex once told me that originally the Bryngarw springers were splendid dogs but that Tom Evans 'messed about with them and got hard mouth into the line'. I don't quite know what Joe meant but I have a suspicion that he introduced Irish setter blood. Many of the 'Garwgarreg' dogs, as Tom Evans's line was called, and their descendants, showed a dark red coat rather than the more conventional liver, and were tremendously fast. From experience I can testify that although Irish setters are dogs of the open country, they are tremendous in punishing cover like brambles and blackthorn, given half a chance, but whereas I have known several Irish setters that were excellent natural retrievers with perfectly good mouths, the breed has not been bred deliberately for good mouths. Perhaps this is where Tom's problem arose, one which we are still not wholly free of.

The O'Vara dogs were a different proposition. Much thought and money went into the strain and current thinking suggests that Selwyn Jones was a brilliant breeder and puppy rearer and Greatorex was an exceptional trainer and handler. It has been said that Greatorex hated puppies but Selwyn Jones loved them, that he was a great 'humanizer' and could produce the goods in the form of 9-month-old prospects for Greatorex to assess and train on. Greatorex for his part would not allow Selwyn Jones to have any of the stud dogs at his home on Anglesey as, being the kindly man that he was, he would have allowed the locals to scrounge cheap or free studs for their bitches – so in no time at all, Anglesey would be over-run by half-bred O'Vara springers! The O'Vara kennel operated a policy of strict line breeding, consistently mating related dogs and bitches but not inbreeding brothers and sisters or parent and offspring. Occasionally an outcross was brought in, but in the old O'Vara pedigrees I have seen, the only outcrosses I could find were the Scottish F.T.Ch. Daud and the bitch Judosa. The policy worked and produced 17 field trial champion springers of which the most influential was Spy O'Vara, who was the foundation stone of all future O'Vara matings.

In present-day terms the two most influential stud dogs were Spark and Sarkie O'Vara. A daughter of Spark O'Vara and Ludlow Gyp, Ludlovian Diana, was mated to Rivington Glensaugh Glean and produced F.T.Ch. Markdown Muffin, winner of the 1962 Championship. Muffin has been very heavily used and although sired by the somewhat capricious Glean, line-breeding policies to Muffin have of course increased the influence of Spark O'Vara, a more consistently bred dog than Glean. Sarkie O'Vara has been an enormous influence through his daughter, the first post-war Championship winner F.T.Ch. Breckonhill Bee. Mated back to her own grandson, Breckonhill Buddie, this union produced my own Breckonhill Brando who was mated to Conygree Simon, a three-quarter-bred O'Vara dog and a great-grandson of Sarkie. The Simon/Brando mating produced the legendary Hales Smut (owned by Arthur Cooke), so far the greatest producing springer sire of all time, with 13 field trial champions to his credit and who, doubtless on account of his sound O'Vara bloodlines, has been line-bred to time and time again with no untoward results, either mental or physical. The present-day springer has received its admixture of Bryngarw blood via the somewhat dubious exploits of Tom Evans and his Garwgarreg dogs. A successful sire of fairly obscure antecedents, F.T.Ch. Burnhatch Soda, was mated to a part-Garwgarreg bitch and produced the prepotent F.T.Ch. Don of Bronton, which figures in many of today's pedigrees, often many times over.

It often has been remarked that in any breeding venture, it is essential to commence operations with really sound females; this is counsel of perfection and frequently honoured in the breach rather than the observance. Let me again quote the late John Nash, himself the most notable breeder of Irish setters in the latter half of this century: 'The bane of the gundog world is poor, well bred bitches, mated to good, or fashionable sires.'

Alas, how often in these degenerate times is this scenario enacted. In the days of the great foundation kennels anything substandard was put down, no matter how illustrious it looked on paper. Unless the genes had come through favourably, the pedigree *per se* was not worth the paper it was written on. The great kennels were not out for financial gain and their common object was to produce shooting dogs which could win field trials. Nowadays with gundog ownership so widely distributed, the temptation to mate a substandard, or even faulty, bitch to a fashionable stud dog must be considerable, in order to produce a litter of puppies for sale. How often do we see advertisements in the sporting press, 'Springer pups for sale. By F.T.Ch. Boozer of Borkindale out of good working bitch'? Just how good she is could be anybody's guess. William Arkwright suggested that the ideal brood bitch should be the favourite shooting companion of its master and it could be taken for granted that a good dog would be found to complement the bitch's excellence. I think Arkwright's remarks may sometimes have been taken out of context, giving rise to the mistaken idea in some quarters that provided the bitch is a good one, almost any old dog would do. I can even quote Joe Greatorex as having said: 'A top class bitch will produce good pups when mated to almost any reasonably good dog.' The interesting point is that if one studied the O'Vara pedigrees it soon became apparent that they had not themselves followed this somewhat *laissez-faire* policy!

To follow the policy in reverse and mate a poor bitch to an excellent dog sometimes can appear to produce spectacular results in the short term, but it is said that if one manages to produce a good dog from a prepotent sire and a poor dam, the dog is most unlikely to prove to be a successful stud dog in its own right. One stands a far better chance of producing a desired knock-on effect if Arkwright's policy is followed to the letter. Certainly in my own case Arkwright's words were vindicated when the exceptionally sound and competent Breckonhill Brando produced the great Hales Smut. The experience was compounded through the bitch Macsiccar Auchtertyre Donna. Like Brando, Donna won an open stake, but though she never achieved her title she was a bitch of exceptional merit and excellent to shoot over under all circumstances. She was not of my breeding but had a line to Conygree Simon which tied up with a son of Hales Smut which I had, F.T.Ch. Gwibernant Ashley Robb. From the first litter Donna produced by Robb, there were three field trial champion bitches, two of which proved to be influential breeders, plus another sister who did not reach their heights in competition. From a repeat mating came two field trial champion dogs, one of which won the Championship; both these brothers each sired a Championship winner and their influences have continued to come down to this day.

Hopefully the foregoing will have given the present-day reader an insight into what has proved successful in the past, as similar procedures could well be effective now and in the future. It seems that policies of informed line breeding are the ones most likely to produce the goods. As for the relationships between prospective mates, it would appear that uncle to niece, half-uncle to half-niece, nephew to aunt, half-nephew to half-aunt, grandsire to grandaughter and grandson to grandam have been consistently successful matings in the past. But nature occasionally flies in the face of such reasoning as often a very good bitch will not produce progeny as good as herself, but these lower quality offspring can make excellent breeders provided they possess no glaring faults. Similarly, if a brilliant dog is a virtual failure at stud, his daughters could well be excellent breeders. This effectively contradicts the John Nash theory regarding well-bred but poor bitches being mated to good dogs, but as it was the great man himself who put forward the alternative view regarding the mediocre daughters of the great quality but unsuccessful stud dog proving to be valuable breeders, it just goes to show that one must always keep one's options open.

27

Breeding a Good Litter of Puppies

There are lots of dogs around. The RSPCA believes there are too many, and shows us horrendous pictures of mountains of dead, unwanted dogs which the Society's inspectors have had to put down. The Kennel Club, on the other hand, although paying lip-service to the condemnation of 'puppy farming', wants lots of pedigree dogs to be born and registered at £7 (currently) per puppy, otherwise it would not frown upon the practice of reducing litter sizes, in those cases where a bitch has too many whelps for her own good, or considering the general tone of the litter. The Kennel Club is badly in need of all possible revenue. Think of the thousands upon thousands of pack hounds, farm and trial sheepdogs, track and coursing greyhounds, working terriers and lurchers, which do not yield a single penny to swell the Kennel Club's coffers. The reader, by now, may have deduced that I don't much care for monopolies.

However, whatever the views of the two official bodies quoted, dogs will continue to be bred for a multiplicity of reasons. The dedicated show or working breeder will wish to continue to obtain replacements, either by breeding or by buying in, as his/her winning dogs near retirement. Someone might own a very desirable bitch, and the owner and some friends might want a pup from her – but be warned, friends can tend to evaporate when a litter finally materializes. The wife is having a baby. They change jobs and don't have the time for another dog. They lose their job. They move to a smaller house. They are getting a divorce . . . the list is endless. Others, sometimes contemptuously referred to by top show or working breeders as 'backyard breeders', sometimes breed the odd litter for pin money, and for the fun and interest a litter of lively pups can create, but in no way should they be classed alongside puppy farmers. Do not despise them. Many a good show or working champion has been bred by a backyard breeder, and as a purveyor of some outstanding stud dogs over the years, I can say that it is these people that have kept me in business.

When it has been decided to breed a litter, let us hope that the bitch to be bred from has as few faults as possible. I will not go too deeply into the matter of hereditary diseases. One could write a whole book on that subject and still end up with many unanswered questions. Even when one has gone in for testing schemes, such practice can only detect clinical problems whilst recessive factors remain undetected. (The exception to this is fucocidosis in show English springer spaniels, where a blood test will identify carriers as well as infected animals.) Obviously, if a bitch was blind or crippled one would not breed from her, unless an identifiable trauma could be isolated as the cause of the defect – a pulled leg muscle, for example.

It is most difficult to advise on the choice of a sire, as the variables are endless. A common rule of thumb is not to breed too close, yet some outcrossed matings are useless, and some closely bred pups turn out to be brilliant. It seems to depend so much upon how sound the ancestors were, and in particular which ones you are doubling or trebling up on. Even then, pups from the same litter can inherit differing gene patterns. A geneticist once told me, 'You can have a brother and sister which are not related.' Another geneticist from a veterinary training college has told me some interesting facts about his work with the Rare Breeds Survival Trust. In rare breeds of farm animals, gene pools tend to be very restricted, but by blood testing and genetic fingerprinting, it is possible to find out which animals it is safe to mate together, even though, by pedigree, they appear closely related.

Certainly it can happen that a dog is a successful sire and his litter brother is a failure at stud. Sometimes one can line breed and duplicate one dog almost *ad infinitum* in future matings, yet duplicate his litter brother and the pups will be nutcases.

If one chooses a 'name' dog as a stud there may be certain advantages. By this definition, I include Champion, Show Champion, Field Trial Champion, Obedience Champion, and Working Trials Champion, and moving on beyond the remit of Kennel Club controlled competitive activities, Sheep Dog Trials Champion. One of the main advantages in using such a sire is that it is bound to possess SOME of the qualities one seeks, bearing in mind that the *perfect* dog or bitch has yet to be whelped. Additionally, it is a fair bet that the proprietor/proprietrix of such a stud will have a fair measure of experience when it comes to mating a bitch, so the chances of the encounter being a successful one will be enhanced. If the bitch's owner can tell the stud's owner exactly when the bitch first showed in season, a forward calculation of the optimum time for mating can be made, usually from the eleventh to the thirteenth day. It is a useful guide if the bitch can be tried on her own territory with another dog, to see if she will curl her tail to one side. It usually works out about right if the bitch is mated 48 hours after her first positive 'stand'. Very often, and not only in the case of maiden bitches, the bitch will not stand when taken to the stud dog on alien territory. Then the 'Stud Groom Technique' of the dog's owner can work wonders. The bitch's owner holds her head. The dog's owner supports the bitch's hindquarters, and the dog, being experienced, co-operates and does his work. Do not, please do not, believe the old tales that pups from a 'forced mating' will be no good. My most notable stud dog's best results have come from the most difficult bitch to mate. She would even roll a stray collie onto its back, and few bitches will not miscegenate, if given the opportunity. Mating with this bitch took place on three occasions, and each time quality stock resulted which is famous worldwide, so I hope I have laid that ghost.

The stud fee is paid at the time of mating. There is no legal obligation, either to refund the fee or give a free service, if the mating is unsuccessful, but it is common practice to give a free service as a matter of courtesy. You pay for the act of service, not the results. The bitch requires no particular attention until she is six weeks in whelp, except that jumping fences should be discouraged. At this point, her food should be increased by about 50 per cent, and split into a morning and evening feed. Some people like to stuff their brood bitches full of all kinds of mineral and vitamin supplements, but if one is feeding a top quality diet, either raw meat based or a premium proprietary food, additional vitamins might upset the dietary balance.

I provide a whelping box with a bed of newspaper. As her time draws nigh, the bitch will tear up the paper and scratch the bottom of the box. When whelping is imminent, the bitch will pant and appear hot, but her body temperature will actually drop about 3 degrees. Hopefully the pups will be born at fairly regular intervals, but often a maiden bitch will whelp and clean the first pup, then go several hours before she produces another. This can be a most worrying situation. If there is no further progression, it is wise to seek veterinary assistance. After a digital examination, to ascertain whether a pup is presenting itself, the vet will inject pituitrin, to stimulate the uterine contractions, and the next pup should be born 20–30 minutes later. If nothing happens, surgery might be essential, unless the vet can dislodge the pup manually. The majority of pups from active breeds are born without any bother, but in breeds like bulldogs and Yorkshire terriers, it can be another matter. 'Leave her to get on with it' is a good axiom, provided one remains vigilant. Having cleaned the pups and eaten the placentas (afterbirths) the bitch should require no food for 12 hours, but in practice many bitches show hunger sooner. Water should be available at all times, as giving birth is thirsty work.

As the days go by and the pups take more nourishment, the bitch will require more food. It will be better if she can be fed three times a day, as too much complete food at once is difficult to digest. However, they do tend to have a greater tolerance to raw tripe than to other foods.

I give the pups their first solid meal at the age of 3 weeks. Here there is great scope. In the past, pups were reared on weird and wonderful concoctions that might have involved large quantities of cows' or goats' milk, Farex baby food, scraped raw beef and various boiled meats. The whole business was very labour-intensive. Nowadays, so many complete puppy foods compete with each other, the choice is endless.

Beware of the bitch suffering an attack of milk fever, which is usually fatal if untreated. I believe that in the case of cattle, this occurs shortly after calving. The remedy is a massive injection of liquidized calcium and magnesium. In a bitch, this condition is most likely to manifest itself when the pups are 3 weeks plus. The first signs likely to appear are that the bitch drags her feet, and on boards or concrete, the *upper* surface of the toenails make a scraping sound. The bitch pants, her eyeballs glaze, and her temperature may shoot up as high as 107 degrees Fahrenheit. First aid measures are to wrap her in soaking wet towels or sacking. It is best if she can be kept quiet until a vet can make a house call to give her the life-saving calcium, but it is better to drive her to the surgery than to leave her untreated. Never go on holiday and leave a lactating bitch with friends, unless they are really experienced kennel people who can spot the onset of this condition. Thankfully, it is fairly rare, but can catch out the unwary.

A final word about the dreaded parvo virus disease, now rarer on account of the use of modern vaccines, but which can still strike anywhere, anytime. Some people boost the bitch 10–14 days before whelping, to give the pups optimum maternal immunity. I do not boost the bitch but vaccinate all my pups at 6 weeks of age with Nobi-vac Parvo, a live vaccine. This vaccine has been developed to override any residual maternal immunity, as most live vaccines are nullified by maternal antibodies. So far, touch wood, it has worked well for me.

28

The Working Cocker Today

What is an Epigram? a dwarfish whole,
Its body brevity, and wit its soul.
                    (Samuel Taylor Coleridge)

Often I think of this small quote in relation to the working
cocker spaniel as we know it at present. Its body is brevity
because there is not much of it when compared to the larger
springer spaniels and English setters with which, historically,
it shares some common ancestry. Most cockers are highly
amusing little dogs and many possess a devilish sense of
humour, so wit can most certainly be said to be its soul. To
succeed with a cocker, particularly in the sphere of field trial
competition, it is absolutely essential that the handler should
also have a good sense of humour, otherwise he or she could
be in for a pretty miserable time on those occasions when
their charge decides that Kennel Club Field Trial Regulations
are strictly for the more staid retrievers and springer spaniels.
I have a sneaking suspicion that some cockers would prefer
to subscribe to the view of a Belgian sportsman of my
acquaintance who believes that to be effective, a spaniel
should bark when it finds game to warn the shooter of
the game's presence, then chase it as it flushes so that it is

closer to the quarry should it be shot but only wounded! I can imagine many cockers would find such a shooting or field trial regime enormous fun, but we must strive to instil more decorous behaviour in our cockers, whatever their personal preferences might be.

When discussing the origins of any breed of dog it can be tempting to dismiss its early history as being 'shrouded in mystery', certainly in the case of older breeds as opposed to those of fairly recent manufacture such as the labrador retriever, the flatcoated retriever and the golden retriever whose origins are reliably documented. Note well that these breeds have all evolved since game shooting became popular and the need for recoverers of shot game arose. Game shooting is a comparatively new sport compared to coursing, falconry and the more mundane taking of gamebirds by net for the table, the two latter activities requiring the services of either flushing or pointing dogs, the former sometimes employing flushing dogs to start the hares from cover for the sight-hounds to pursue. It follows that the pointing and flushing breeds are of greater antiquity than the retrievers and consequently their evolution can be more difficult to chart, though not necessarily impossible. Without any question the cocker spaniel is of very mixed origins but I think it may be possible to trace what I believe is its oldest bloodline.

When the Celtic tribes migrated westward across Europe from what is now southern Germany, between the years 500 and 150 BC, they took their cattle and horses with them and, without any doubt, their dogs. It is well documented that there existed at that time a large 'Celtic hound'; possibly descended from the ancient molossus and in all probability the main ancestor of the Old English mastiff, later to find fame as the war dog which fought the invading Romans in Britain and afterwards as a fighting dog in the arenas of ancient Rome.

The Celts also would have possessed herding dogs and my belief is that these people had smaller red-and-white hunting dogs. Falconry is a very ancient sport and it is highly probable that the Celtic chieftains flew hawks and falcons, particularly the short-winged goshawks, at rabbits, the natural quarry of the goshawk, which were present in Europe long before their introduction to Britain. What better could a high-born Celt wish for to flush rabbits and woodcock for his hawks than a spaniel-like animal? My belief is further compounded by the Celtic settlement in Brittany, Wales, Cornwall and Ireland. To this day, all these areas produce red-and-white hunting dogs. Brittany has its *épagneul Bréton*, known to Britons and the Americans as the Brittany. The original *sang pur* Brittany was only red and white but at the end of the 1939–45 war, so few Brittanies of breeding age were available in France that crossing with other local pointing spaniels took place which introduced black and liver colouration. Ireland has its ancient red-and-white Irish setter and later the more familiar Irish red setter came into being, frequently with accepted white markings on nose, chest and legs; and as far back as the tenth century, red-and-white spaniels were present in Wales which were the undisputed ancestors of the Welsh springers of today. Then there existed for a time the enigmatic 'Welsh cocker'. There is confusion to the present day over the Welsh cocker as many working cockers are bred in Wales and frequently the uninitiated believe these products of the Principality to be Welsh cockers, which they are not. To the best of my knowledge the 'Welsh cocker' never was a Kennel Club recognized breed. It has been mentioned by various earlier writers and cynologists like Clifford Hubbard as being red and white, which would suggest that it evolved as a smaller sub-species to the Welsh springer, just as we have miniature poodles, schnauzers and dachshunds. It is said to have become extinct; however, I believe the Welsh cocker was simply absorbed into the breed of cocker spaniel prior to the Kennel Club's formation in 1873 as we still have both red, and red-and-white working cockers to this day which are distinct from the lemon-and-whites and orange-roans. 'Stonehenge', in his *Book of the Dog* (1859), mentions the Welsh cocker and there is an illustration of a 'Welsh' and an 'English' cocker standing together.

A difficulty that arose during the latter half of the nine-teenth century was that although the cocker was becoming established as a breed in its own right, around the turn of the century the Kennel Club brought in a 'weight classification' whereby any dog 25 pounds or under was a cocker and anything over was a field spaniel or a springer. What hap-pened was that, although some breeders strove to establish the breed, others crossed their cockers with springer spaniels and registered the larger ones as springers and those under the weight limit as cockers. Even Mr C. A. Phillips, doyen of the spaniel movement of his day, crossed a cocker with a springer to produce F.T.Ch. Rivington Sam, the first spaniel ever to gain a field trial title. Those of us who breed cockers today have inherited this genetic to-ing and fro-ing – genes do not just disappear. Recently there has been some rather uninformed comment in the sporting press about variation in type regarding cockers, with suggestions made that many cockers of undesirable springer size, action and colour are currently emerging. I can do no better than quote a brilliant ex-scientist friend who states: 'Some of these people are naive beyond belief, and know nothing of the history of anything. In fact they believe that the history of everything began on the day they themselves became interested in it.'

I saw my first working cocker in December 1945. She was a clear liver and white but with a good cocker action. My real experience began in 1957 at the Kennel Club Cocker Championship when a large, springery liver-and-white dog, F.T.Ch. Carswell Solomon, was beaten into second place by the very cockery F.T.Ch. Jordieland Bunty. This was to be repeated in the Cocker Championships of 1962, 1964 and 1974 when a large, springery animal was beaten on each occasion by a very typical cocker. Doubtless these large cockers had put up excellent performances in the body of the stake but in the final analysis, the experienced judges exercised their preferences for the true cocker type. Nevertheless, in 1960, 1965, 1969, 1970 and 1980, very large cockers won the event.

So for as far back as I can go, there has always been a vast difference in type within the ranks of the working cocker. It might be easy to blame the breeders for departing so far from the breed standard, but that would be unrealistic if we take a backward glance into the history of the show, and earlier still, the dual-purpose cocker. The disparity in type as depicted in old pictures and photographs is both amazing and enlightening. Ch. Obo, born in 1879 and probably regarded as 'The Father of the Breed', was a long, low dog and I am certain he would not have gained his title under the show judges of today. His daughter, Miss Obo, born in 1882, was of positively dachshund-like proportions. Moving into the twentieth century, Mr C. A. Phillips's Ch. Rivington Reine (born 1904) was short-legged and long-bodied yet the same owner's Ch. Rivington Gunner (born 1906) was tall and leggy and of very workmanlike proportions. Bearing in mind that show and working cockers of the present time both stem from the same root stock, is it all that strange that a disparity in type sometimes occurs?

The situation is further compounded by the various outcrosses which quite legitimately have been brought into the breed in the past, before the Kennel Club placed an embargo on this practice *circa* 1969. I am fortunate to have had as one of my mentors Miss Peggy Brown, of the 'Headland' cockers. A notable historian of the breed, Miss Brown has a vastly extended pedigree of one of the old Rivington cockers which in the last generation shows outcrosses of both field and Sussex spaniels. Miss Brown also told me that, in the past, springer outcrosses have not been good, as springer blood is so dominant that when it is introduced it tends to 'mask' cocker characteristics and is persistent over the generations. Apparently she considers the English setter outcross as beneficial, with which I would agree, but as English springers and English setters apparently both originated from common stock of the 'land spaniels of Europe' about 400 years ago, a far back setter outcross can still produce characteristics which the uninitiated could mistake for recent springer ancestry. Only very recently I discovered, via a close member of his family, that one of the greatest show cocker breeders of this century used an English setter outcross, doubtless quite legitimately and via the now defunct Kennel Club Class 11 registration.

Having observed the working and field trial cocker scene for nearly four decades I can state quite categorically that the proportion of untypical cockers which can be seen today is less than that which manifested itself in the late 1950s to the mid-1970s. In many cases a good type has been maintained along with the bold, lively, mischievous cocker temperament. I am proud that, partly through good luck, I have been able to render the breed assistance, mainly through my F.T.Ch. Speckle of Ardoon, who won the Cocker Championship three years in succession in 1972, 1973 and 1974, plus nine open stakes, all before she retired aged only 4 ½ years. Speckle was sired by a working Irish show dog of 'Sixshot' breeding and her dam carried the best of 'Elan' genes. Speckle has revitalized the breed and her line-bred descendants are still winning well today. The line has been further strengthened by F.T.Ch. Rhu of Migdale, another dog I bred and a great-grandson of Speckle. Sound as a bell and a great stud force.

The working cocker is in an enviable position. It is more free from hereditary physical defects than any other gundog with the possible exception of the working pointer. Working ability is excellent and there are now many gifted cocker trainers. Nobody involved with working cockers need hide their heads in shame.

Dorothy Morland Hooper makes an interesting though wholly inaccurate statement regarding working cockers in *The Springer Spaniel* (p.131), where she states: 'The working and trial cocker . . . unless it comes of a big strain it cannot retrieve a big hare or pheasant with the ease and speed with which a springer can do so.'

The author obviously had little experience of working cockers. Admittedly the F.T.Ch. Heath-hill Lad, who could throw a blue hare around like a mouse, is a big black cocker, but my own triple Championship winner, Speckle of Ardoon, weighed only 23 pounds in fit condition and could handle the larger brown hares, dead or wounded, far better than most springers.

But most interestingly Miss Hooper acknowledges the fact that big strains of working cocker existed in her own pre-1963 era. Perhaps those who own present day cockers which are little larger than black tomcats and believe this type of animal is the only correct one to produce, should do their research a trifle more carefully.

29

The Fall and Rise, and Rise of the Cocker

The working cocker spaniel is the Dickensian steet urchin of the gundog group, and will pick your pocket whilst smiling in your face. It is loved or hated by its *aficionados*, according to which side of the bed it – not they – get out of on a particular morning.

Over the past few decades, the cocker's fortunes have run on similar lines to those of the Gordon setter. From that auspicious and historic occasion in 1865, which heralded the dawn of official field trials, when Gordon setters swept the boards, to the dark days of the 1960s, by which time its death knell was sounding, the Gordon rose phoenix-like from the ashes of its former glory and became a real force to be reckoned with, within the limited confines of the field trial circuit.

When trials were resumed after the 1939–45 war, the cocker quickly got on its feet again, and a plentiful supply of rabbits nationwide provided some excellent quality stakes. There were some good cockers about, albeit somewhat head-strong by all accounts. The late Colin Thomson, whose father, James, saw the advent of spaniel trials in 1900, when he was trainer for Mr C. A. Phillips of the Rivington Kennels, told me an amusing story of a visit he paid to the veteran trainer

George Curle, of the Breckonhill Kennels. George offered to show Colin a good cocker in his rabbit pen, but before he even let the dog out of its kennel, 'He armed himsel' wi' a damned great whupp'.

The advent of myxomatosis in 1953 had a serious effect upon the cocker. The dogs which had developed their skills on rabbits before the disease struck maintained their abilities until the end of their careers, and in the first Cocker Championship which I witnessed in January 1957, some really good, though somewhat mischievous, cockers presented themselves. The F.T.Chs. Buoy of Elan, Jordieland Bunty, Stockbury Elizabeth and Carswell Solomon were real quality animals, to name but a few. Thereafter, the quality of cockers fell away at a truly incredible rate. It seemed that few could accept the scarcity of rabbits, whereas springers took the changeover to pheasants in their stride, and the 1960s saw a tremendous upsurge in the quality of the English springer spaniel. Where are their like today?

Cocker numbers fell away drastically, and the breed was kept alive by a somewhat autocratic body of wealthy patrons, who seemed unable to appreciate that the breed was deteriorating to a dangerous level. Most cocker stakes only fielded about eight or nine dogs. Yet even in the darkest days of the cocker, a few quality animals still manifested themselves, cockers like Whisper of Corsewall, Exton Monty, Headland Hazel of Monnow, Simon of Elan, Swift of Elan and Debdenhall Terra.

My own involvement in cockers, which was to have a profound effect on the breed, began more by accident than design. Harold Timms, a Monmouth dentist, and owner of F.T.Ch. Headland Hazel of Monnow, wasn't happy with his trainer and asked me if I would train a couple of bitch pups out of Hazel for him. Both were very sound in the essentials. The lemon-and-white Mayfly was the better competition animal and became a F.T.Ch., also taking a 3rd and a 4th in the Championship. Her sister, Elizabeth, was good in thick cover but slow on open ground, but ultimately proved an important brood bitch.

Shortly after I had commenced to run Harold Timms's bitches, Speckle of Ardoon arrived from Ireland. She was sired by a show dog, out of a granddaughter of F.T.Ch. Jet of Elan, a sound, brilliant gamefinder, but slow, and described by one of our local Welsh keepers as 'like a black cat walking about'. Speckle was unbelievably brilliant and won everything there was to win, including an all-time record of three Championship wins in a row. She didn't produce competitive stock as spectacular as herself, but some of her sons and daughters proved to be very influential breeders.

Others were doing their homework too. Jack Windle, winner of the 1957 Championship, although no longer competing, had kept his 'Jordieland' breeding lines going. Bill Bremner, an Aberdeenshire farmer, had seen Speckle and decided cockers were worth trying, so he acquired Jordieland stock and did well with it. Bill wasn't much for breeding, but when he was winning, he helped keep the standard up. Lady Auckland's Wilfred of Cromlix sired Templebar Blackie, who, when mated to Speckle, produced some very influential lines. His son, Ardnamurchan Mac, was an important sire and produced some successful bloodlines when mated to Monnow Elizabeth.

Denis Douglas, from Kincardineshire, along with his wife, Dorothy, bred some very good cockers. Denis also ran and made up the wicked Carswell Zero, a truly evil dog but a very influential stud force, siring the famous Bunter of Jordieland, who proved himself a prepotent sire.

A son of Ardnamurchan Mac, out of a daughter of Swift of Elan, came in for ordinary shooting training, and I judged him first rate. Mated to my Ginger of Gwibernant, closely related to Speckle, he produced F.T.Ch. Rhu of Migdale, a tremendously sound cocker and a brilliant sire, particularly when mated to F.T.Ch. Gwibernant Snake, the greatest bitch of the 1980s, of a line going back to Mayfly, Blackie and Speckle. I once saw a trial where eight of Snake's progeny were running. They took 1st, 2nd and 3rd and two certificates of merit.

Through the influence of the dogs and bitches I have quoted beyond Mayfly, courage in cover had improved dramatically. Patronage also had changed in many cases. Instead of landed gentry, we had several working men owners and gamekeepers, who needed a cocker which could do just as good a job in a rough place as a springer, so they have tended to select down to such mettled animals as breeding stock. The prepotent sire of the present day is F.T.Ch. Jade of Livermere, who goes back to a Blackie/Speckle son. He is sound in all departments and has sired about ten F.T.Chs. His most notable achievement was the siring of the 1st, 2nd and 3rd prizewinners at the 1963 Cocker Championship at Sandringham. His granddaughter took 4th place, sired by his own father, such close breeding verifying the soundness of the bloodline. So cockers are now at a high standard, and a most important bonus is that the standard of sportsmanship among the human participants is pleasingly high. Long may this remain so!

30

Woodcock and 'Cocking' Spaniels

My three favourite quarry species are the Welsh red grouse, the rabbit and the woodcock, not necessarily in any particular order, although the not-so-humble rabbit is certainly the most useful to me. It teaches my young spaniels to hunt, provides them with shooting experience later on, fills my freezer with low cholesterol meat, and provides skins for my training dummies. It will be noted that all three are truly wild quarry and herein lies their major appeal. The late Sir Charles Clore was hardly cognizant of this fact, when after a pleasing number of woodcock figured in the bag on a driven pheasant day on his Berkshire property, he remarked to his headkeeper: 'Wonderful birds these woodcock, we must rear 500 next season.'

I have always lived in woodcock country – East Yorkshire, Norfolk, Lincolnshire and North Wales, but none of these areas are what I would class as *prime* woodcock territory. In this exciting category I would include Cornwall, the Scillies and Lundy Island, West Wales, the Llyn Peninsula in Gwynedd, Mull, the Hebrides and of course several parts of the Irish Republic and Ulster. Although I have consistently shot woodcock throughout a fairly long shooting career, they have figured more in my bags as incidentals, rather than as the mainstay of my venture with dog and gun. This is typified by my best bag on my home shoot, of a dozen head consisting of six rabbits, four pheasants and two woodcock, shooting alone and all over spaniels.

The Scandinavians and Europeans are absolutely mad about woodcock. In Sweden they hold heavily sponsored pensioners' field trials. The pensioner smokes his pipe and strolls along the forestry road while his pointer or setter quarters the forest on either side of him. The quarry is blackgame and woodcock, which the handler shoots over his own dog. Great stuff. Some Continentals believe it is impossible to shoot woodcock without the help of a pointing breed. They say the birds erupt too quickly in front of a questing spaniel to allow a shot to be taken. The *épagneul Bréton*, a pointing breed, evolved in Brittany as a woodcock dog and is believed to share common ancestry with the Welsh springer spaniel and our own cocker spaniel. In common with most of our gundog breeds, the early history of the cocker is not well documented. Early records tell us that there were linguistic and cultural ties between Brittany and West Wales. Certainly there were red-and-white spaniels at the court of Hywel Dda in AD 900, and many others belonging to the King's subjects. It is said that these spaniels were used for flushing game for the King's falcons or into nets. King Hywel's realm was good woodcock country and remains so to this day. Although it would not be impossible to take them with an agile short-wing hawk, strategically placed nets would take far more woodcock, when flushed from their haunts with the *tarv ci* or 'dispersing dog'. I am, therefore, rather stubborn in my belief that it was from this period, well before the advent of gunpowder, that the name 'woodcock spaniel', later simplified to 'cocker', derives.

Assuming that many of our present-day cockers do derive from this ancient Welsh heritage, many other spaniel breeds have been added to this original stock, including English springer (a very mixed-up dog itself and not at all 'of pure and ancient lineage'), field spaniel, Sussex spaniel, cavalier

King Charles and even English setter and border collie! The net result is that we have, in its pure working form, a small, very active spaniel, from about 17 to 25 pounds in weight and in a bewildering selection of colours. True to its name, it is ideal for woodcock shooting, but not because its small size means that it is incapable of retrieving any quarry larger than a 12- to 14-ounce woodcock. The best of the breed are capable of handling any game, no matter how large, and many can handle a hare, dead or wounded, better than some much larger springer spaniels. The major strength of the cocker as a woodcock dog lies in its hunting method, but I am of course assuming that the dog is properly trained and under control, and not prone to bore on ahead with its nose on the ground.

Having disposed of that negative point, it can be said that a cocker should work a closer pattern than a springer. Some springer purists consider them 'fiddly', when comparing them to some sweeping, wider-running springer. Certainly this can be spectacular to watch but with woodcock as a quarry, it is very much horses for courses. I have already mentioned that some Continental sportsmen consider it virtually impossible to shoot cock over spaniels. In some parts of the British Isles, such as the Western Isles, these birds can be found in fairly open situations of heather and gorse clumps where a pointing dog can come into its own, but in much of mainland Britain, and certainly where I shoot, woodcock generally favour fairly heavy cover. They have a penchant for hawthorn, holly and laurel bushes, often squatting in bracken, bramble or dead leaves within a yard or two of the base of a bush. This can mean that when a woodcock flushes, the friendly bush can often act as a shield. It should be a simple enough matter for a competent shot to kill a woodcock at 40 yards, but in many woodcock shooting situations, a 40-yard woodcock will be safe behind bushes and tree branches. Most woodcock in cover have to be taken much closer in, and this is when the close hunting method of the cocker maximizes one's chances. Woodcock are tricky and unpredictable in their habits. Sometimes they sit quite tight and allow a spaniel to make the classic check, turn in and positive flush. On other occasions they can be quite restless and will flush in front of a questing spaniel before nose contact can be made. But whatever the mood of the birds, a spaniel no more than 10 to 15 yards from the gun puts the shooter more in command of the situation when a bird rises.

Sometimes a woodcock will run a surprising distance before flushing. Woodcock are seldom seen walking about, but the birds' rolling 'sailor's' gait has been remarked upon. I have witnessed this method of locomotion and believe it is a feature of tired, recently landed birds. When rabbiting in a Norfolk 'carr', many years ago, I was waiting in an open space for my dogs to drive rabbits to me, when I spotted a woodcock hurrying towards me. It ran as tidily as any partridge, stopping every now and then to listen to the deep baying of the dachshund, and showing no sign of the rolling gait. Nearer home, I once worked a spaniel the whole length of a shallow gulley, through birch and bracken. The bitch was onto moving game the whole way, and at the very end, a woodcock broke cover and was shot. That bird must have been moving at a fair rate to keep ahead of a hard-going spaniel for such a distance.

Although the woodcock is a wader, and closely related to snipe, with similar feeding habits, they usually prefer drier situations as daytime resting places and are seldom flushed from marshland, except perhaps where a clump of sallow bushes have colonized a bit of higher ground. An oak wood, with bracken undercover, is often considered ideal but a sunny aspect is not always sought, as it is in the case of pheasants, and hens in particular. Freshly arrived woodcock can be found in all kinds of peculiar places, but once they have rested for 24 hours or so, will move to more conventional woodcock territory. When one gets to know one's ground, this unpredictable bird can be better predicted. Year after year, as with hares and grouse, certain areas of the ground will be more favoured than others. With woodcock, this can sometimes be narrowed down to individual bushes. There are several such places on my own mountainside where the chances of finding a woodcock are enhanced through prior knowledge, and I am always extra vigilant when working the cocker towards such known haunts.

When shooting woodcock, they are not always easy birds for the cocker to mark when shot. Often the dog will have its head buried in cover, the bird rises silently and when the shot goes off, the dog will accept a bit of rudimentary handling: not 100-yard blind retrieve working test stuff, but if the dog's gun-sense takes it in the general direction of the bird, it is useful to be able to stop it on the whistle and signal it left or right a few yards. The scent spread of a shot woodcock is usually fairly localized, so the meticulous, 'feathery' method of search of the cocker might well prove more effective than the bigger sweeps of the springer. I am also convinced that the quieter the dog can be handled the better – bear in mind the archaic expression 'Ears like a woodcock'.

Whatever purpose one requires a cocker for, it will be found that many possess the most pleasing temperaments. On average, they are bolder than springers, many of which show the more shy 'collie' temperament. Most require less 'humanizing' and have an inbuilt confidence. They are 'fun dogs' as well as competent workers, but it is most essential to choose the right, pure working source of supply. Several of my colleagues can oblige. Readers interested in contacting these gentlemen can write to me via my publisher and I will pass on their details.

31

The Changed Face of Field Trials

The first official field trial ever to be held predates the Kennel Club itself; this body was formed in 1873, whereas the first field trial, for pointers and setters, was held on 18 April 1865, on the estate of Sir Samuel Whitbread at Southill in Bedfordshire. The trial was held on paired grey partridges, and black-and-tan setters did exceptionally well.

Surprisingly, retriever trials did not come into being for another 34 years when, in 1899, the first retriever event was held on the estate of Mr Warwick, near Horsham in Surrey. Mr Warwick was a keen spaniel fancier, and some spaniels actually took part in this first venture. It seems that in the early days of retriever trials, handlers carried guns loaded with blanks. Apparently the first ever lady handler to take the field was the Duchess of Hamilton. Spaniel trials also started in 1899, on the estate of William Arkwright, at Sutton Scarsdale in Derbyshire. The ground donor was an interesting and controversial character. Described by one of our contemporaries, a descendant of Joseph Lang, the famous gunmaker, as 'a man of inherited wealth', William Arkwright was a direct descendant of that Arkwright who invented the 'Spinning Jenny', and made the family fortune during the Industrial Revolution. William Arkwright wrote

The Pointer and Its Predecessors, a mammoth tome regarded by some as THE definitive work on the pointer, but debunked by others who consider that Arkwright misrepresented the breed's origins to a certain extent, because he deliberately chose to ignore evidence which did not appeal to him. The German author Waldemar Marr was particularly scathing, safely after Arkwright's death in 1925; it is thought by some that as Arkwright had been, at times, particularly critical of the Kennel Club, Marr, who was a creature of the Establishment, wished to ingratiate himself with his fellow members.

In the early days of field trials, all trial grounds were donated by persons with their own kennels of dogs, and who, by this token, had a vested interest. A typical patron was Mrs Quentin Dick, later Countess Howe, who, year after year, donated her estate at Idsworth, Hampshire, to the Labrador Club. This trend has all but died out now, but persisted well into my own trial career, which commenced in October 1956. There can be no doubt whatsoever that these patrons did an awful lot for the trial movement, although at times it did create a 'Them and Us' situation; however, a certain *noblesse oblige* prevailed which ensured that reasonable standards of behaviour, dress and sportsmanship were maintained, which, regrettably, are not invariably present in today's climate.

Even though large numbers of the officer class were killed in the 1914–18 war, with a subsequent impoverishment of many estates due to death duties, field trials were resumed after the Armistice, much as they had been in the past, but it was during the period following the 1939–45 war that subtle changes began to manifest themselves. We still had interested donor/competitors, people like Lord Rank (labradors and pointers), Lady Auckland of Cromlix (labradors, cockers, pointers and Gordon setters), Captain Parlour (English setters), Countess Howe (labradors), Talbot Radcliffe (spaniels), Harry Blackburn (spaniels), Neill Lamb (spaniels) and Charles Williams (labradors and spaniels). The latter gentleman merits particular mention. For many years, Charles Williams was the Duke of Bedford's shooting tenant at Woburn Abbey.

He was fortunate to have Dick Male as his private trainer and handler. For at least 20 years he gave his ground at Woburn, selflessly and unstintingly, for retrievers, and springer and cocker spaniels. He hosted championships for all these breeds and invariably provided excellent teams of guns. Dick Male won the Retriever Championship for him with F.T.Ch. Berrystead Bee at Cromlix in Perthshire and the Any Variety Championship But Cocker (for which read springer) with F.T.Ch. Berrystead Freckle at Wherwell in Hampshire. Mr Williams never attempted to project himself politically. With more push he could have judged both the Retriever and Spaniel Championships, but he preferred to keep in the background and shoot over the dogs, in which sphere he was a more than competent shot.

During the post-war period quite a bit of ground was donated by shooting syndicates, which produced its own set of problems. Many of the guns had never shot over dogs, and had done only a limited amount of driven game shooting. Consequently, under such circumstances, a lot of game was missed and too many runners were put on the ground, which rendered the trials more hazardous for the competing dogs. Then an improved situation arose whereby ground was given but the keepers were asked to organize the guns. This saw a vast improvement in trial shooting. Quite a few clay pigeon shots were invited to shoot, many of whom have what it takes when it comes to shooting at field trials. Many gamekeepers have shot at trials over the years, and generally they give an excellent account of themselves, particularly as rabbit shots.

Since the late 1980s we have seen an innovation with which I have had close personal connections. This has worked very well in conjunction with commercial shoots, where game is sold on a per capita basis. Several of us who are in the field trial movement have bought shooting by the day and donated the day to a field trial club or society, sometimes inviting the other guns as guests, or in some cases a group of guns have shared the expense between them. Another way has been for the field trial society to buy the day, then sell the guns off to

15. David Pope (left) judging a February rabbit trial in North Wales with the respected professional trainer Jack Davis. David Pope won the 1987 Spaniel Championship with F.T.Ch. Drury Girl, a daughter of the 1977 Champion, F.T.Ch. Ashley Buster, 'A very nice dog ... did a lot of good for the breed'. (*Author*)

16.   David Chudley accepts a cock pheasant at a North Norfolk cocker trial judged by the author. David is the son of the famous trainer Keith Chudley, of Harpersbrook Kennels in Northamptonshire. (*Author*)

17.   A French springer delivers a wounded Chinese/American cock pheasant at a spaniel trial in the La Sologne district of France. In France, 'shooters are excellent and the sportsmanship and good manners of competitors are beyond reproach', although the quality of the dogs is probably not yet up to British field trial standards. (*Author*)

18. (*Left*) Bonnie of Cilcraig, trained by the author, twice winner of the Coupe d'Europe; (centre) a winning cocker, Norleigh Mayfly; (right) Bonnie's daughter, Brown Speedy of Dashill, another winning springer. (*Joep van der Vlasakker*)

19. Springers in Holland: Janni van Stuyvenberg-Los, wife of the successful Dutch trainer Rokus van Stuyvenberg, with a good-looking team of working springers from British bloodlines. (*Rokus van Stuyvenberg*)

20. Arthur Cooke, owner of the legendary stud springer Hales Smut, which the author bred in 1960.(*Author*)

21. British-bred working spaniels are in demand all over the world: George Okamoto of Japan collects a working cocker from the airport. (*Author*)

22. (*Above*) American
hunters with their spaniels
on Long Island. These
dogs are American-bred,
from original British stock.
(*Bobby Penn*)

23. (*Left*) Montagu
Christopher, for eighteen
years Head Gamekeeper
to HM the Queen at
Sandringham, and a great
supporter of the field trial
movement. (*Author*)

24. Olov Axelsson, a Swedish forest keeper, with a cock capercaillie he shot after 'good dogwork' by his springer bitch, Zicka. At nearly 3 feet long, and weighing up to 12 pounds, a cock caper presents a challenge to any dog. (*Author*)

25. The Danish F.T.Ch. cocker Neseborne Toft, handled by Mrs Egelund Faddersbøll, the only Field Trial Champion cocker spaniel in Denmark. The Danish Kennel Club has now agreed that (as in Britain) working spaniels may now have a separate registry from the show dogs – an advance that is bound to improve the quality of the working strains. (*Marianne Faddersbøll*)

26. A dual-purpose French-style cocker spaniel which works wild boar for Steve Horn – the ultimate demonstration, perhaps, of the spaniel's versatility? (*Steve Horn*)

27. A Swedish cocker, again of the French type, with a roe deer foot, which is used in blood trailing exercises. (*Hans Ahlner*)

interested parties. The former, more personal, approach gives some of us the chance to put something back into trials when we don't have a shoot of our own which we can offer to the movement.

Another viable alternative, where retriever trials are concerned, is for the trial to run in conjunction with a day's commercial driven shooting. For this kind of venture, it is essential to have a strong-minded host or shoot manager, who understands thoroughly what is required and will firmly and tactfully keep the guns in order. A first class team of pickers up is essential to deal with unwanted birds. I have judged on such an occasion and I found the venture a perfectly viable one. We had a very interested host, who was running his own labrador, and after a drive, when there were plenty of birds to keep us occupied, the guns moved on to another drive, where they were attended by the picking up team.

So far I have dealt only with the way trials have been conducted, but in the light of recent events, I feel I should mention the winds of change which have been blowing in high places. In 1991 I was interviewed by *The Field* magazine. I remarked that if the Kennel Club would allow some field trials to be held beyond its remit, without penalty to competitors or judges, it could be 'regarded as less of an ogre and more of a father figure'. In May 1994 the Club's General Committee, prompted by the Office of Fair Trading, made provision for unlicensed trials to be held. This is something which many people have believed should be permitted, and letters to the sporting press have supported such a view for many years. Now that this has finally come about, many people seem unable to believe it; others are critical even though they have not thought the matter through. For example, in a fairly recent press interview, one professional trainer remarked what a bad thing it would be for trials to move away from the Kennel Club. No such thing is envisaged. Kennel Club licensed trials will still fill to overflowing. The Club will not lose one penny in revenue. It simply has granted us more freedom of choice and has moved closer to the twenty-first century, or so it would appear.

32

Spaniel Trials in Britain

Considering that the first field trial for pointers and setters took place in 1865, it is surprising that the first official spaniel trial did not take place until 34 years later. I use the term 'official' advisedly, as the first spaniel trial really took place in 1871 at the Vaynol Estate in Caernarvonshire. Why this trial is not recognized is somewhat anomalous. The fact that it was not held under Kennel Club rules should hardly be significant as the Kennel Club was not formed until 1873, yet the 1865 event for pointers and setters is part of recognized gundog history despite this trial not being held under Club rules either. It is said that this delay in getting spaniel trials off the ground was caused by the fact that it seems no two gentlemen could agree on precisely what should be required of a spaniel. A die-hard faction of shooters believed that a spaniel should never be allowed to retrieve, lest it should become unsteady to flush, reasoning that if a spaniel never tasted the delights of handling its shot quarry it would be less likely to attempt to rush forward when game was shot. Here there is logic, but it was soon discovered that with good training and discipline instilled on the flush, it was quite feasible to allow a spaniel to retrieve its shot game. A similar hide-bound tradition persists in Britain to this day regarding pointers and setters. Some trial people believe that if a bird-dog is allowed to retrieve, it will become unsteady on point and flush its birds unbidden, or run in whenever a shot is fired. Practically every country in the world where pointer and setter events are held proves how wrong we are in this premiss.

Two judges officiate. All stakes must have a minimum of one 'A' panel judge. In open stakes which qualify for the Spaniel Championships the second judge must at least be on the 'B' panel. In novice or all-age stakes, neither of which qualify for the Championships or the title of Field Trial Champion (F.T.Ch.), a non-panel judge can officiate with an 'A' judge. To be eligible to run in open qualifying stakes a spaniel must first win a novice or all-age stake; or should it manage to secure a run in an open qualifier in the rare event of under-subscription, or a competitor not turning up on the day and no qualified reserve dog being available, if it won a second or third place in that trial, that would qualify the dog to run in open stakes for the rest of that season and the next two seasons following.

At the present time, and bearing in mind that the regulations change quite frequently, an aspiring judge must judge a minimum of four novice or all-age stakes before he or she can be added to the 'B' panel. A 'B' panel judge must judge at least four open qualifying stakes before being considered for the 'A' panel. There is absolutely no formal training for judges and I believe the system to be seriously flawed. When a judge is recommended by a society or club for whom they have judged, the Kennel Club writes to all the 'A' judges the person has officiated with for a recommendation (or otherwise). What happens then is something of a mystery. The matter is debated behind closed doors before the Kennel Club Field Trials Sub-Committee. Some judges who are considered excellent by grass-roots opinion are rejected, and it seems that others whose credentials seem flimsy are appointed. No reasons are ever tendered in the case of a rejection.

It is argued by some that a first class piano teacher does not necessarily have to be a brilliant concert pianist; however, if a person wishes to lecture in, shall we say, ancient archaeology, in order that his or her students ultimately can obtain degrees in the subject, such a lecturer must first hold such a degree before they can teach others, and doubtless, from a practical angle, will have been on a few 'digs' themselves. For some obscure reason a similar set of logistics does not seem to apply to gundog matters, although there are rumours now afoot that some persons in high places are in favour of a big rethink over the matter of non-winners being allowed to judge field trials. I sincerely hope that the powers-that-be will give this matter further serious thought.

From their inception until myxomatosis decimated the rabbit population in 1953, more spaniel trials were held on rabbits than on any other game, with the occasional pheasant or woodcock figuring in the bag as incidentals. Stakes were held for single dogs, braces or teams. In the case of team stakes, only one dog in the team was required to retrieve, so theoretically at least, some non-retrievers would be eligible for taking part as team members. To succeed in these rabbit trials, often held on ground teeming with rabbits and where other rabbits frequently were shot during the act of retrieving, spaniels had to be trained to a very high standard to cope with these often exacting conditions. Several top class professional handlers ran spaniels for wealthy patrons, with men like John Kent, Joe Greatorex, John Forbes, Reg Hill, Jack Curtis, Tommy Gaunt, James Thomson and Mr Church proving to be formidable forces to reckon with. As regards breed quality, there seemed to be little difference in competence between cockers and springers. On one memorable occasion a field spaniel handled by Dick Male placed second in the Any Variety Championship But Cocker, but the Welsh springers, Clumber and Sussex spaniels lagged behind in open competition.

The dread rabbit disease myxomatosis proved to be the watershed of spaniel trials. We had the pre-myxy era and the post-myxy era. For many years pheasants became the main quarry at spaniel trials. One effect of this situation stems from the fact that pheasants will disclose hard mouth to a greater extent than will rabbits. They are harder to handle than rabbits, particularly live cocks, and so with the pheasant trials came a necessity to breed spaniels with more reliable, or at least better-educated, mouths.

Sixteen dogs in a stake is the allowable maximum nowadays. Two judges officiate on parallel beats, unlike pointer and setter trials where the judges walk side by side and a brace of dogs cover the same ground. By tradition the senior judge takes the odd numbers on the right-hand side and his opposite number takes the even numbers on the left. Normally two guns shoot over each dog, one on either side of dog, handler and judge. There is no allotted period of time for a run in Britain. The judge simply works the dog until he has seen enough. This can vary between two or three minutes to over an hour, but either of these extremes I would consider exceptional.

Finding the unshot game should be all-important and an experienced judge can differentiate between a positive find and a flush by bodily presence. If the find is a pheasant or woodcock, it is highly desirable that the dog should mark well to save disturbing ground, but owing to the variable nature of ground on which trials are held, to make a good mark is not always possible. Often a spaniel's vision is obscured by heavy brambles, gorse or laurels, so in such an event a spaniel must be capable of being handled to the fall. A spaniel should pick up cleanly and retrieve with alacrity, but common sense should be exercised with regard to conditions of heavy cover and how exhausting the hunt has been which has made the find and shot possible. Nevertheless it seems that some modern judges are nowhere near as meticulous over retrieving and delivery as the judges of yesteryear, and today we frequently see some very poor and sloppy retrieving.

After all dogs have been seen by one judge each, the dogs which have not committed eliminating faults are switched over to the opposite judge and the process is repeated. After all 'clean' dogs have been seen a second time, the judges compare notes; if from two to several dogs are standing equal, the dogs are run off against each other. Some judges require shooting in a run-off. Others dispense with shooting and judge the dogs solely on hunting. Here many variables of personal choice enter the picture. Some judges go for the easiest handling boot-polisher (i.e. too close a hunter) and will favour an inferior dog if it gives the least trouble. Others will go for the hardest-going dog and will tolerate a certain amount of whistle provided the dog obeys instantly. Such judges usually prefer a bold dog which will get out and take in a fair bit of ground. Dogs are usually worked closer together in a run-off than in the body of the stake, and frequently it can be seen that a bold dog can demoralize its opponent by cutting it off from potential game-holding ground, causing it to drop its nose and potter.

Spaniels should be judged as shooting dogs with just that bit more dash, style and polish. I have always maintained that when I am out working a spaniel and hoping to shoot a rabbit for the cat's supper, the dog is not doing anything so very different from what would hopefully earn it a good grade under a trial judge.

33

Past and Present

Some time ago there appeared in *Shooting Times* an excellent article by Adrian Blundell on the veteran spaniel breeder, trainer and *genuine* amateur field trialler, Bernard Dutton. Although we are a generation apart, age-wise, we are contemporaries in the competitive sphere, as I have just 11 months' seniority over Bernard. By this token, our trial experiences and observations on changing patterns within the movement have been virtually identical. Of tremendous significance is the list of 10 top 'Names' Bernard quoted as being established when he first entered the lists of competition: John McQueen, Tom Laird, Talbot Radcliffe, Joe Greatorex, Jack and Keith Chudley, Jimmy Wylie, Dick Male, Mason Prime and John Kent. To these, I would add John Forbes, William Edwards, Hal Jackson, Reg Hill, Gilbert Smith, Tom Ellis, Reg Goode, Tom Lauder, Janet Wykeham–Musgrave, Frank Bell, Danny MacKenzie, George Curle, Dr Douglas White, Dr Tom Davidson, Major Hugh Peacock, Grant Fiske and Jimmy Scott. These top people constituted a formidable body of handler/judges, and appeared to newcomers such as Bernard and myself as a virtually insurmountable barrier, if we were to beat them in competition or sufficiently impress them when we ran under them, so Bernard's testimony unwittingly gave the lie to any reckless claims that trials were easier to win in those distant days.

It is tempting to speculate on how great sports personalities and competition animals of the past would measure up to their more modern counterparts. Could Bob Fitzsimmons, Britain's only world heavyweight boxing champion, beat Lennox Lewis? No, he was 5 stone too light. Could Golden Miller have beaten Red Rum? Could Red Rum have beaten Desert Orchid? Could Master McGrath get the winner's handkerchief, in a tight finish with the current Waterloo Cup holder? But without some sort of time machine, we can never really know.

The history of spaniel trials can be sub-divided into three identifiable phases. From 1900 to 1954, take away 10 years or so for the two World Wars, spaniel trials were conducted almost exclusively on rabbits. To win rabbit trials, a spaniel must be absolutely sound in the basics, it must work a tight pattern, be an exceptional gamefinder, must have a nose which is educated to respect unshot body scent, so it drives in on its quarry but makes no attempt to catch it. It must stop to its game directly it flushes. It must not persist on the footscent of a missed rabbit, but must take the line, accurately on command, of any shot rabbit. The ability to take 'legged' rabbit lines is a big bonus. Occasionally a pheasant or woodcock would be shot, but if the dog did not mark the bird, considerable latitude would be allowed over its collection. Few trainers taught a spaniel to handle out on blind retrieves. It was not deemed necessary, although handlers of the calibre of John Kent, Joe Greatorex and Dick Male could handle their labradors any distance.

As I mentioned in the previous chapter, when myxomatosis decimated the rabbit population in 1953–4, spaniel trials were radically altered and pheasants became the main quarry, with quite a few hares featuring in the bags, particularly in Scottish trials. It took a few seasons before the situation was stabilized. I actually took part in one trial in Bedfordshire where the first event of the day was a drive, with several spaniels in line, and we were asked to pick birds, retriever fashion, when the drive ended. Several judges were more retriever- than spaniel-minded, and expected spaniels to handle out long distances on blind retrieves. Some coped surprisingly well, and handlers like the Chudleys, Dick Male and John Kent could get their spaniels out anywhere. Jimmy Wylie never could, but produced a better *basic* animal than these handlers. However, the sensible people on the Kennel Club Field Trials Committee eventually wrote into the recommendations to field trial judges that spaniels should be taken within 'reasonable gunshot' of blind retrieves, and recommended that no more than two spaniels should be tried on the same retrieve, should the first dog fail to collect.

Throughout the 1960s the standard in springer spaniels was very high, and we had some terrific, hotly contested Championships. Stakes always filled, with some reserves, so it was much easier to get into trials than it is today, but if you were beaten by a certain dog in the last trial, there was an excellent chance that you would have to face it in the next, and the next . . . Nowadays, with such pressure of entries, there is far more chance of not meeting such 'danger dogs' trial after trial, so often one can win now against a weaker opposition. Then, so many really good dogs were held down by peer pressure, and never gained their titles, dogs like Brockhill Pim, Saighton's Streamline, Saighton's Slash, Saighton's Seat, Meadowcourt Mistress, Meadowcourt Soda, Hales Smut, Micklewood Smock and Auchtertyre Donna. Had these springers been running today, probably all would have gained their F.T.Ch. status.

About 1980, spaniel trials entered a third phase. The rabbit returned to northern areas. Many trials are now won in grass and rushes, and no dog need scratch its nose. All need not be doom and gloom, but a worrying number of first places are now withheld by the judges, which is hardly indicative of a high general standard.

The most fatuous remark I have heard is that the standard of spaniels is higher now than ever before, as no one thinks anything about handling a spaniel on an unseen retrieve of more than 50 yards, and dogs are expected to handle a wide variety of cover, and face it bravely. What the blazes does anyone think spaniels were doing with cover 30 years ago? Circling it and pussyfooting around? And since when was blind retrieving ability the *sine qua non* of a spaniel? The truth about the position today is that, speaking purely mathematically, there are more people capable of bringing out a *reasonable* spaniel than ever before, because there are more aspirants. There is a dearth of truly great dogs, the ones which are 'almost too much dog', the stallions which become pillars of their breeds. Such animals require a gifted professional breathing down their necks, five days out of every seven. The talented amateur with a day job, dark mornings and early nightfalls during the trialling season, cannot keep on top of such a spirited animal and requires a much more amenable dog, often lovely to watch but lacking true stallion quality. Today we only have two young full-time professionals who are doing the full circuit.

It would be seemly if those who are winning today acknowledged the debt of gratitude they owe to those who came before. The winning bloodlines of the present era did not ooze out of a hole in the ground!

34

Field Trials in Europe

Holland

I have had contacts with The Netherlands for many years. In the early to mid-1970s, I ran an excellent springer and potent stud force in British trials for Paul Huet, a banker from The Hague. When the dog retired from trial competition, aged 6, I took him over to his owner to use as a shooting dog, and picked up at a unique snipe and duck shoot, not far from Delft. Some years later, I sold a springer puppy to a Dutchman to work with a goshawk, then his son took it over and ran it in field trials with considerable success. I also recommended a bitch I had trained for a Welsh client to another Dutchman who wished to purchase a fully trained bitch – one from the top bracket is never easy to come by. The eventual outcome was that I was invited to watch and report the Coupe d'Europe in early October 1988.

This was an international event, held in rotation in France, Italy, Belgium and Holland. Dogs from all these four countries competed, plus a few Danish dogs, both springers and cockers. The year I attended, the trials were held on the island of Texel, in North Holland, below the chain of Friesian Islands. The first two days were occupied by a cocker and a springer stake on the first day, on different parts of the island, under different pairs of judges, and the process was repeated on the second. Individual dogs won and were placed, but points were accrued by the various countries for ultimate team awards according to how the dogs from these five countries fared. The judges also picked worthy contenders from the first two days' events to compete in the Coupe d'Europe, or European Championship, on the third day. The trials were fascinating and a great personal triumph, as my host, Joep van der Vlasakker, took a first and second on the first two days, making my export, Ci of Gwibernant, an International Field Trial Champion; the dog also placed fourth in the Coupe d'Europe. An Italian dog, sired by one of my stud dogs, Black Rod of Gwibernant, placed second in this prestigious event, which was actually won by Bonny of Cilgraig, which I had trained.

Alas, the Coupe d'Europe is no more. After Bonny won it a second time in France, the Italians pulled out as they could not agree on rules and policy, so international events are now held minus Italy.

In late September 1991, I was honoured to be invited back to Texel to judge in this excellent sand dune country for a couple of days. The trial ground is donated by Government shooting tenants and the gamekeeper is an excellent shot, really keen and interested. He drives to the trial ground in traditional yellow Dutch clogs, then dons green wellies to shoot, and evenings in the restaurant bar see him back in his clogs again.

The Continental system differs from the British as dogs are run singly under a pair of judges. Each dog is allowed one minute's grace in which to settle, and if it is so inclined, can commit every crime in the book without penalty, although positive work is credited. The dog runs for a further fourteen minutes, and to complete its run, must have a minimum of one positive find and one retrieve. The quarry on Texel is exclusively rabbits, with the odd partridge shot, if a dog is really pushed for a retrieve. Neither hares nor pheasants come into season until 15 October.

There is a most interesting, stockily built character who wears a gold earring and who carries and paunches the shot rabbits. As he is somewhat shifty looking, my ex-gamekeeper's instinct registered 'poacher', in which assumption I was apparently correct. He is a great friend of the gamekeeper and the local police grant him a hunting licence, as he then proves very useful in keeping other poachers off the ground!

Dogs are not allowed to hold a solid point on game, on the assumption that a pointing spaniel can allow game to slip away in heavy cover. The odd squeak, or even bark, is tolerated, but a spaniel is eliminated if it babbles like a beagle. Dogs are eliminated if they catch unshot game.

If, after its fifteen minutes, a dog still lacks a find, or a retrieve, or both, the judges will take the dog or dogs so lacking for a further unlimited period until the deficiency is rectified. In the event of no retrieve being forthcoming, judges are empowered to give an artificial, thrown retrieve, although this is rarely necessary. The most important event is the actual find. If a spaniel enters cover and game departs, this does not suffice unless at least one judge can positively identify the acknowledgement and drive-in to flush. Dogs are also graded according to performance as 'Excellent', 'Very Good', 'Good' or '*Non Classé*', i.e. ungraded, if the dog completes its fifteen minutes without elimination but is too poor to merit consideration.

There were four judges in operation, Mr Bart Boers, Mrs Tineker Antonisse–Zijda, Mr Arnaut Faber and myself. I judged cockers on the first day with Tineker, a charming and knowledgeable Friesian, and springers with Bart on the second. Arnaut Faber is a local shooting man, a bit of a rebel, and will judge nowhere but Texel. He regretted we did not judge together and hopes this will be rectified at some future date: 'With no rules', he said, 'only those we make up as we go along.' Could be interesting!

The first dog to run under us in the cocker stake was handled by an outstanding lady of 82, Dr T. van Loon–Wierenga. Tineker warned me that there would be little contact between dog and handler, but Dr van Loon was very popular on the island and knew all the shoot proprietors, so it was 'just good local fun'. Her prediction was correct. The little dog hunted the dunes at its own range, and as the Scots would say 'took a loan of its handler'. The good Doctor was followed by several French and Belgian cockers. These were absolutely useless, allegedly dual-purpose but falling between two stools: no hunting ability and ugly as sin. One French dog did a little better and kept going, albeit with no style. It had a blank run, but when we took it in again after the first round, it had an exciting hunt on a moving pheasant in marshland, and when the bird finally flushed, the dog chased it to kingdom come! I was beginning to feel rather depressed, then we got into better dogs. A tiny little black and white Scottish-bred bitch, owned by a Dutchman who shoots over pointers and flies falcons in Scotland, and handled by the wife of one of the top Dutch springer handlers, did a superb piece of hunting. She had an average retrieve, then had another find and a top class retrieve across a valley, using a combination of gun-sense, rabbit line and wind.

A young Danish handler was let down by his useful type dog, but his father fared better, with a very good hunt in buckthorn, moving several rabbits but without the essential positive contact. This bitch then had an outstanding retrieve, winding the rabbit at a surprising distance. Her find materialized in the second round, when she flushed a very dark grey rabbit from marsh cover. She was followed by a big black bitch with great drive and style. She moved rabbits in her first run without a real find or retrieve but made up for it afterwards. She was close to Tineker, out of my vision, when a shot was fired by the keeper. A hare drifted across my front towards the left-hand gun, who did not fire. A muted murmur arose from the gallery: 'The gun had shot at a hare out of season.' He had not. The cocker flushed a rabbit and a hare from the same seat. The gun took the rabbit but properly left the hare, and the bitch had her retrieve.

Results: (1) Fritz Kleyn's bitch Norleigh Mayfly (Excellent); handler, Jannie van Stuyvenberg-Los. (2) Bjorn Ovesen's bitch Madonna of Jordieland (Very Good). (3) Jan Biemans' bitch Mallard (Very Good); handler, Nellie de Haan.

The Any Variety (for which read springer) had better hunting dogs than our also-ran cockers, but again the French dogs were disappointing, being half-wild or bullied into submission. Most are a dual-purpose type spaniel but though they penetrated cover well enough, they lacked style and control. One English-bred dog did very well but had to be downgraded on account of the handler's bad behaviour towards his dog. The Dutch produced a better type of entry and I cannot speak highly enough of the sportsmanship, camaraderie and decorum of the Dutch handlers. Their dogs are largely stylish and reasonably well controlled, if a little on the hot side, but I was impressed with their drive, style and gamefinding. HRH Prince Bernhard of The Netherlands' keeper, Gerit Visscher, ran his International F.T.Ch. Hauk's Donald, but it had an 'off day' under Bart and myself. Gerit supplies the dead ducks for the water test. The cockers could swim with no problem but the water was too shallow that year for the taller springers, so for the second day, we had to use a drain. All went well until the President of the French Spaniel Club's dog, which we had provisionally awarded the grade 'Good', decided to eat the duck, so was demoted forthwith!

France

My first acquaintance with French field trial spaniels took place in 1988 in Texel, North Holland, where I watched the Coupe d'Europe as a privileged spectator, walking with the judges. On this occasion, Dutch, French, Belgian, Danish and Italian spaniels were in contention with each other. The French dogs did not fare too well. In the final Championship event, Mlle Yvette Chavernac's springer spaniel Va Tout des Vorgines performed very well and took an award, and her 16-month-old Casanova of Gwibernant performed in promising fashion for the future but was eliminated for missing a rabbit on this occasion. No other French dogs distinguished themselves. The next time I saw French spaniels was again on Texel in 1991, when I had the honour to be invited to judge another international event. This time I judged springers and cockers and we were unable to classify any French dogs of either breed. All honours were won by Dutch and Danish dogs, apart from one dog living in Belgium which was handled by a Frenchman.

It seems that there is some concern in spaniel circles that the French dogs do not do so well in international competitions, so in January 1994 I was most grateful and honoured to accept a very kind invitation from the French Spaniel Club to attend their Championship Trials in the district of La Sologne, to carry out a 'watching brief' and report my findings on the quality of the dogs and give any advice which I felt could be appropriate.

I could see that one of the major difficulties experienced is that there are very few venues in France where trials can be conducted on natural game, whereas in Britain, Ireland, all four Scandinavian countries, Holland and I think perhaps Belgium also, spaniel trials are always held on ground where the game lives naturally, even though in some cases it may have been artificially produced some months before the trials are held. On this natural ground, game establishes a presence. Rabbits and pheasants live in the cover and make natural pathways which a spaniel can identify and gain access by. Even when no game is in the immediate area, there is always a faint permanent ground scent which will tell an experienced spaniel that game lives in the region. In their contrived trials, the French have a similar situation to the Americans, the Canadians and their close cousins, the Québecois: these have no natural game on their trial grounds, so they place birds on the ground ahead of the advancing dogs and people.

They use ground with very open, easy cover which requires speed and a setter-like quartering method but requires no courage on the part of the dog. The French, on the other hand, use tough cover like that found in many places in Britain. British dogs have the advantage of knowing that game lives on the ground and this gives them encouragement, whereas French dogs are expected to go through tough cover with no incentive. The dog must hunt the tough places because the cover is there, and this is a spaniel's job, but according to my observations, the released birds do not penetrate the thickest cover but seem to be found on the edges of the bushes. In most cases, even the good dogs had to be given strong commands to get into the cover but I am sure that in a natural game situation, they would have entered cover without any persuasion. It would not be realistic for me to say 'Only conduct the trials on natural game' when I understand the difficulties existing in this respect, and I do not know if the situation in France would permit natural game reserves to be created where outside hunters would be forbidden to hunt. One system which works very well in Britain is that we can buy trial ground by the day from a commercial shooting ground and we pay the owner an agreed sum for every natural bird which is shot. I wonder if such shooting grounds exist in France where this system could be used?

It seems that the French believe a spaniel should search a wide area to give it more chance to find game when game is scarce, and that a wide-running spaniel shows initiative. This is a good theory in the case of pointers and setters but I am not so happy with this procedure in the case of spaniels. I saw some of the dogs run about 50 metres in a straight line up an easy path, ignoring thick cover at the sides of the path, then begin to hunt when they found easy ground ahead. I do not condemn a spaniel which hunts fairly wide to the flanks of the handler, but I do not wish to see a spaniel boring ahead. For me, a classic manoeuvre would be that a spaniel would go across easy ground to the left or right of the handler, then enter a piece of demanding cover without handler encouragement. This is my definition of showing initiative. However, I would not require that the spaniel should go more than 30 metres from the handler. It was pointed out to me that as quite a lot of pheasants were shot, the spaniels must have been carrying out their functions correctly. To this I would say yes, if field trials are just an activity in their own right with no thought of spaniels as practical dogs for the hunter. The trial shooters were placed on the flanks and sometimes were in a position to shoot a bird which the handler, had he been a hunter, could not possibly have reached. Hunting spaniels need to hunt their ground more carefully to be truly effective.

The best spaniel I saw in France was Finbarr's Fancy dit Lereuk, handled by M. Baudry. This spaniel was very bold in quest, made three excellent finds and three good retrieves but had not by this time done the 15 minutes. After the third retrieve, he cast out in front very boldly but left a significant area of ground behind which was not hunted. Unfortunately, this piece of ground held a fourth pheasant which a judge trod on and flushed. A spaniel must hunt the ground at his handler's feet. He must not stay at the handler's feet but must get out and quest boldly, but should never leave a gap between himself and his handler as this is where game can be hiding. This is particularly important when the wind is blowing from behind. The spaniel should swing out in an arc, 25 or 30 metres in front of the handler. The handler should stand still and the dog should hunt the ground back to the handler, right to his feet. If game should rise between the dog and the handler, before the spaniel has had the chance to reach the area where the game has flushed from, the dog should not be penalized as the game has not waited long enough for the dog to make the point. Of course the dog cannot be credited for finding the game, so must hunt further for the chance of a real find.

We now come to the individual quality of the French spaniels. For international competitions, it seems that trying to keep close to a breed standard causes the most difficulties when competing against spaniels which have been bred only for work. A book published in Britain in 1993 on gundogs is *Pointers and Setters* by Derry Argue. Mr Argue has this to say about breed standards: 'Nor do I believe the ideal can be described in words or that all dogs in a certain breed should adhere to some committee's idea of what constitutes a standard for the breed. I have never understood that. Do such people go home from their committee meetings to be greeted by standard spouses, a row of children each conforming to a standard, and with standardised cats and dogs asleep on the hearthrug?' These are my sentiments, and something which I am sure every Frenchman will understand is that the world is full of beautiful women of different sizes and colouring. There are blonde Swedish girls 180 centimetres tall and black-haired Japanese ladies of 140 centimetres. Both are female human beings but they do not conform to the same standard and gentlemen who appreciate variety would not wish that they should. So too with dogs. I believe a spaniel can be good-looking if it looks nothing like the breed standard. Remember too that racehorses are bred to win races and some are very beautiful animals, but they would not win conformation classes at horse shows.

Now we come to the actual quality of the dogs I saw, both the natural quality and the man-made presentation. For the good of the breed, the former is the most important but without good presentation, the dogs cannot win. The essential mix is good natural ability and competent presentation.

In every country in the world where field trials are held there are some good dogs, some not so good and some bad. I am not going to say that all spaniels in Britain are good because this would be a lie. I judged a trial in October 1993 of 16 spaniels and gave classifications to nine, which was very good. In November I judged another 16 dogs and we were not able to classify one dog, so British dogs are not good all the time – but on average, I think the British still lead the world in quality of work and good behaviour. Some of the French dogs I saw were weak on hunting and were afraid to enter cover. Some would enter cover when strongly commanded and a very small number hunted the cover naturally and well. Some of the French-bred dogs were short of style and many tails were cut too short. A trial spaniel needs at least 23 centimetres. I noticed that some did not have a correct set-on to the tail, causing the tail to be carried too high, and sometimes a tail would curve upwards. I was disappointed by lack of control. In series Springer A on 9 January 1994, the first five dogs all ran to the birds when they were shot, or chased the bird after the find. This was very bad. It makes it too easy for the judges and lowers the standard of the trial. I can see the logic from a breeding angle of classifying a dog for natural ability when it has done wrong, but I wonder if this can make the handlers too complacent if they can still get some recognition with a badly trained dog, whereas in most other countries, unsteadiness means no recognition at all. One matter which pleased me very much in the French trial was that although the judges did not examine the pheasants for dog damage, when I examined the birds myself, I found that the dogs had not damaged any of them. This was very good. Perhaps in France they value the game so much on the table that they exercise care in breeding and only breed from dogs with gentle mouths.

In future, the main improvements the French should look for are more style, better courage in cover (in some cases) and much better training and steadiness to game and gun-fire. From the human side, shooters are excellent and the sportsmanship and good manners of competitors are beyond reproach. The know how to enjoy themselves and this is what trials should be all about. *Bonne chance*!

Italy

Unknown to many British gundog people, Italy is a hotbed of gundog activity, particularly where the pointing breeds are concerned. It has been remarked that Italians seem to have a natural affinity with any breed that ranges wide and points, and Italy produces many first class pointers and English setters, plus German pointers, Brittanies, Spinoni and Bracchi Italiani. Italy also produces trainers and handlers of a calibre to equal its better dogs with names like Francesco Morando and Gino Botto springing immediately to mind. I think in Britain we are apt to underestimate the Italian sportsman. Some individuals have earned themselves a bad press in Britain, Holland and the vast wheatlands of the Canadian prairies on account of their shooting excesses, but none the less Italy produces some excellent sportsmen and gundog handlers, particularly from the northern half of the country.

Spaniels are not so populous as the pointing breeds but there is a thriving field trial movement catering for springers and cockers. Italian spaniel people frequently invade France, Holland and Belgium, often taking home a fair amount of loot with spaniels which are mainly of British bloodlines.

In their own field trials, the Italians follow the example of the rest of Europe and Scandinavia in running their dogs singly under two judges. Rabbits are scarce in Italy so trials tend to be run almost entirely on pheasants. Judges look for speed and wide ranging and do not mind if a dog goes out of shot every now and then. Dogs must not catch unshot game or point although, unlike in America, a slight indication of game is tolerated. The find is all-important and when game is shot, the spaniel must collect it from where it has been flushed. No latitude is allowed regarding the handler leaving his position and moving forward to help the dog, as I have seen allowed in France. Dogs must be absolutely steady to flush and must ignore missed game but can run in to collect directly a bird is down. I have even seen Italian spaniels run in at a water test in Holland during an international event, for as it was the European Championship, Dutch rules (almost identical to British) did not apply.

In Italy some spring trials are held where dogs are judged on hunting and gamefinding, with gunfire accompanying the flushes, then the best dogs are graded out at the end of the series and each dog is given a thrown retrieve of a surplus game farm cock pheasant which is killed before it is used.

Fine limits of control or behaviour are less common in Italian spaniel trials than would be expected in British, American and Scandinavian events, but to win in Italy a dog must still have the basic spaniel qualities of pace, drive, style and gamefinding ability. Their handlers are very quick, reactive and good company. Personally I have a lot of time for them and would pay good money to see them perform!

Denmark
By courtesy of Henrick Vilendal

The following is a short survey of working spaniels in Denmark since the late 1970s. By 'working spaniels' we are talking about English springer spaniels and cocker spaniels with pure field trial pedigrees whose bloodlines go back on every line to British imports of trial-bred spaniels. I could not have written this chapter without the help of various field triallers in Denmark who have been part of this story from the late 1970s, when the most significant imports entered the country. Especially I would like to thank Mr Niels Egelund Faddersbøll for allowing me to use his splendid articles over the years in Danish shooting magazines, *The Spaniel* magazine and the Spaniel Club's 60th Anniversary book.

English Springer Spaniels

The evolution of working springers in Denmark began in the late 1970s but the working springer was seen here for the first time many years before this period. For example, back in 1950 estate owner C. Juul Johansen Langeskov bought a springer from no less a person than the late John Kent, and as Mr Johansen still owns and shoots over his own springers, he has had the breed for over four decades. There must have been other imports of working springers in Denmark of which the Spaniel Club is not aware, some of which will have been bred from on a small scale, but it was during the late 1970s and early 1980s that the number of imports increased and springer breeding on Danish soil really got under way. To paint a picture of the bloodlines that laid the foundations for these spirited animals I will mention some of the imports that had a major impact on the breeding programme in Denmark.

Mr Allan Mattison from Jutland imported two dogs, Parkmaple Domino and Chasers Arabbit (FTW Bricksclose Mark × Hyppolyta Brown) and two bitches, Sunstar Saint and Chaser Diana of Harwes. The two bitches and the dog Chasers Arabbit were the foundation of Mr Mattison's breeding under the prefix 'Chaser'. Mr Jørgen Lycik from Lolland imported the bitch Hedenham Park Sherry (Flint of Berrystead × Slipper of Hedenham Park) and later the bitch Tess of Gwibernant (F.T.Ch. Robbson of Gwibernant × Gwibernant Shilluk). They were the foundation of Mr Lycik's breeding under the prefix 'Lycik' from the beginning of the 1980s. On Fionia, Gamekeeper Holm imported a couple of springers from Ireland and the bitch Bricklemor Colleen founded his breeding under the prefix 'Rosendal'. In the 1980s Mr Peter Laursen imported five springers, among them the bitch F.T.Ch. Sealpin Speedwell (Badgercourt Rufus of Sealpin × Abbeyoaks Canna), later also to achieve the title of DK F.T.Ch. She only had two litters in Denmark, but two of the four dogs Mr Laursen imported had a major impact on the breeding in Denmark. They were Gorsty Gavel (Parkmaple Blackberry × Gorsty Gruach) (influential mainly through his son DK F.T.Ch. Lycik Brief, see later), Trioaks Toby (F.T.Ch. Raffle of Rytex × F.T.Ch. Rytex Ria), known as 'Brumble'. Mr Lycik had Brumble for a period and then sold him on to a gamekeeper, Frank Storgaard. He is now retired from trials and is enjoying life with Mr Storgaard who describes him as one of the best shooting dogs he has ever seen, shot over or trialled. The trial dogs in Denmark today show a lot of Brumble, his sons and daughters gaining awards and winning trials. In the mid-1980s Mr Leif Stov Petersen imported the dog Scot of Porsholtvej (F.T.Ch. Parkmaple Zip × F.T.Ch. Parkmaple Honey Bee) and Mr Niels Egelund Faddersbøll the dog Spinner (F.T.W. Gwibernant Rovdjur × Swedish & Norwegian F.T.Ch. Sherrys Sheena) from Sweden, which in the male line is Gwibernant and in the bitch line is the Swedish lines Sheenas and Woodcock.

Mr Niels Kristensen's dog DK F.T.Ch. Lycik Brief (Gorsty Gavel × Tess of Gwibernant) is the only Danish-bred dog that has had a major impact on the breeding of working springers in Denmark and we see quite a lot of very good Brief progeny on the trial circuit today.

New imports over more recent years worth mentioning are a bitch, Webbswood Glory (F.T.Ch. Gorsty Gester × Magpie Faux), which was mated to F.T.Ch. Barrowden Willow before being brought over to Denmark by Mr Ole Rasmussen who has also imported a bitch by F.T.Ch. Badgercourt Moss, two dogs by F.T.Ch. Rytex Rod and a bitch out of F.T.Ch. Poppet of Balscote bred by Mr Jørgen Lycik, and a bitch by F.T.Ch. Cortman Lane bred by Mr Henrik Vilendal.

Springers in Danish Field Trials

After a weak period in the 1970s with dogs like Greatford Fizz, handled by Mrs Marrianne Juel Brockdorff in 1975, and Rivirets Flimsy, handled by Mrs Hardy Jensen in 1978, something important began in the 1980s when Mr Leif Stov Petersen ran a bitch which was later to become the first springer to become a Danish F.T.Ch. – Lycik Getty (Chasers Arabbit × Hedenham Park Sherry).

The Spaniel Club was founded in 1933; English springers had been bred since then but virtually only out of show lines. Many triallers later on began to realize the qualities of the alternative bloodlines and the logic of buying stock for trials from the earlier mentioned breeders. From the mid-1980s the number of working-bred springers increased by leaps and bounds and we saw dogs of much higher quality and trained to a higher standard than ever before. The rise in standards and quality came from the 'new' breeders and several good new handlers made their marks. More inspiration followed at field trial meetings and the working springer was then recognized as the trial spaniel supreme. To mention anyone in particular would be invidious but Lycik breeding was absolutely the most dominant. Three Danish F.T.Chs were made up from Lycik breeding: DK F.T.Ch. Lycik Flynn (Scot of Torsholten × Tess of Gwibernant), handled by Leif Jacobsen; DK F.T.Ch. Lycik Brief, handled by Mr Niels Kristensen; DK F.T.Ch. Lycik Caprino (DK F.T.W. Rytex Raffle of Drakeshead × Tess of Gwibernant), handled by Mr Henning Rasmussen. This kennel up till now has produced at least 20 springers which have run in trials. The highly significant brood bitch Tess of Gwibernant was sired by F.T.Ch. Robbson of Gwibernant × Gwibernant Shilluk. Shilluk was sired by the prepotent F.T.Ch. Don of Bronton × F.T.Ch. Emma-Lene and was bred by the author in North Wales.

A smaller number of springers on the trial scene has emanated from the 'Go Get It' kennels with approximately 15 springers running in trials of which seven have won either open stakes or open stake awards. The 1993–4 trial season saw two springers being made up to DK F.T.Ch., Harrocks Fly (Pele of Rynllwyn × Harrocks Hebe), which also won that year's Championship (handled by Mr Jørgen Lycik, who most certainly can lay claim to be one of the best trainers of both spaniels and retrievers in Denmark), and DK F.T.Ch. Go Get It Kit (Spinner × Brit), handled by Mr Carsten Ovesen. Incidentally, the author judged this bitch in Holland in 1991.

Cocker Spaniels

Like the working springer there have been working cockers in Denmark for many years, some of them being from fashionable bloodlines. However, they have not made their mark on the trial scene and thus did not have any major impact on the production of working cockers in Denmark until the mid-1980s when some field trial handlers/breeders started to import some. Some seven or eight have been imported mainly by Mr Bjørn Ovesen, but Mr and Mrs Egelund Faddersbøll also brought in a couple.

Eight cockers have been run in trials and won first prizes, and four have qualified to run in open stakes – Madonna of Jordieland and Jagtcocker Barney, handled by Bjørn Ovesen; Ingelsøs Freja, handled by Mr Carsten Ovesen; and the only DK F.T.Ch. Neseborne Toft (Blackie of Jordieland × F.T.Ch. Morborne Nese), handled by Mrs Egelund Faddersbøll.

Working Spaniels and the Shooting Man

Even though the working spaniel can claim to have taken over completely on the trial scene, this reveals only part of its development. As in Britain, field triallers are only a small percentage of those guns who shoot over spaniels and the majority does not take part in any of the activities run by the gundog clubs. The escalation of the working spaniel in its wider sense in Denmark has been quite incredible, and in a period of about ten years shooting over spaniels has changed from being a minority interest to being a widely recognized and respected branch of field sports.

Working Spaniels and the Future in Denmark

Does the future then look bright for working spaniels in Denmark? The answer to such a question will depend on a number of factors. The Danish Kennel Club is a member of the FCI (Fédération Cynologique Internationale) and because of their 'show-attitude' to dogs in general much pressure is being put on the different breed clubs and also on those clubs which cater for the gundog breeds. There is the question of minimum show awards and a preoccupation with breed standards, etc. As there is only one set of conditions concerning registration, with which triallers as well as show breeders have to comply, this means that the two groups have to co-exist within the same breed clubs. This of course creates a schism in the gundog clubs and a lot of mud has flown through the air over the years. We need to establish respect and acceptance of each other's dogs and of the different views and ways of breeding gundogs. Breeding sound and healthy, biddable gundogs worth shooting over ought to be to the fore of the intentions of any person who takes an interest in any one of the gundog breeds, for the sake of the shooting man and his working gundog.

Danish field triallers really do get a lot of inspiration from Britain, by reading books and watching Championship or training videos. They are usually encouraged by and definitely learn from British judges who sometimes accept invitations to cross the North Sea and judge Danish spaniel trials.

Author's Note

On reading the foregoing, breeders in either Great Britain or North America should be grateful that we are never in any way subservient to a show-orientated gundog regime, and can breed our gundogs as and how we wish with no 'Big Brother' breathing down our necks!

Postcript

Since writing the foregoing I have received interesting and welcome news from my friend Bjørn Ovesen. Although the Danish Kennel Club is a member of the Fédération Cynologique Internationale, with its preoccupation regarding breed standards and its insistence that dogs should have won a minimum show award before they are allowed to run in field trials, as is the case in Finland, the Danish Kennel Club now has yielded to pressure from the hunter/triallers and has agreed that working spaniels now may have a separate registry as distinct from the show spaniels. Thus the breed in Denmark is now officially divided and there is no longer any pressure put on working spaniels to have any kind of show award. This is surely a victory for common sense, and it will be interesting to see if in future any other European and Scandinavian countries follow Denmark's lead.

Sweden

Sweden has several native breeds of hunting dogs, more usually slanted towards larger game such as moose and roe deer. Gundogs for use with winged game tend to have been imported from Germany and Great Britain. A typical example is the English springer spaniel. The first specimens to be imported were all show dogs. As there is great interest in Sweden in all forms of hunting and shooting, it comes as no surprise that attempts were made to work these show specimens, with varying success. Before long, field trials were instituted but seemingly with the accent on retrieving rather than hunting. There is a vast amount of water in Sweden and quite a lot of duck shooting takes place, so it is hardly surprising that exhaustive water tests featured heavily in the past. Another feature was the 'Obligatory Rabbit' (often called the 'Silly Rabbit' in some quarters). This was a test whereby a dead rabbit was dragged quite a distance and the spaniels were expected to follow the artificial line and complete the retrieve.

For all I know this type of trial may still be run, but it seems that during the recent past, several Swedes have visited Britain for the Kennel Club Spaniel Championships and have abandoned completely the show type of springer and have imported pure British field trial stock, along with British ideas of how spaniel trials should be conducted. There is now a movement which is concerned with promoting the superior hunting-type spaniel (to which the show spaniels cannot hold a candle), and though the Swedes still recognize the necessity for all spaniels to face water with no hesitation, the accent is now on land work with no artificial tests featuring in any of their new-style field trials.

Over the years, I have met several of the 'New Look' Swedish field triallers, including Herr Rolf Lindgren, who lives on the estate of Count Thott who, with his brother, Baron Erik Thott, manages a beautiful 7,000-acre estate a few miles north of the city of Malmö.

Early in 1993, Rolf, on behalf of the Svenska Spaniel och Retrieverklubben, wrote to ask me if I would judge the Swedish Spaniel Championship. I was most honoured to receive this invitation. With typical Swedish efficiency, Rolf sent me a list of eliminating faults beforehand and, what was even more interesting, some photographs of the trial ground we were to work on the first and second days. Rolf assured me that there would be plenty of rabbits on the first day and that he had counted over 50 sitting out on the day he took the pictures. In deference to the trial, the official Malmö City rabbit shooters had agreed not to shoot any rabbits for some weeks prior to the event, and would act as guns at the trial.

The second day was to take place on farmland, some distance from the city. According to the photographs, this ground looked quite demanding and Rolf assured me there would be plenty of pheasants and rabbits. I was to discover that Rolf had not exaggerated.

At the end of October, I set out on my epic journey from Manchester Airport. The plane dipped down through cloud cover as we crossed the coast of the large Danish island of Sjaelland, on the eastern side of which is situated the city of Copenhagen. The country was dead flat and agricultural with rectangular fields of almost geometrical precision. It also appeared that every farmstead had its own pond. Approaching the suburbs of Copenhagen, the farms gave way to small, quaint, box-like dwellings, rather like dolls' houses. Taking a backward glance into history, it seemed almost inconceivable that this tranquil, rather uninspiring land could have given birth to one of the fiercest warrior nations the world has ever known.

Rolf, a latter-day Viking if ever there was one, met me at the airport with his 4 × 4 Isuzu and after a brief exchange at customs, where he managed to convince the young Danish policeman that I was not an international terrorist, merely an irritant in my own country, we proceeded to the ferry. Denmark and southern Sweden are close together – so close in fact that two intrepid Danish girls, resenting the German occupation during the Second World War, swam from Denmark to Sweden. However, the ferry must have taken a different route as the journey took an hour and we sailed right out of sight of land, but eventually arrived at our destination, Malmö, a city of a quarter of a million inhabitants and principal town of the province of Skona. After dinner, I was escorted to my hotel at a suburb named Jagersro, which, rather appropriately, means Hunter's Rest.

The event was scheduled for two days, the first day to be held on city land, within half a mile of my hotel. The field trial meet was the most urban I have ever seen, close to my hotel in a huge car park, backed by the imposing bulk of a McDonald's. After the introductions, there was a somewhat lengthy debate. It was the Vikings who instituted the first parliaments, where every free-born man, or 'Carl', had an equal voice, and the old traditions are by no means dead. One of the top handlers had quite a few reservations regarding the guns, who he said were labrador men and would shoot retrieves too far out for spaniels. I am not sure that he approved completely of an overseas judge, as apparently I was the first judge from beyond the Scandinavian countries ever to be invited to judge spaniels in Sweden. In the final analysis, subsequent events proved these reservations to be groundless.

The first day's trialling was to be conducted entirely on rabbits. We did move a couple of hares and there was quite a nice showing of wild pheasants but, for some unknown reason, they were not to be shot. We had four guns on the first day who shot two at a time, turn and turn about, and couldn't they just shoot! The course we worked was dead flat, cover being a few isolated patches of buckthorn but in the main rushes and thick clumps of yellow marsh grass. Cockers and springers competed together, and to qualify, must have won either an open or an elite stake. Skona abounds with all kinds of game but further up country there are no rabbits, so the local dogs were at a distinct advantage. I had one beautifully stylish and polished bitch under me which had no experience on rabbits and soon missed one. Others found their rabbits extremely well but scent was very poor on shot rabbits, and it was not until after lunch that I saw a spaniel put its nose down on the track of a wounded rabbit and take a really good line – and this was the youngest competitor, a 13½-month-old cocker puppy! This was real hunting, with the spaniels providing superb sport for the guns, just as they would be expected to do in any hunting situation, except that most displayed more decorous manners than one might expect of average hunting spaniels.

I finished the first round shortly after lunch. Every 'clean' spaniel had a minimum of two and a maximum of four retrieves and there were many more flushes, where some rabbits were missed and many slipped safely away into cover. We had plenty of ground and daylight left, so I gave all the clean dogs a second round with just one retrieve each. So well did the game come to hand that the first three contestants were only down about a couple of minutes each. It didn't matter. Stamina had been well tested during the morning.

There was a drive of several miles to the north for the second day. Skona is flat, rich agricultural country with extensive broadleaved woodlands, completely different from the coniferous regions further north. It was a province of Denmark until the 1600s and there was little wonder that the Danes were so loath to give the region up; in fact Rolf told me that in Skona, they regard themselves as more Danish than Swedish. Whereas my hotel at Jagersro was ultra-modern, with acres of glass and futuristic decor, my next hotel, though perfectly adequate, was more on old-fashioned rooming-house lines.

We all assembled for dinner at a nearby restaurant. Guest of Honour was Herr Olov Axelsson, a stalwart of the field trial movement but sadly now afflicted by Parkinson's Disease. Olov was a former forest keeper and hunter of larger game, and although no longer able to participate, turned up very smartly attired in the most expensive English Savile Row shooting suit. He brought with him a pile of photocopies of an article I had written about him in an English magazine, many years before, with a photo of him and a 5-month-old springer pup I had sent over, with a roebuck which the pup had trailed for 60 yards after it had been shot. My caption was rude: 'Who needs a German Shorthair?'

One of my rabbit carriers on the previous day was a young landowner, Bosa Nilsson, whose wife, Britt, was one of the contenders. Bosa had arranged the second day's trial ground with his neighbouring estate owner at Dagstorp. I would describe it as a top class farm shoot. The agriculture is sophisticated and profitable; crops include blackcurrants and aubergines, but many acres are set aside for game and there are strategically planted areas of game cover. Rabbits and wild pheasants do well but there is also a modest rearing programme. I wouldn't have known it. Every pheasant had the appearance and habits of a true wild bird. Throughout the trial, I never saw a bird running ahead of us. Either I saw nothing, or I saw a spaniel dive into the cover and a pheasant erupt. Every cock was a ringneck, with mauve wing coverts and rump. They were released at the end of June and every bird was full-tailed and strong. I formed the distinct impression that the Scandinavians have managed to stay closer to nature with their rearing programmes than anyone has done in Britain.

Bosa was my right-hand gun and a young gamekeeper covered my left. Both were excellent shots and hardly missed a thing. There was only one cripple shot throughout the trial, and that didn't go far before being apprehended. A deep, slow river with very heavy cover on its banks proved interesting and we had retrieves both in and over water.

The day commenced in a spinney which provided a pheasant and a rabbit for last year's winner to retrieve, then we were into currant bushes which held a lot of rabbits but were difficult to deal with. Dogs could be credited with the finds but mostly the rabbits dodged and doubled; but three were shot for different dogs, so it was a useful exercise. Then we were onto the riverbank and really began to get into the pheasants, although rabbits continued to create a diversion and the occasional retrieve. Rolf's springer had a bird in the river and Britt's bitch made two perfect flushes and marks on pheasants, one of which fell across water. Without doubt, the fastest springer I have seen for years was a very white bitch, 'Date' (pronounced 'Darter'), which was handled by a young pro trainer, Bengt Rodseth. Despite her blinding speed and American-style quartering, she never over-ran her nose. Her gamefinding was deadly but unfortunately she broke on her third pheasant.

By lunchtime, there was little left to do. Our youngest contender needed to finish its run but this little cocker, although performing excellently on rabbits and a hare, came to grief in a patch of heavy cover from which it was unable, or unwilling, to pull out a big cock pheasant. By this time I had the winner and runner-up decided and had a 9-year-old cocker bitch and last year's Springer Championship winner standing equal. I ran both together side by side in heavy cover and instructed the guns not to shoot, as I had seen enough retrieving over the two days with 60-odd head of game shot. The hunt in heavy cover was inconclusive. Both dogs faced it with courage, then we were out into some lighter stuff with the wind behind us. The springer arced out downwind, turned back towards us and made a perfect find and drop to flush on a hen pheasant, so beating the cocker to the find and gaining the advantage.

First place went to Jörgen Sandberg's 8-year-old cocker dog, Skenchall Mark, a most efficient golden dog which had about 20 flushes and eight retrieves over the two days. Runner-up was Britt Nilsson's springer bitch Vekabodas

Cookie: fast and stylish and under good control. Third was Christer Janérus's springer bitch Vekabodas Jacky: a very efficient gamefinder but a little plain in hunting style. Fourth was Hans Sjöblom's cocker bitch Ebony Slice: a very experienced, polished bitch that found a large quantity of game and retrieved to perfection. Award of Honour went to Rolf Lindgren's springer dog Sheena's Major: an excellent shooting dog but lacked a little pace.

Immediately after the trial had finished, the awards given and pleasantries exchanged, which included the presentation of an engraved heavy glass decanter to myself as an appreciation for judicial services rendered, Rolf thrust a nice Spanish 12-bore into my hands with the words, 'Now you will go and shoot some pheasants', which I did, but that merits a story of its own.

Finland

Finland is a wonderful, wild land of lakes, forests and arctic tundra. The Finns are a nation of hunters and pursue a wide variety of quarry species from the snipe to the moose, making extensive use of both local and British hunting dog breeds. Winged game consists of wild duck, snipe, woodcock, capercaillie, black grouse, hazel grouse and willow grouse above the treeline.

Finland is another country where there is great interest in dog-showing. The local breeds of hunting dogs are the elkhound, the Finnish spitz and the Finsk Stövare, all workers first and foremost. The elkhound hunts the moose, the Finnish spitz hunts and chases capercaillie and blackgame up trees and barks until the hunter, guided by the sound of his dog's baying in the dense forest, stalks carefully to the tree and shoots the bird sitting, as the dense tree canopy precludes a sporting flying shot. The Finsk Stövare is a beautiful lemon-and-white hound, tall and graceful, trained to ignore deer and moose and to concentrate on hare or fox only which it hunts towards its master's gun. These breeds are bred in the main for work and there are no specific strains of show dogs, so it is a simple matter for any of these native dogs to become a bench Champion without the working ability becoming diluted in any way. Unfortunately the Finnish Kennel Club is of the opinion that the imported British gundog breeds should conform to a dual-purpose standard also, which can make life rather difficult for owners of imported English springer spaniels as the Finnish Kennel Club could be said to put the cart before the horse by requiring that an aspiring field trial spaniel should be awarded a minimum of a second place in a show before it can be entered for field trials.

Despite this handicap, several British working springers have managed to collect this essential qualification, including a little bitch I exported a few years ago. There are two differing types of spaniel trials in Finland, lakeside trials and forest trials. In lakeside trials, the handler, wearing a pair of waders, hunts the waterlogged cover around the margins of a lake, the dog alternatively hunting or swimming in front of him as conditions dictate. The dogs are worked singly, according to Continental and Scandinavian fashion, and the handler is accompanied by two judges. The quarry species are snipe and duck which the dog flushes or which rise of their own volition, the handler is his own official gun and shoots over his own dog. Another contrived exercise is to retrieve duck from a boat, as this is an exercise a Finnish spaniel would have to accomplish frequently throughout its hunting career. The judges make their assessments but if they should be at variance over the performance of any of the contestants, their notes are read by a judge who is senior to both of them and he has the casting vote.

The forest trials are self-explanatory. On this subject, some time ago I received a phone call from Carl Blomqvist, a Swedish-speaking Finn whose English also is impeccable, to inform me of the progress of the bitch I sent him, Gwibernant Astra, Kennel name 'Star'. Here I must digress as the manner in which 'Star' received her name is worthy of the telling. She was sired by Cortman Lane and bred by a local gamekeeper who originally was a valley boy from South Wales, known as 'Merthyr Mike' as he came from Merthyr Tydfil. The litter was born and one pup appeared to be dead so Mike wrapped her in our local Border rag, the *Shropshire Star*, and put the pup in the dustbin. Some time later Mike heard squeaks coming from the bin and there was the pup, alive and well (which speaks volumes for the therapeutic properties of the *Star*) and this is how she became known as 'Star'. Carl told me Star had done particularly well in forest trials 'where we hunt the little black birds with the funny tails'. I was nonplussed. What kind of little black birds live in forests and have funny tails? Was it some peculiar Finnish species of which I was not aware? Eventually it transpired that Carl was referring to blackgame and the blackcock in particular, but 'little'? A mature blackcock can turn the scales at three pounds four ounces, cock pheasant size in fact, but I suppose these things are relative. As Finland is the home of the king of the grouse family, the mighty capercaillie, perhaps by comparison a blackcock is 'little'!

35

Spaniels – A Continental Sportsman's View

During the course of writing this book, it was suggested to me by the President of the English Springer Spaniel Club of France, along with the President of the French Spaniel Club, that I should give my views on the methods currently being advocated by a Belgian journalist and spaniel owner, Monsieur Jean de Roo. Although M. de Roo has competed in spaniel trials (and won!), it seems that his ideas are somewhat unorthodox and, it is feared, might lower standards if they were widely adopted. The two presidents felt that a respected international authority should refute these ideas and I am flattered that they approached me. All I can say is that I have worn out quite a bit of shoe leather behind a fair few spaniels, good, bad and indifferent.

Who Is to Blame?

This was the title of an article by M. Jean de Roo in *Chiens de Chasse*, from which it became apparent that he was unhappy about the current situation relating to working spaniels, both on the Continent of mainland Europe, and in Great Britain. Through my four decades of association with spaniels, and my experience of judging field trials for spaniels in Britain and all over the Continent, I think I have a fairly good idea of what I am looking for and, equally important, what I am looking at, and so am in a good position to comment on his views.

By his radical ideas, M. de Roo has placed himself in the category of a maverick, flying in the face of all accepted traditions except possibly those of Germany, where I believe a spaniel must give tongue and chase the game. What worries me is that M. de Roo is a very able journalist and can put his points of view forward in such a persuasive manner that many persons who are beginners with spaniels might be converted to his way of thinking, which could be very damaging to the spaniel breeds.

M. de Roo's first points concern giving tongue and unsteadiness, for which most field trial judges will eliminate dogs but which M. de Roo believes actually make the best dogs, those of the greatest service to the ordinary hunter. In such a case it is a matter of what the hunter has been educated to expect from his spaniels. Often we require different performances from the various breeds of hunting dogs. Hounds which hunt wild boar, deer, hares or foxes must give tongue when hunting and so must terriers and dachshunds when working underground, or when driving deer to guns. In most countries, spaniels are expected to work silently, although the occasional small bark is tolerated in some countries but not in others. The exception is the Sussex spaniel. Nowadays there are very few of this breed which are capable of normal spaniel work but it is accepted that any Sussex spaniels which do work are allowed to give tongue without penalty. Many years ago, the English Kennel Club would allow crossing between various breeds and I have competed against a field spaniel crossed with a Sussex. This dog also was allowed to give tongue in a field trial because of its part-Sussex heritage but, apart from these few examples, most spaniel owners in Britain and elsewhere require a spaniel to be as silent as possible.

Rare exceptions can still occur. I have some friends in

north-east England who went to shoot rabbits in late summer with a gamekeeper. The rabbits lived in large areas of tall bracken and the hunting technique was for the gamekeeper to disturb the rabbits with his spaniels and drive them to the shooters who stood at strategic points. All the spaniels gave tongue, which my friend said was quite useful as it warned the guns of the approach of a rabbit. Afterwards, the guns, who were all field trial competitors, told the gamekeeper that they had enjoyed the shooting but mentioned that although his spaniels had done a good job, they would not be suitable for field trials because of the noise factor. The gamekeeper was very puzzled. He understood nothing about field trials and said, 'But how do you know when a rabbit is coming if your dogs don't bark?'

What was conducted on this occasion was not true spaniel work. It was more like driving roe deer to guns with dachshunds, drevers or wachtelhunds, as is done in Sweden. In true spaniel work, the shooter walks behind the spaniel which covers a systematic beat, either side of the shooter or handler (in a field trial). The object is not to drive game to guns. It is to flush game, which flies or runs away from the shooter. It is better if the spaniel never hunts more than 20 metres from the shooter. To ensure that the spaniel hunts within these limits it must be 100 per cent responsive to command. If it is not, it will hunt too far away. Some game will be flushed out of shot. Some will be shot at extreme range and will be more likely to be wounded than dead. It is very nice if a spaniel is good at finding wounded game. It is far better if it flushes game within comfortable reach of the gun, so more game is killed than is wounded. If a spaniel is working correctly and flushing all its game within shot, there is no need for it to bark to warn the shooter of the presence of game. The shooter has eyes to see with!

I would say to M. de Roo that in Britain we have no trouble in filling our game bags. I would also point out that where most of us use spaniels for shooting, there is not the large quantity of game present which is seen at some of our field trials (which, even when in large quantities, is either wild or released some months before). In Britain, Holland and all the Scandinavian countries, this situation regarding the status of the game applies.

M. de Roo observed, and I agree with him, that some people see field trials as an end in themselves and that this is the greatest heresy, but in all countries of the world where spaniel trials are held, there is always a hard core of persons like myself who see spaniels as shooting dogs first but where the better specimens compete in trials. In trials, it cannot be avoided that spaniels only work for a limited period of time. It would be impossible, because of the time factor, to run every contestant for as long as a spaniel would work in a shooting situation. It should be the aim of every responsible trial breeder to breed spaniels which are capable of working far longer, but at a reduced pace, than ever they are required to do under trial judges. Apply this situation if you will to thoroughbred horses. A racehorse covers a limited piece of ground at the fastest possible speed, then his work is done. But from the blood of this racehorse, or his close relations, horses can be produced which one can ride when stag or boar hunting which will have to gallop at a more normal pace for much longer periods than their racehorse ancestors.

The spaniel that flushes game, then sits and looks at it, is not engaging in useless theatricals, as M. de Roo has suggested; rather, it is doing a piece of work which, far from being useless, or even optional, is absolutely essential. Particularly in the case of a rabbit and often when the game is a woodcock, if the spaniel chased the game, as M. de Roo favours, the dog could be shot. It MUST stop for its own safety. I can understand that in the case of a pheasant, if the dog chases the bird as it flushes, if the bird is only winged, the dog will be so much closer to the bird when it hits the ground; but steady dogs, on a good scenting day, often find good runners even when the bird has a good start. Quality of the dog's nose is of considerable importance.

I feel I must challenge M. de Roo's statement that 'mechanical spaniels without any initiative as we see them in British field trials seem to us totally inefficient from a hunting point of view.' True, we do have this type of spaniel in Britain but these are mainly of the working test type which do a lot of competition work in spring and summer on gameless ground and only retrieve dummies or game out of deep freezers. The example he quotes is interesting, of the spaniel in Britain that flushed a pheasant inside a wood which then flew out of the wood and was shot by the left-hand gun, who was walking on the edge of the wood. M. de Roo complains that the dog took too long to find the bird, which was dead, but had it been a runner, it would have been lost. This is a typical trial situation where a bird shot by a trial gun frequently is far more difficult to find than one shot by the handler. In woodland, birds are often more difficult to mark than in the open, simply because of the trees which can obscure the dog's vision. A dog can mark a bird so far, but if it falls outside the wood, as in this case, then because of the spaniel's low eye level, it cannot see that the bird is in the field, as its vision gives the wrong message and the dog believes the bird is still in the wood. These are the most difficult retrieves we have to contend with, when the dog is in cover but the bird is beyond the cover and in the open. It is within the nature of any spaniel to stick to the cover under such circumstances and it requires sophisticated handling to convince the dog otherwise. In a shooting situation this would not have occurred: the handler would have shot the pheasant which would have fallen closer in, and inside the wood.

When we organize field trials, we must have a starting point. In most cases this starting point demands that dogs are steady and don't give tongue. Coming down from this point, we have the shooting dogs which their owners can educate as they wish, or not at all. People who think on the lines of M. de Roo can allow their spaniels to chase the game when it flushes and the excitement which this regime engenders is most likely to ensure that soon the dog will give tongue also.

It seems as though M. de Roo would consider trials to be more realistic if they started at what is actually his finishing point! We must respect his views on what he expects of his spaniels but he must not expect to win trials with them, except perhaps under German rules or perhaps under some Belgian judges who are looking for the same performance which he considers to be correct.

Some years ago I saw M. de Roo run a springer on the island of Texel in North Holland. His dog was given the usual one minute to settle down, but at the end of the minute the dog refused to return within gun range and was correctly disqualified. I believe it was some little time longer before he was able to find the dog. I doubt that this performance would have been much use in an ordinary shooting situation either. I have also judged some Belgian cockers in Texel which refused to hunt, so I don't think that handlers in Britain or the rest of Europe need worry too much over the doom and gloom which M. de Roo has attempted to cast over the spaniel scene. For the record, I have a Papillon which will chase rabbits and bark. From my spaniels I expect more decorous behaviour!

36

Transatlantic Spaniel Trials: USA and Canada

Dorothy Morland Hooper's book *The Springer Spaniel* provides an interesting and valuable insight regarding the early days of the English springer spaniel in North America but has some slight inaccuracies. It is correctly stated that the first spaniel trial in America was held on Fishers Island in 1924 but, as I have quoted elsewhere in this book, according to Eudore Chevrier, this was not the first spaniel trial to be held on that continent as an event held in Canada preceded the Fishers Island event by a few years. Eudore Chevrier is credited by many with the title of 'the father of the springer spaniel in North America', but there are some who believe that William Humphrey of the Horsford Kennels in Shropshire is more deserving of this accolade. Certainly he participated in the Fishers Island inaugural event, taking first and second place, and exported many notable dogs before he gave up springers and concentrated on Llewellin setters from 1927 onwards, having purchased the entire kennel of the late Ll. Purcell Llewellin from the latter's housekeeper, Llewellin having been a lifelong bachelor.

An anecdote regarding Llewellin and Humphrey might bear repetition. Humphrey was walking down the High Street in Shrewsbury one day when he espied Llewellin gazing into the window of a ladies' outfitter with rapt attention. Humphrey tried to avoid Llewellin by surreptitiously slipping across onto the opposite side of the road but the eagle eye of the great setter man registered Humphrey's presence. 'Come here quick, Humphrey,' said Llewellin, pointing his finger at several articles of female apparel (which in the early 1920s must surely have been far less scanty than their counterparts of today). 'What silly, frivolous things women must be to wear such impractical garments. Small wonder that they are forever becoming afflicted with ailments and incurring doctor's bills. What do you think, Humphrey?' With as straight a face as possible Humphrey replied that he had absolutely no experience of such matters, which some of Humphrey's contemporaries later told me was a monstrous lie!

However, from this small beginning on Fishers Island, the popularity of springer trials in North America escalated beyond belief, culminating in a record entry of over 100 quali-fied dogs in the 1993 American National Championship.

The first trials in both Canada and America originally were held on wild game, pheasants and rabbits on Fishers Island and pheasants and prairie chickens in Canada, but the format was soon to change and pheasants which are 'planted' on the trial course ahead of the dogs became the quarry in open and Championship stakes. Miss Morland Hooper mentions 'Licensed' and 'Sanction' trials. The latter are no longer held. All trials nowadays are run under the auspices of the American Kennel Club (AKC) and consist of Open, Amateur and puppy stakes, plus of course the National Championships. In Canada there are no Amateur handler stakes, so Canadian clubs usually hold two open qualifying stakes at each field trial meeting. In the past great fun was enjoyed with 'shooting dog stakes'. In these events the handlers shot over their own dogs and either planted feral pigeons or pheasants were used. When pigeons were used it was necessary to kill the bird otherwise it would simply hightail it back to the nearest city. In the case of planted pheasants one old-stager found a kill unnecessary.

His name was Val Dervin of California and at one time he had a dog that was an absolutely brilliant marker. When the dog flushed a pheasant, Val would deliberately shoot over the top of the bird to miss. Eventually the bird would plane down and he would send his dog. There is only one flight in a game farm 'planted' pheasant, which upon alighting would squat and allow Val's super-marker to effect a retrieve; the dog would be credited by the judges with a brilliant long retrieve!

I am not aware that shooting dog stakes are held any more, although perhaps some are ultra-curricular and the results do not appear in *Spaniels in the Field*, the only publication in America devoted purely to spaniel matters. Miss Morland Hooper includes rabbits as quarry in open stakes but these have been disregarded within living memory. Nothing is shot but planted pheasants, not even quail if encountered. Another error in the Morland Hooper narrative is the inclusion of the double National Championship winner Staindrop Breckonhill Chip (1957 and 1958) as a British-bred bitch. In fact she was American-bred, but the British affixes 'Staindrop' and 'Breckonhill' were plagiarized by her American breeder. This is confusing and the practice has not altogether died out, to the annoyance of some affix holders in Britain, so it is understandable that Miss Hooper made this error.

American trials differ from British trials in many respects. Seldom, if ever are trials run in what one would term real spaniel cover where courage and penetration are prerequisites, although I am told that the 'Valley Forge' trials in the Eastern States are held in more British-type cover than any of their other events. It is little use planting reared birds in heavy bramble-type cover – they would simply push in and allow themselves to be caught, and although catching a bird is no crime in an American trial, as allowances obviously are made for the often unsophisticated behaviour of game farm birds, unless at least a proportion will flush and provide a mark and retrieve, a trial would be impossible to judge. Hence more open cover is in the most common usage, such as weedy ground or alfalfa. Often these planted birds require a strong inducement to become airborne and a spaniel that goes in gently on the flush is likely to induce a bird to take to its legs rather than its wings.

It seems that in all disciplines of competitive gundog work in America, a performance well beyond the norm is sought. Retrievers must mark further and swim greater distances than anywhere else in the world. Their major circuit pointers and setters and sometimes German pointers and Brittany spaniels must run so far and wide that handler, judges and spectators require horses to keep up with the contestants. Small wonder that in American spaniel trials certain aspects are, by British standards, exaggerated. The 'hard flush' is a prime example and has been described as 'cosmetic' by one of their most intelligent and successful handlers. Judges really love to see a dog driving in hard on a bird and leaping in the air to speed its departure. Spaniels are required to run far wider than would be consistent with a handler shooting over his own dog, and to do so at top speed. Conversely to British requirements where so many judges will downgrade a spaniel which hunts with a high head, American judges demand a more setter-like head carriage and will discard a low-headed hunter. Marking a shot bird seems to have become something of a fetish. An American judge requires a spaniel 'to hit the fall on the head' whereas judges in Britain would credit a dog with a good mark if it arrived a few yards beyond a bird but right for the wind, then turned into the wind, used its nose and quickly found the bird.

Another essential difference is the American attitude to 'runners'. In British terminology a 'runner' is a winged bird. These are 'cripples' in America. This is something of a misnomer as there is little of the cripple about an old wingtipped cock, which will defeat a great many dogs and whose wound frequently heals, enabling it to fly again provided it can keep out of the way of the local fox. The American spaniel trial 'runner' is a bird which, after being planted, leaves its 'nest' and takes to its legs. In Britain we disregard such birds and keep our dogs quartering at all times, and if a spaniel takes the line of a moving bird more than a few yards without producing, the dog is pulled off the line and put back into its hunting pattern. The Americans have developed a whole trial scenario around 'the runner'. It is the epitome of a classic performance if, when a dog breaks its pattern, drops its nose and begins to 'trail', it can be stopped by whistle until judge, handler and one gun can catch up, then the dog is laid on the line again and the performance repeated until the bird is successfully flushed, shot, marked and retrieved. Often it happens that in a stake of really high standard a spaniel will run an impeccable trial with a copybook performance of fine hunting, hard flushing, excellent marking and good retrieving but still receive no award apart from the distinction of having 'completed all series', simply because it had no opportunity on runners whereas other dogs did. This is a similar situation to a retriever trial in Britain where a dog has a succession of perfect marks and retrieves on dead birds but has no opportunity to execute eye-wipes after other dogs have failed, and has collected no 'runners' (our shot variety!). Should a spaniel fail on a retrieve in America, its bracemate is never tried on the retrieve as usually happens in Britain.

American judges don't seem to mind how much whistle is used to control a hunting spaniel provided it responds whenever the whistle is blown. This was once remarked upon by a highly intelligent handler from Oregon, the late Paul Diegel. Paul had visited the British Spaniel Championships and, writing about his experiences afterwards, remarked how much less whistle was used by our handlers. He said: 'British spaniels are *trained* to stay within shot. Try that on the next half dozen field trial champions you judge.' Another essential difference is that the British prefer a competing spaniel to appear calm and collected whereas it seems that many American judges like to see a dog just on the edge of control. Recently I had a visit from a well-known American journalist who writes extensively on wildlife and game shooting. He shoots over a springer bitch of mainly American field trial breeding which has given him a great deal of satisfaction but is not content to switch off and sit quietly when not actually hunting, as he discovered that my springers will. It seems that, temperamentally, British and American trial spaniels have evolved on different lines. Perhaps this reflects more exacting requirements in Britain regarding breeding stock, which at the end of the day have produced a more stable temperament.

Virtually all I have written regarding American field trials can be applied to Canadian springer trials. I was told in the 1950s that a dog was allowed to point its game in Canadian trials whereas this is an eliminating fault in America. I don't know if this was true or not but certainly this would not apply today. The Canadians are by no means the poor relations of the North American field trial circuit and the Canadian National Championship is a hotly contested affair with many of the top American professional and amateur handlers competing. I am fortunate to have supplied the Canadian National with three winners over the years: Windmillwood Storm, who in addition has open and amateur titles in the USA; Whitlocks Warrior, who also has an open USA title; and the best of all in my opinion, Pel Tan Roly, who has his open and amateur American titles.

One significant difference between American and Canadian spaniel trials is that whereas the Americans can throw live birds out over water to be shot for their water tests, this would be contrary to the Criminal Code of Canada so is proscribed accordingly. Canadian water tests consist of dead birds being thrown into water, which works well enough. There are strong feelings in America that perhaps it would be a better idea to follow the Canadian example and stage water tests which might be more 'meaningful', such as a retrieve over a river or wide ditch or perhaps even a double retrieve across water, to simulate a right-and-left shot over water and onto land in an ordinary shooting situation.

37

Spaniels Today

If any person should ask 'Which is the best breed of gundog?', I would have to reply that a fatuous question can only produce a silly answer. If, however, the question was rephrased to 'Which is the *most useful* gundog breed?' (or, more properly, group), then the floodgates would be open for more intelligent debate. We could interpret the term 'useful' as meaning having the widest range of uses for the widest spectrum of shooters. If we were to believe all the claims which are made for them, the Continental hunt, point and retrieve breeds would win such a contest hands down. Theoretically, at least, there is no job in the shooting field which is beyond the scope of these paragons. They should hunt thick cover, and many can. They should hunt fast and wide in more open country, such as stubble, beet or heather, searching for air scent and freezing instantly on point, at the first hint of game-tainted breeze. They should retrieve any game, dead or wounded, which is either shot over their point, or shot at a stand, when they fulfil the retriever breeds' function at driven game shoots. They should be competent water dogs; I know of one young Thuringian vorstehhund (an East German variety of the German shorthaired pointer) which made a long retrieve of a goose on an ebb tide when its owner happened across a dogless wildfowler (shame on the latter). The HPRs should work with short-winged hawk or long-winged falcon and a good German pointer should walk quietly to heel, whilst its owner is woodland deer stalking, and be reliable on the blood scent of a wounded deer.

Most certainly, all these skills lie within the brief of these 'Versatiles' (as they are known in the USA), so it could be argued with some conviction that for any person who requires a gundog for a multiplicity of purposes there would be no need to look beyond the HPR group. Alas, but all that glisters is not gold. The sad reality is that to find an animal which can adapt to each and every one of these situations is extremely rare. It is not impossible, but having found such a paragon, after the dog's demise the owner could well spend the rest of his or her shooting career in vain pursuit of a worthy successor. Many HPRs excel in one or two departments but are weak in others. A German shorthair might range far and wide on the sparsely stocked hills of Sutherland but be an indifferent retriever. An excellent retriever might lack range and hunting drive. Many are vociferous if made to wait at a drive and many are not of compliant temperament. A Greek friend tells me that most Greek shooting men use German shorthairs of German or Austrian origin, wild, macho dogs which are prone to rip out the interior furnishings of their Fiat Pandas (the only vehicle a Greek is not taxed on). Most British shooting people aspire to something a little more manageable.

This is where the spaniel fits in. He is not so versatile as the ultimate, though seldom found, HPR, but within the brief of his individual versatility, is more predictable and consistent, so whereas the HPR owner might have that one dog of a lifetime, the spaniel owner could have a long succession of animals all more or less equally competent. What is it that makes a spaniel so universally useful? There is really only one job it cannot do, and that is to quarter wide and out of gunshot, take air scent of game and hold a steady point. Despite its close kinship with the English setter, the spaniel does not handle air scent, although through exposure to grouse shooting, they certainly can become aware of it. A spaniel seeks footscent and body scent. According to the manner in which spaniel work is conducted in Britain, the tendency is to concentrate on teaching a spaniel to ignore footscent and seek body scent of squatting game, whereas the Americans rate a spaniel very highly which can accurately 'trail' moving pheasants, particularly in their artificially contrived field trials. The spaniel finds body scent close in, often between one and three feet in the case of a pheasant, and sometimes within inches of the game, where close sitting rabbits in 'seats' are the quarry. Some spaniels point, but it is a direct, low-headed point, at close range. Body scent becomes air scent when it is carried on the wind for some distance, rather, I imagine, as shot spreads into a cone as it comes out of a gun's barrel. The further shot or scent travels, the more dispersed it becomes, and at the greater distances, only the sophisticated noses of the true pointers and setters, or the more competent HPRs, can profit by it and establish the true point which will enable the shooter to walk at leisure to the point, to take the shot. When spaniels are used in conjunction with pointers and setters, as pure retrieving dogs, walking to heel until something is shot, some quickly become aware of air scent as one walks them in to the point behind the locating dog, but this can be more of a hindrance than a help. They walk in high-headed, winding the air scent of the grouse at far greater distances than when engaged in their own true spaniel function, and often they show a great desire to go in and flush the grouse themselves, which would be most annoying to the dog on point and distracting to the shooter.

But if one is content to leave bird-dog work to the bird-dogs, there is little else of which a good spaniel is not capable on or around any shoot. Its main function is to hunt game-holding ground at such a distance from the gun that anything which the spaniel finds can be taken comfortably by the gun at a range which precludes the taking of long, potentially wounding shots. I judge a spaniel trial as a shooter, and I would give a higher mark to a spaniel which did a tidy piece of hunting, found within comfortable shot, then made a nice retrieve of a dead bird, than I would to a dog which pulled to the limits, causing the gun to take a long shot, then making a good job of the ensuing runner. But if in spite of the spaniel putting its game up with decorum, the gun still shot a runner, obviously the dog would receive full credit if it rectified the gun's shortcomings by collecting his runner.

A spaniel should come into its own where game is fairly scarce and should possess the stamina to hunt for long periods without game contact, finding what little game happens to be on its beat. But so many modern spaniels possess a temperament so equable that they can cope with large flushes of game, either whilst hunting, or in the vicinity of the shot game which they are expected to retrieve.

Granted that the main purpose of the spaniel is to perform as a personal shooting dog, when its handler is rough shooting, its uses are many and varied. A spaniel under good control is an invaluable asset in a beating line and this is often how many of our splendid, present-day, artisan field triallers gain experience on game for their charges, although a danger can arise when a dog has so many flushes, and no direct retrieves, that its marking may suffer in field trial competitions. Spaniels, particularly English springers, can make marvellous picking-up dogs on driven game shoots. I have done quite a lot of picking up over the years and no matter at what stage of its career a dog was introduced to picking up for the first time, even at 5 years of age, I have never had a springer which failed to adapt to sitting quietly at a drive, then retrieving as bidden. The same should apply to the spaniel which is used as a driven game dog by its owner. Not every shooter has the aptitude to keep a spaniel calm and stable whilst he addresses his birds, but not every shooter fares better with a retriever. It seems one can either keep a gundog quiet and steady, or one cannot. An example of what an ordinary non-trialling shooting man was capable of was given by the great Welsh squire, the late Col. Sir Watkin

Williams-Wynn, who always shot over two or three spaniels when shooting driven grouse or pheasants. I never knew his dogs ever to make a sound or attempt to run in.

Taking the sedentary functions of the spaniel further, I have found them ideal for waiting for pigeons to flight in to roost, for shooting pigeons over decoys and for waiting by fed ponds for duck to flight in at dusk. Some shooters seem quite happy to use spaniels for marsh and coastal wildfowling, but it must be remembered that the smaller body of the spaniel loses heat more rapidly than that of the larger retriever, so one should be circumspect over how much immersion in cold water a spaniel should be subjected to.

Certainly the spaniel is an ideal gamekeeper's dog, performing a multiplicity of functions around the shoot, including driving wandering poults back to covert. For the austringer, who flies short-winged hawks, they are ideal for flushing rabbits for Harris hawk or gos, or even blackbirds and moorhens for the sparrowhawk.

Finally, most springers are complacent dogs and have an inbuilt faculty to 'switch off' when not working, with no desire to wreck the car or travelling box. Without any question, for the title of the most useful gundog, even though it may lack the aristocratic grace of our native pointer, or the dignity of the well-trained retriever, the spaniel gets my vote.

38

A Review of Spaniel Championship Winners

It is said, 'Those that can, do. Those that cannot, teach. Those that cannot do either, administrate.' Often I think of this amusing little quote when pondering questions related to the giving of gundog advice and, as I discussed earlier, the judging of field trials. Sometimes I wonder what qualifies some persons who aspire to reach dizzy heights in one or the other of these spheres, and very frequently both.

In the British sporting press recently we have read various strange things relating to gundog matters, from the supposed origins of the flatcoated retriever, to the matter of why some persons seem to have encountered, in the last year or two, several young English spaniels which are reluctant either to hunt or to retrieve. According to some of the answers we have seen, I am very much reminded of a quotation attributed to the great American writer, Mark Twain: 'The research of many commentators has already thrown much darkness on this subject, and it is probable that, if they continue, we shall soon know nothing about it.'

The questions regarding the spaniels remain unanswered, so I think we must go back into history and consider the spaniel situation in years gone by, in comparison to today's position. Immediately following the Second World

War, the most influential springer sires were Pinehawk Roger (soon exported), Silverstar of Chrishall, Silverstar's son Rivington Glensaugh Glean, Spark O'Vara, Sarkie O'Vara, Searle O'Vara and Slam O'Vara (little used but of enormous significance, right through to the present time). All were descended from strains which had been heavily culled of sub-standard stock. The Spaniel Championship is the supreme accolade. It is not the be-all and the end-all of the spaniel situation but is a tangible yardstick by which to measure the scenario.

My own involvement in this event began in 1957. For the next nine years, it was won by dogs on six occasions. Over the next 20-year period, dogs won 11 times, just maintaining their ascendancy, but from 1987 to 1993, bitches won six times out of seven, with no dog from mainland Britain winning at all. In my view, this was a direct result of the 'bitch boom', with more bitches being trained and entered for trials than dogs, so giving the bitches a numerical advantage on the law of averages. This has left field trial champion dogs in somewhat short supply, in addition to there being no Championship-winning dog in existence this side of the Irish Sea. There are at the moment about 15 F.T.Ch. springer dogs in Britain, not a large number to start with, but the gene pool is further reduced when one considers that only four or five can be considered 'fashionable' and are in regular use. So now we have an element of over-use of the few. Despite the importance of brood bitches in a breeding situation, stud dogs tend to be highly influential, particularly in the sphere of passing on faults. It is possible for a dog to sire a number of successful trial progeny, but still be prone to pass on faults. Cream rises to the top, but some dogs' also-ran progeny can consistently exhibit faults. I know that this is happening at the moment regarding retrieving faults. One very competent professional will not accept for training dogs sired by a certain fashionable sire. I have given awards to two of this dog's progeny when judging, and there were no problems, but several handlers have reported that more of his stock are bad, or non-retrievers, than otherwise. If the total number of bitches put to F.T.Chs in the recent past had been equally divided between the 15 or so F.T.Chs available at stud, the problem would have been in no way so concentrated.

The actual success as breeding prospects of the 35 springer dogs and bitches which have won the Championship since 1957 makes an interesting study. Quite a limited proportion have been influential and frequently 2nd or 3rd prize winners in the Championship have proved to be the more valuable breeders. Let's have a look.

1957: Gwen of Barnacre. A lovely stylish bitch by Searle O'Vara, who was put to an earlier daughter to produce Gwen. Very headstrong, she proved a great breeder when mated to Conygree Simon, but her several F.T.Ch. progeny were quite useless as breeders.

1958: Criffel Snipe. Not impressive, but lucky, and won on a brainy retrieve. Exported immediately. The 2nd prize winner, F.T.Ch. Breckonhill Brave, proved a prepotent sire in Northern Ireland.

1959: Willie of Barnacre. A son of Gwen. A tremendous dog when he behaved himself, but very headstrong (a bit insane). Widely used at stud and produced not one winner.

1960: Micklewood Slip. Very classy but a bit sly. Produced two spectacular F.T.Ch. dogs, but neither were notable studs.

1961: Harpersbrook Reed. Big, slow and clumsy. Very sound but the win was highly controversial and he was little used, producing no successful trial progeny.

1962: Markdown Muffin. Brother to Micklewood Slip, but with a better dark eye. A class dog, one of the pillars of the breed. Most influential, produced nine F.T.Chs, including two Championship winners. We could do with him today.

1963: Ruff-in-Tuff. A brainy, honest, class dog. Won while still a puppy. Exported right away. Left no stock and never made the grade in America.

1964: Berrystead Freckle. A nice classy little bitch, but won by default by sounder behaviour over Hales Smut. Left influential stock behind her.

1965: Saighton's Stinger. A brilliant performer on pheasants but couldn't find rabbits. Lacked true spaniel method and was never at public stud. A most successful sire of American trial dogs.

1966: Meadowcourt Della. Not a nice bitch at all. Disliked by her owner and the guns in his syndicate. Exported after win. Did no good in America.

1967: Hamers Hansel. Very classy, forceful and stylish. Light-eyed and could be dishonest. Left no notable stock behind him.

1968: No Championship held.

1969: Joss of Barnacre. Very stylish but no stamina. Not a good stud. Sired two F.T.Chs, one very poor with no stamina, the other, out of a class bitch, quite a reasonable dog, but a bit settery.

1970: Layerbrook Michelle. Very stylish but poor in cover. Won on white grass and bred no decent stock.

1971: Coppicewood Carla. A class bitch who could do it all. Said to be hard to handle, but so well handled, it didn't show. An influential breeder.

1972: Robbie of Barnacre. Very stylish but a terrible dog with no brains. Good handling and good luck got him through. Virtually useless as a sire. Gwibernant Ashley Robb ran 3rd to him, one of the most influential stud forces in the whole period under discussion.

1973: Harwes Silver. Not the most impressive bitch but good on the occasion and picked a good runner in each run. Not a successful breeder. 2nd to her was Rytex Rex, a most influential son of Muffin.

1974: Crowhill Raffle. Plenty of style and drive and brilliant on his retrieves, but could be weak on gamefinding. A disappointing sire, siring two F.T.Ch. bitches of only fair quality.

1975 and 1976: Sport of Roffey. A spectacular dog. Very

well handled and brought to a high peak of fitness. A light-eyed dog, which only sired one novice stake winner.

1977: Ashley Buster. A very nice dog who had the lot, and dead easy to handle. Sired five F.T.Chs, one being a Championship winner. Did a lot of good for the breed.

1978: Cleo of Coppicewood. A good class bitch, very well handled, but could be hot in a shooting situation, according to her owner, who did not handle her in trials. Not a successful brood bitch.

1979: Judy of Runwell. A class bitch with tremendous courage in cover. Did not leave any notable stock behind her.

1980: Macsiccar Mint. Another performer with a lot of class. Did not make a very successful sire but some good stock has come down the line from him.

1981: Inler Harryslin. A very classy bitch which had a lot going for her. Has been influential as a breeder.

1982: Sandvig Triumph. Quite a good dog but lacking the true class of some. Won the Championship on an easy eye-wipe. Sired a few good dogs, but left a lot of hard mouth behind him.

1983: Parkmaple Jolly. An exceptional bitch who retained her winning quality well past middle age. Very influential in the breeding department.

1984: Dandelion of Gwibernant. A bitch who swept all before her for a time. Sensitive but could be very hot. Some excellent lines have come down from her.

1985: Cortman Garry. A very stylish, forceful dog, well above the commonplace, but has not proved to be a very consistent sire.

1986: Cortman Lane. A brother to Garry. Had enormous quality and was dead honest, his only fault being that he needed an experienced handler to hold him onto his ground. The only dog over this period, besides Markdown Muffin, who was a prepotent sire, with seven British F.T.Chs sired and possibly more in the pipeline. Also has sired a whole generation of good, trainable shooting dogs.

1987: Drury Girl. Sometimes underrated, she was a most

consistent, efficient bitch. Did little as a brood bitch until mated to Lane, when she produced two F.T.Chs.

1988: Simonseat Slip. A small, stylish bitch who beat a heavily fancied opponent by superior honesty. Too early yet to comment on her abilities as a breeder.

1989: Penny of Housty. A very good mover and brilliant gamefinder. A daughter of Lane with many of his qualities, but easier to handle. Nothing of note has been produced by her, then she was exported before her true worth could be assessed.

1990: Tops of Castlings. The only black-and-white contender under review apart from Judy of Runwell. Very polished and classy, with tremendous ability on a runner. Too early yet to comment on her progeny.

1991: Rytex Racine. A small, very stylish bitch with an automatic 'windscreen wiper' hunting pattern. Very fast on dead leaves but not one of the most favoured winners. Did not run to defend her title. Uterine problems precluded her breeding career.

1992: Tanya's Bass Special. Shrouded in mystery. Won the Championship in two runs in heavy cover where only the judges could see him. As he was not called into the run-off, the spectators never got a look at him. Mike Thomas reports seeing him run a very good trial in Northern Ireland. His progeny have not yet been seen.

1993: Poppet of Balscote. A very spectacular bitch which was made up very young. Terrific drive in cover and very stylish. Some judges have queried her gamefinding, saying she sometimes appears to flush by bodily presence. Comes from a most illustrious female line, so might breed well, but too early yet to tell.

Only about 14 of the Championship winners under review have proved themselves as influential breeders, with time yet for those from 1988 onwards to prove themselves. Other highly influential breeders have been Berrystead Factor (2nd, 1969), Don of Bronton (3rd, 1978) and Macsiccar Auchtertyre Donna (4th, 1970), who produced five F.T.Chs, four of which have proved most beneficial to the breed.

The English springer spaniel is a great working dog. The current tragedy is that its field trial movement is so bedevilled by politics and riven by internecine strife. We can only hope that the situation will ultimately improve, to the benefit of the spaniels themselves and our own enjoyment.